FOAL

"YOU'LL NEVER KNOW"

by C. Tyler

BOOK III

SOLDIER'S HEART

OTHER BOOKS BY C. TYLER

THE JOB THING (FANTAGRAPHICS BOOKS, 1993)
LATE BLOOMER (FANTAGRAPHICS BOOKS, 2005)
YOU'LL NEVER KNOW BOOK I: A GOOD and
   DECENT MAN (FANTAGRAPHICS BOOKS, 2009)
YOU'LL NEVER KNOW BOOK II: COLLATERAL
   DAMAGE (FANTAGRAPHICS BOOKS, 2010)

FANTAGRAPHICS BOOKS
7563 LAKE CITY WAY NE
SEATTLE, WA 98115

DESIGNED BY C. TYLER
PRODUCTION BY PAUL BARESH
EDITED BY KIM THOMPSON
ASSOCIATE PUBLISHER: ERIC REYNOLDS
PUBLISHED BY GARY GROTH AND KIM THOMPSON

TO RECEIVE A FREE CATALOGUE OF COMICS, CALL 1-800-657-1100, OR
VISIT THE FANTAGRAPHICS WEBSITE: www.fantagraphics.com .

DISTRIBUTED IN THE U.S. BY W.W. NORTON AND COMPANY, INC. (800-233-4830)
DISTRIBUTED IN CANADA BY CANADIAN MANDA GROUP (410-560-7100 X843)
DISTRIBUTED IN THE UNITED KINGDOM BY TURNAROUND DISTRIBUTION (44 020-8829-3002)
DISTRIBUTED IN THE U.S. TO COMIC BOOK SPECIALTY STORES BY
DIAMOND COMICS DISTRIBUTORS (800-452-6642 X215)

C. TYLER WEBSITE: www.bloomerland.com
FACEBOOK: CAROL TYLER
caroltyler.blogspot.com

FIRST PRINTING: August 2012

ISBN: 978-1-60699-548-8

PRINTED IN SINGAPORE

C. TYLER PERSONAL THANKS TO:
THANKS TO EVERYONE I MENTIONED IN THE TWO PREVIOUS VOLUMES,
BUT AN EXTRA SPECTACULAR SHOUT-OUT, 100% TO MY MOM.
I LOVE, LOVE, LOVE YOU.

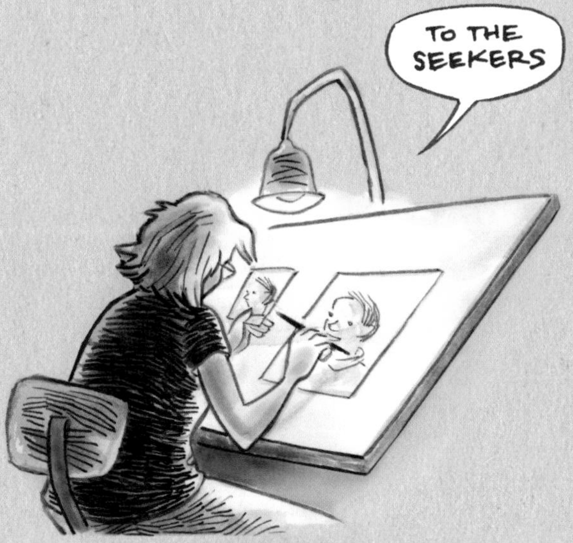
TO THE SEEKERS

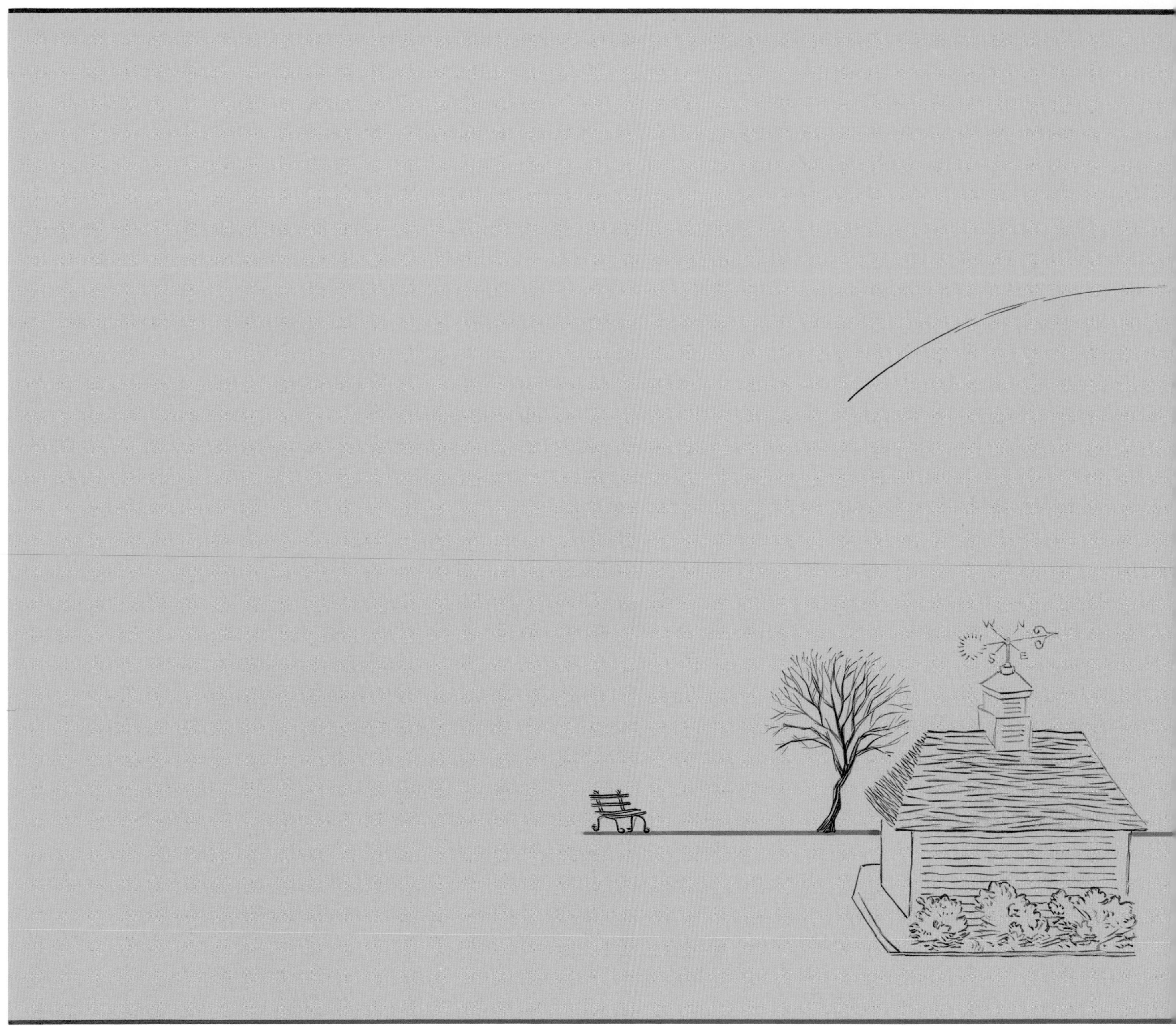
W
N
S
E

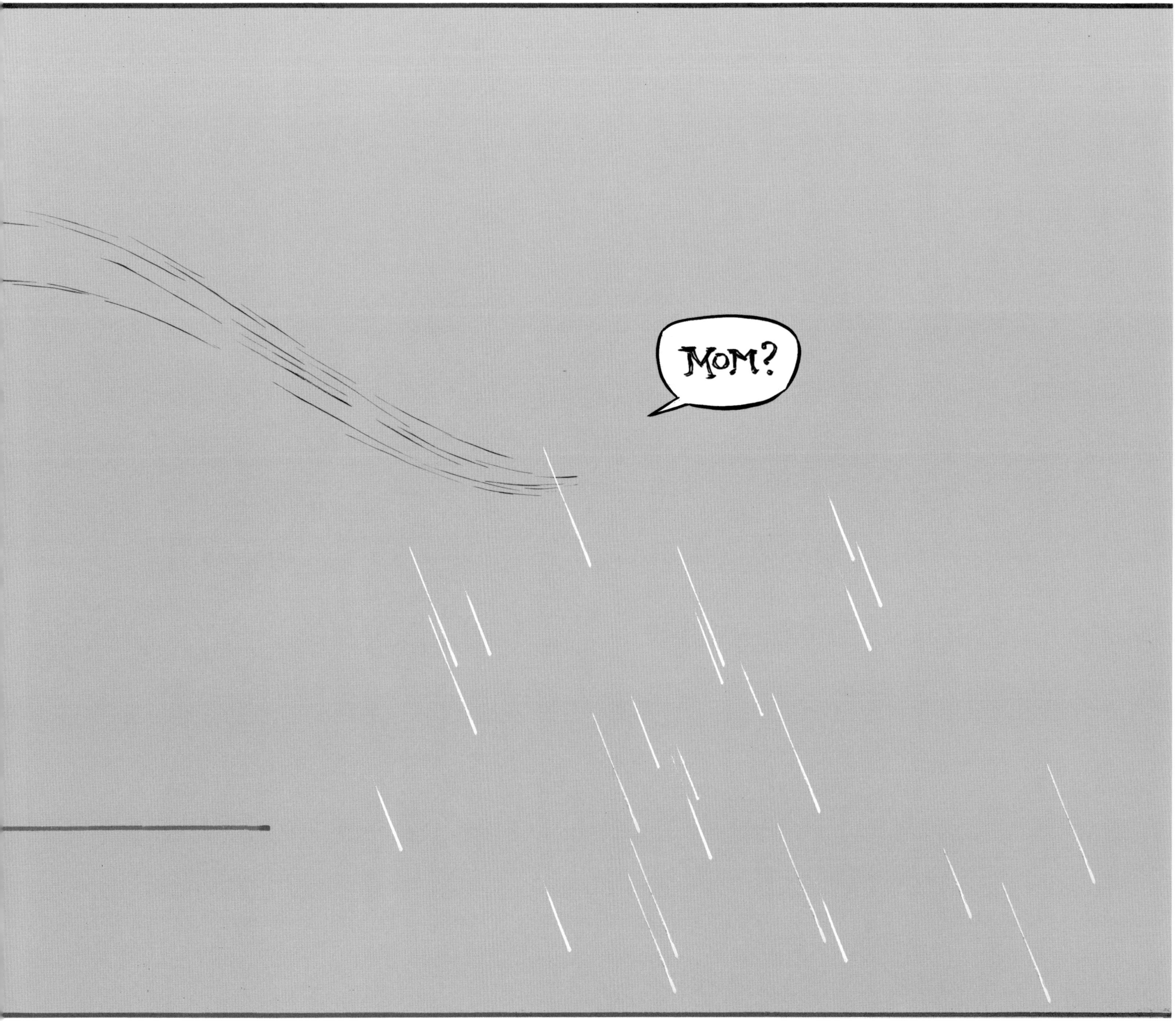
MOM?

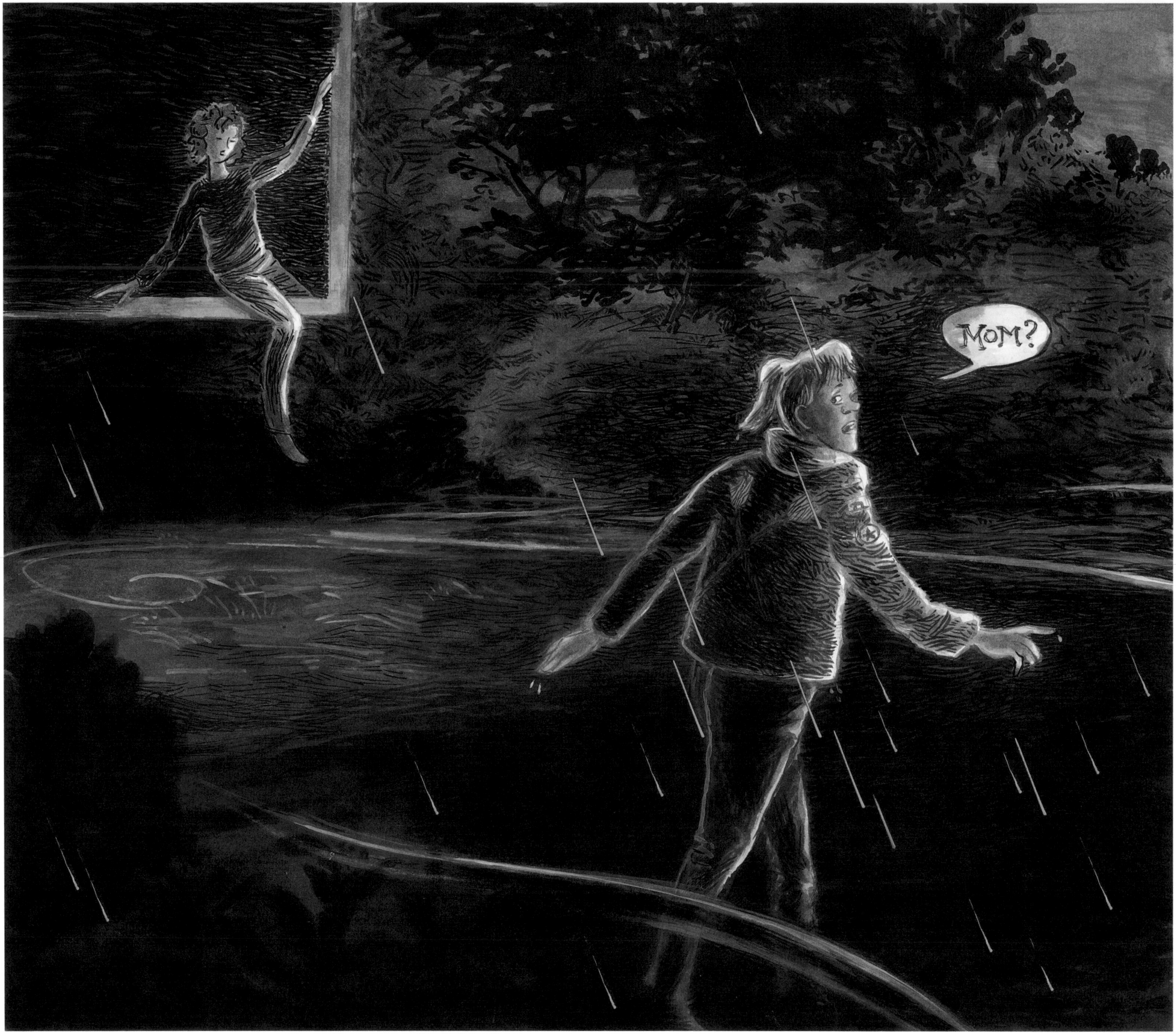
MOM?

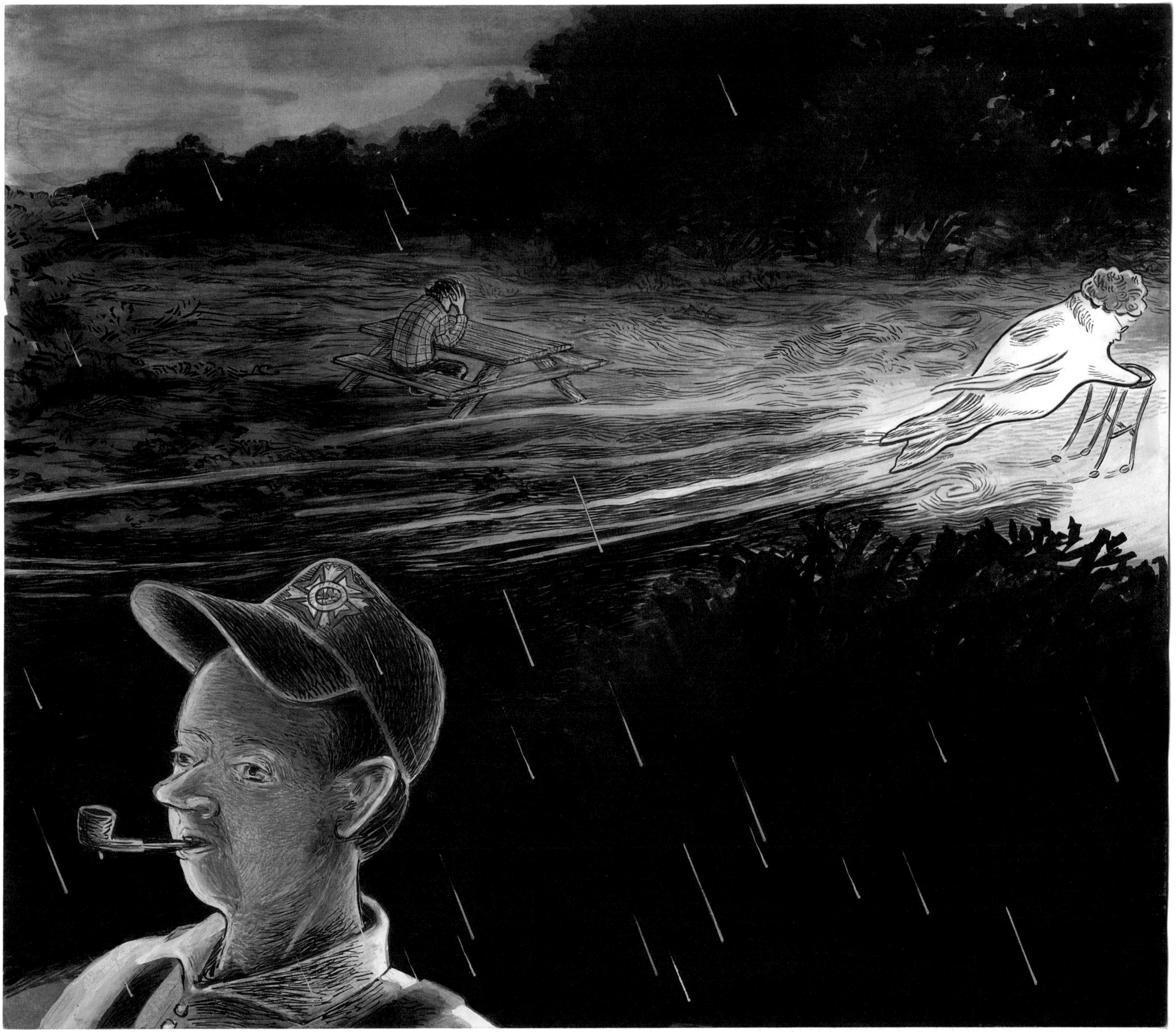

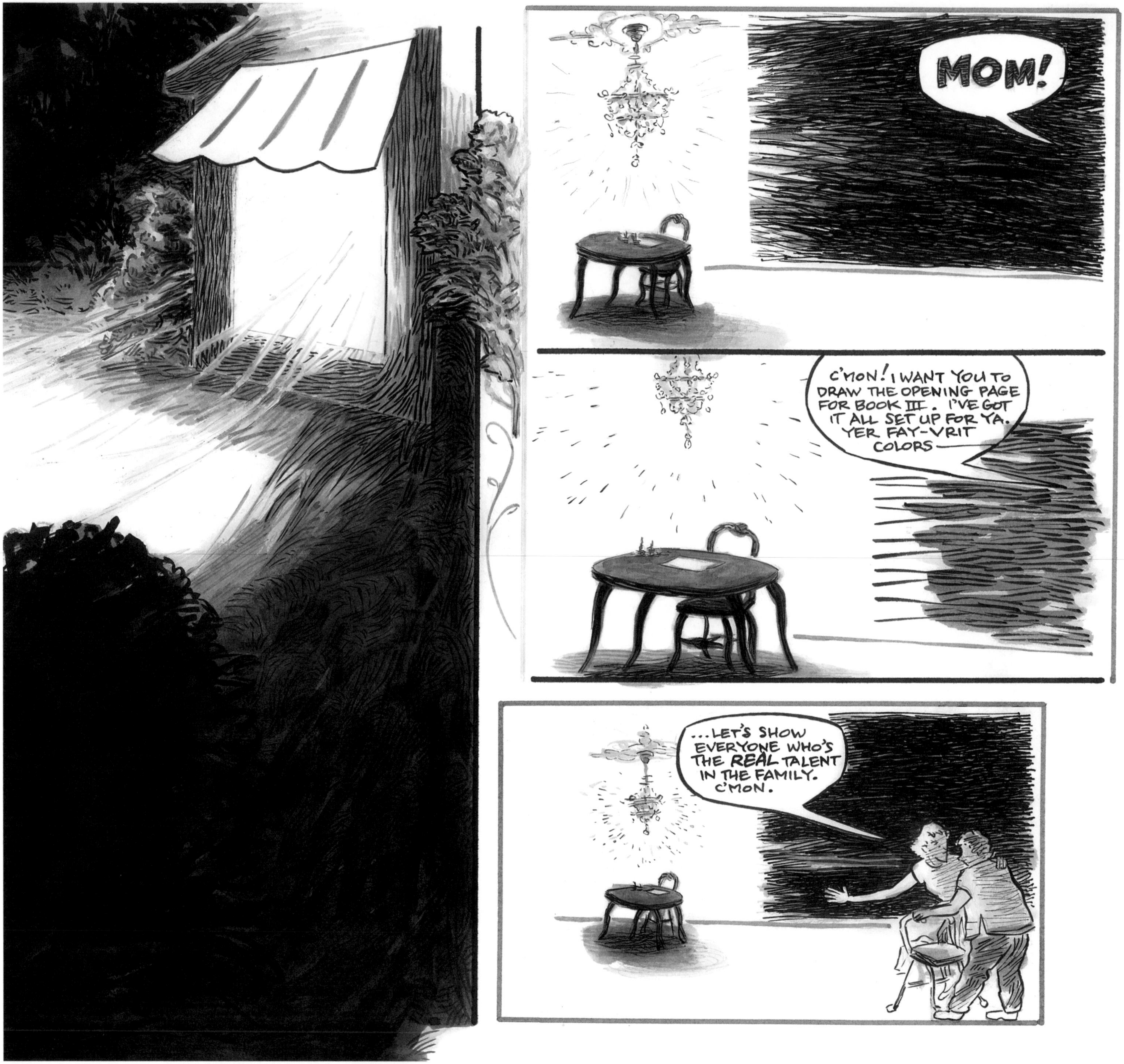
MOM!
C'MON! I WANT YOU TO DRAW THE OPENING PAGE FOR BOOK III. I'VE GOT IT ALL SET UP FOR YA. YER FAY-VRIT COLORS—
...LET'S SHOW EVERYONE WHO'S THE REAL TALENT IN THE FAMILY. C'MON.

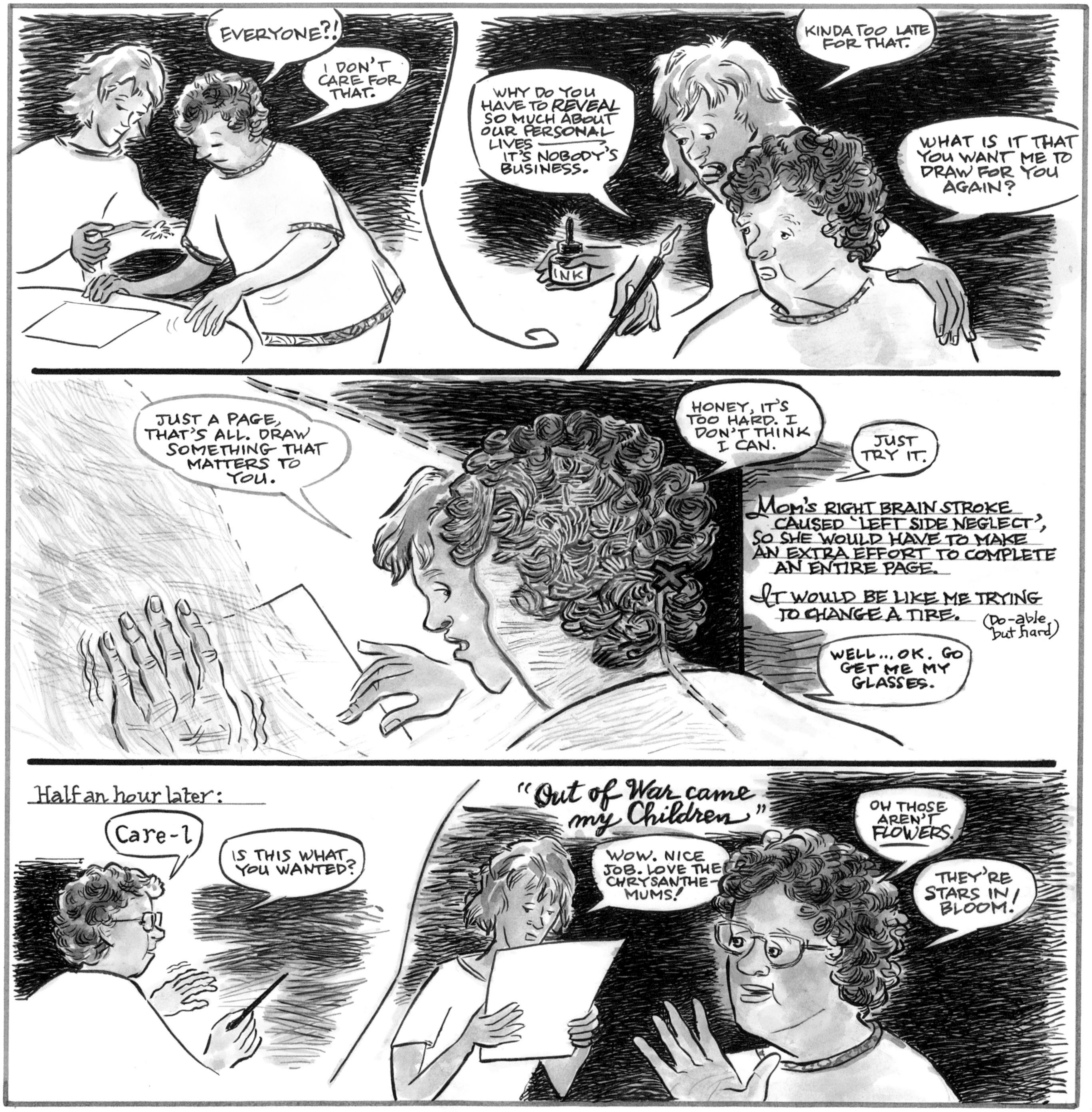
EVERYONE?!
I DON'T CARE FOR THAT.
WHY DO YOU HAVE TO REVEAL SO MUCH ABOUT OUR PERSONAL LIVES — IT'S NOBODY'S BUSINESS.
KINDA TOO LATE FOR THAT.
INK
WHAT IS IT THAT YOU WANT ME TO DRAW FOR YOU AGAIN?
JUST A PAGE, THAT'S ALL. DRAW SOMETHING THAT MATTERS TO YOU.
HONEY, IT'S TOO HARD. I DON'T THINK I CAN.
JUST TRY IT.
MOM'S RIGHT BRAIN STROKE CAUSED 'LEFT SIDE NEGLECT', SO SHE WOULD HAVE TO MAKE AN EXTRA EFFORT TO COMPLETE AN ENTIRE PAGE.
IT WOULD BE LIKE ME TRYING TO CHANGE A TIRE. (Do-able but hard)
WELL... OK. GO GET ME MY GLASSES.
Half an hour later:
Care-l
IS THIS WHAT YOU WANTED?
"Out of War came my Children"
WOW. NICE JOB. LOVE THE CHRYSANTHE-MUMS!
OH THOSE AREN'T FLOWERS.
THEY'RE STARS IN BLOOM!

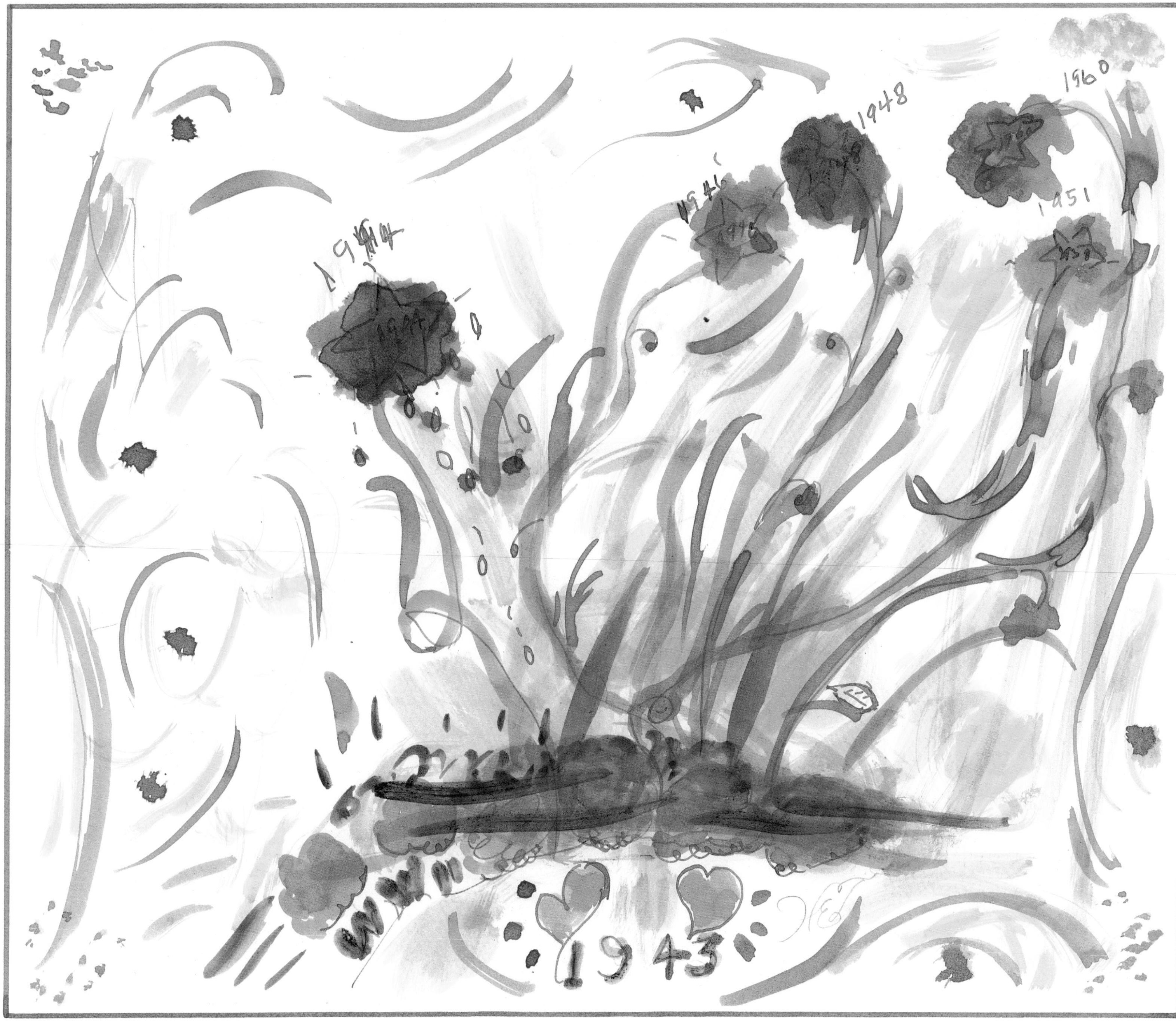
1948
1960
1951
1943

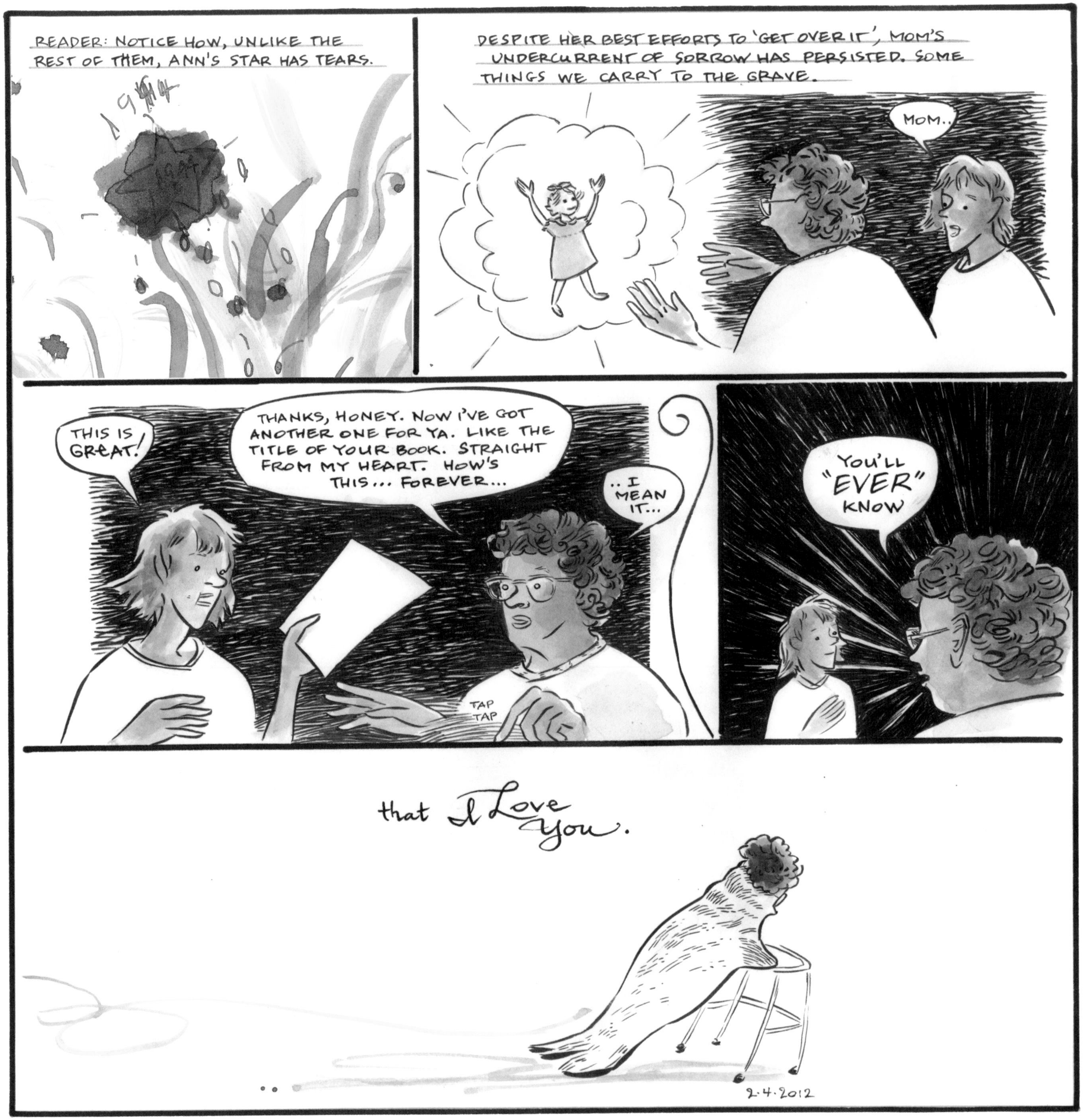
READER: NOTICE HOW, UNLIKE THE REST OF THEM, ANN'S STAR HAS TEARS.
1944
DESPITE HER BEST EFFORTS TO 'GET OVER IT', MOM'S UNDERCURRENT OF SORROW HAS PERSISTED. SOME THINGS WE CARRY TO THE GRAVE.
MOM..
THIS IS GREAT!
THANKS, HONEY. NOW I'VE GOT ANOTHER ONE FOR YA. LIKE THE TITLE OF YOUR BOOK. STRAIGHT FROM MY HEART. HOW'S THIS... FOREVER...
..I MEAN IT...
TAP TAP
YOU'LL "EVER" KNOW
that I Love You.
2·4·2012

O.K....

SO NOW YOU KNOW FROM READING BOOKS I + II THAT I WAS RAISED BY A NICE COUPLE WHO HAD SUFFERED SIGNIFICANT EMOTIONAL TRAUMA DUE TO WAR AND TRAGIC LOSS. AND THAT THIS TRAUMA STAINED MY CHILDHOOD. I DID NOT WANT THIS PATHOLOGY TO CYCLE THROUGH YET ANOTHER GENERATION AND STAIN MY CHILD. BUT SADLY, BECAUSE OF THE DRAMA BETWEEN ME AND HER DAD, IT HAPPENED. SO I'M GOING TO CALL HIM IN N.Y. AND INSIST HE COME HERE *Now!*

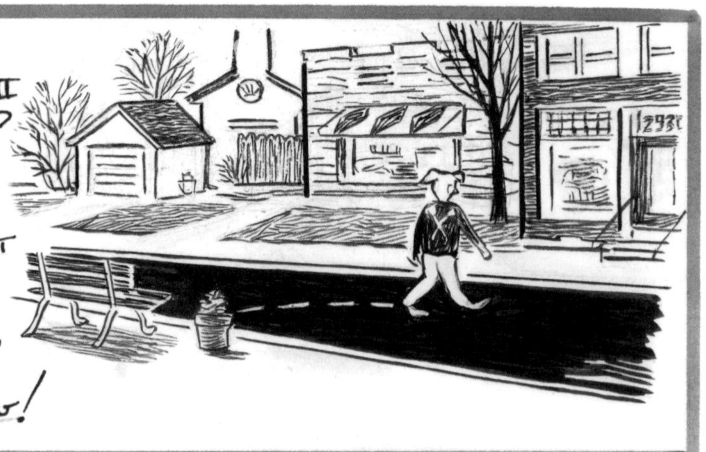

ALRIGHT. SO ONCE I GOT TURNED AROUND, I HEADED BACK OVER TO BE WITH MY GIRL. WHATEVER SUBSTANCE SHE WAS ON, WELL... SHE SEEMED BETTER. SO MUCH WAS BEING REVEALED: THE EXTENT OF HER RISKY BEHAVIOR AND ITS BASIS IN HER SADNESS OVER THIS WHOLE DAMN MESS WITH HER DAD LEAVING, AND ME YANKING HER OUT OF HER CALIFORNIA LIFE. BLESS HER HEART, SHE HELD IT TOGETHER AS LONG AS SHE COULD.

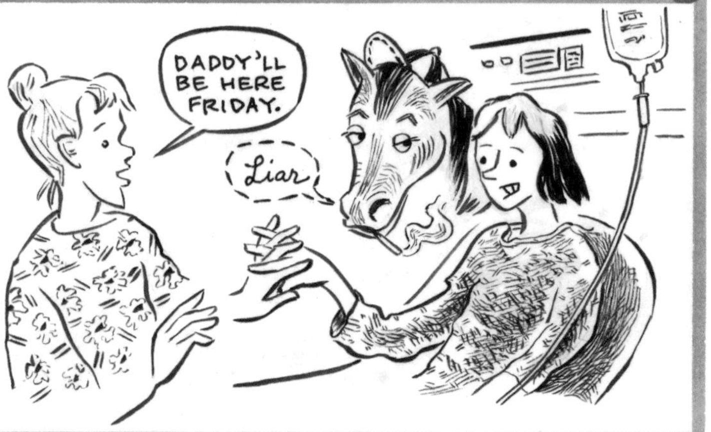
DADDY'LL BE HERE FRIDAY.
Liar

GOING ON DAY 3 AT CHILDREN'S AND THE DOCTORS WERE STILL NOT READY TO PUT A LABEL ON HER CONDITION. MY MOM HUNCH, AFTER ALL THESE TESTS AND EXCEPT FOR THE VOICE — I'D SAY SHE HAS DEPRESSION. I SHOULD'A SEEN IT COMING. I MEAN I WENT **NUTS** FOR AWHILE THERE. BUT THEN I THREW MYSELF INTO PARENTAL RESPONSIBILITIES. AND DAD'S ***BOOK*** — I MEAN, DAD'S **CLAIM**.

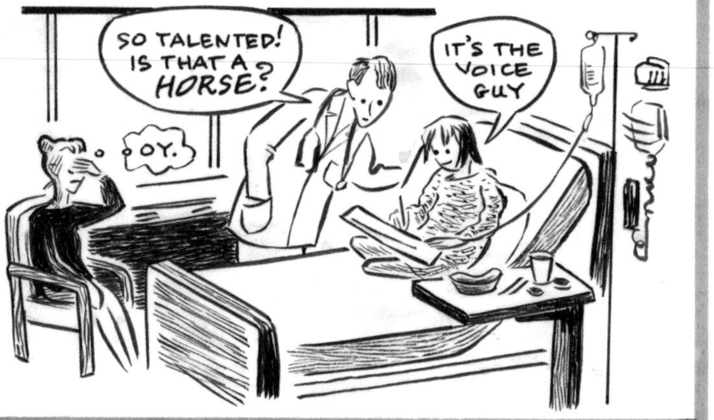
SO TALENTED! IS THAT A HORSE?
OY.
IT'S THE VOICE GUY

SEEING JUSTIN THERE AT THE NURSES STATION... AND AFTER SO MANY MONTHS... THE RELIEF I FELT WAS **DEEP**, LIKE NOURISHMENT TO THE STARVED. BUT THEN IT WAS AS IF SOMEONE POURED A CAN OF SALTY BROWN **GRAVY** ON ME, BECAUSE I KNEW WHY HE HAD COME AND I KNEW HOW THE GRAVITY OF WHAT I HAD TO TELL HIM WOULD BREAK HIS HEART — REGARDLESS, I EMBRACED HIM AS ONE DOES POSSIBILITY: WITH HOPEFULNESS AND A **SMILE**.

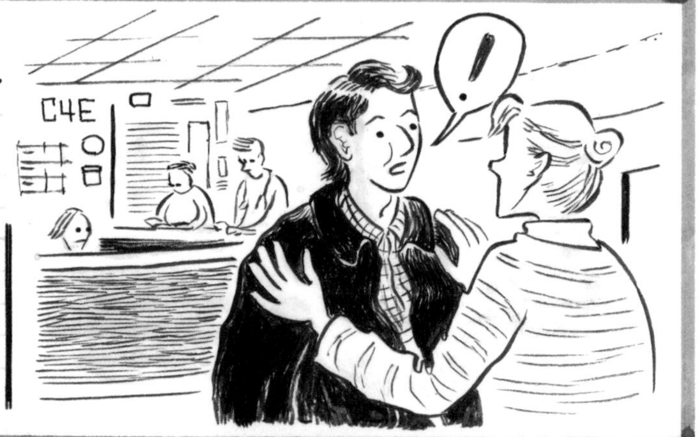
C4E
!

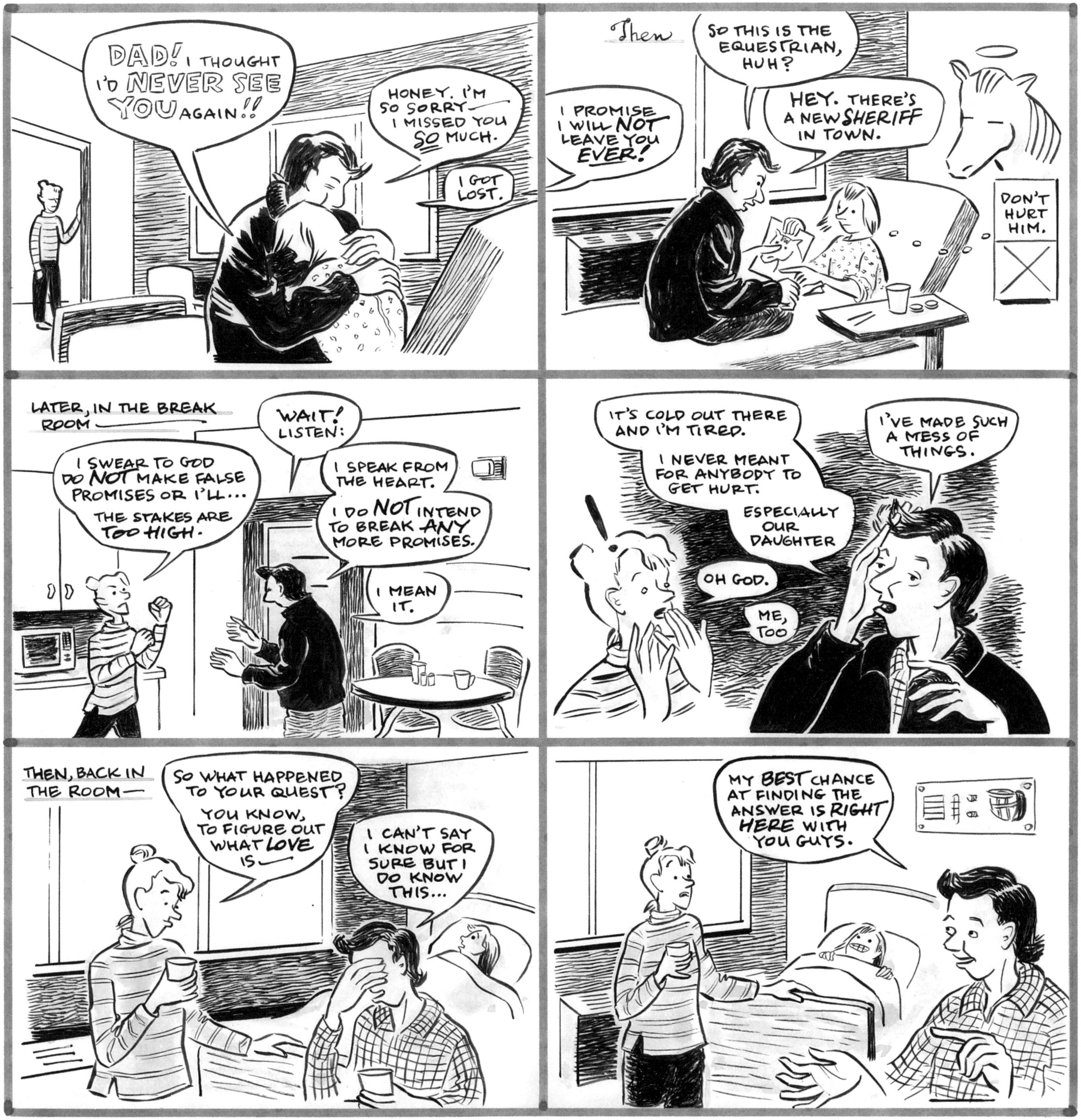
DAD! I THOUGHT I'D NEVER SEE YOU AGAIN!!
HONEY. I'M SO SORRY— I MISSED YOU SO MUCH.
I GOT LOST.
Then
SO THIS IS THE EQUESTRIAN, HUH?
HEY. THERE'S A NEW SHERIFF IN TOWN.
I PROMISE I WILL NOT LEAVE YOU EVER!
DON'T HURT HIM.
LATER, IN THE BREAK ROOM
WAIT! LISTEN:
I SWEAR TO GOD DO NOT MAKE FALSE PROMISES OR I'LL...
THE STAKES ARE TOO HIGH.
I SPEAK FROM THE HEART.
I DO NOT INTEND TO BREAK ANY MORE PROMISES.
I MEAN IT.
IT'S COLD OUT THERE AND I'M TIRED.
I NEVER MEANT FOR ANYBODY TO GET HURT.
ESPECIALLY OUR DAUGHTER
I'VE MADE SUCH A MESS OF THINGS.
OH GOD.
ME, TOO
THEN, BACK IN THE ROOM—
SO WHAT HAPPENED TO YOUR QUEST?
YOU KNOW, TO FIGURE OUT WHAT LOVE IS—
I CAN'T SAY I KNOW FOR SURE BUT I DO KNOW THIS...
MY BEST CHANCE AT FINDING THE ANSWER IS RIGHT HERE WITH YOU GUYS.

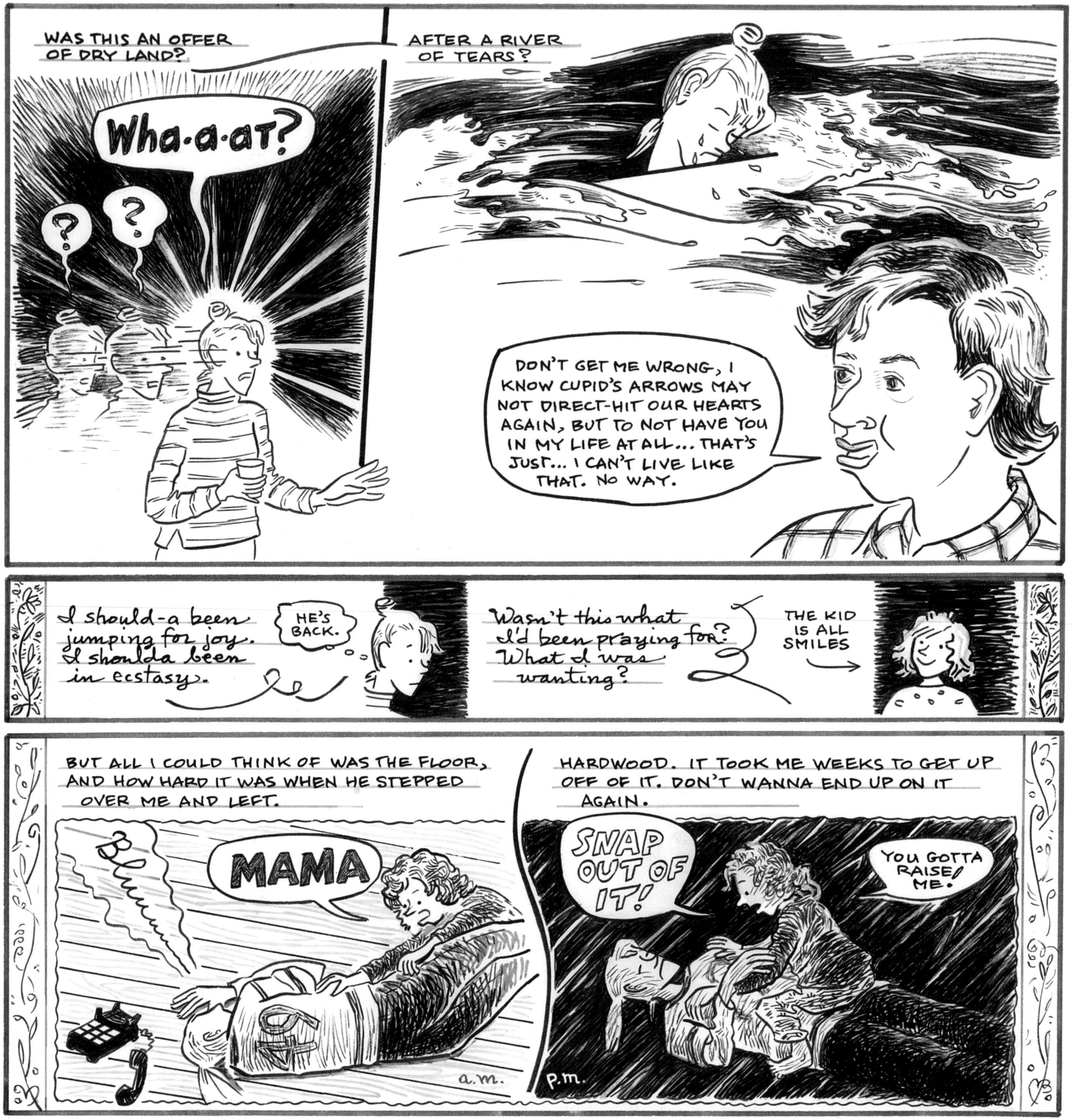
WAS THIS AN OFFER OF DRY LAND?
Wha-a-at?
?
?
AFTER A RIVER OF TEARS?
DON'T GET ME WRONG, I KNOW CUPID'S ARROWS MAY NOT DIRECT-HIT OUR HEARTS AGAIN, BUT TO NOT HAVE YOU IN MY LIFE AT ALL... THAT'S JUST... I CAN'T LIVE LIKE THAT. NO WAY.
I should-a been jumping for joy. I shoulda been in ecstasy.
HE'S BACK.
Wasn't this what I'd been praying for? What I was wanting?
THE KID IS ALL SMILES
BUT ALL I COULD THINK OF WAS THE FLOOR, AND HOW HARD IT WAS WHEN HE STEPPED OVER ME AND LEFT.
MAMA
a.m.
HARDWOOD. IT TOOK ME WEEKS TO GET UP OFF OF IT. DON'T WANNA END UP ON IT AGAIN.
SNAP OUT OF IT!
YOU GOTTA RAISE ME!
p.m.

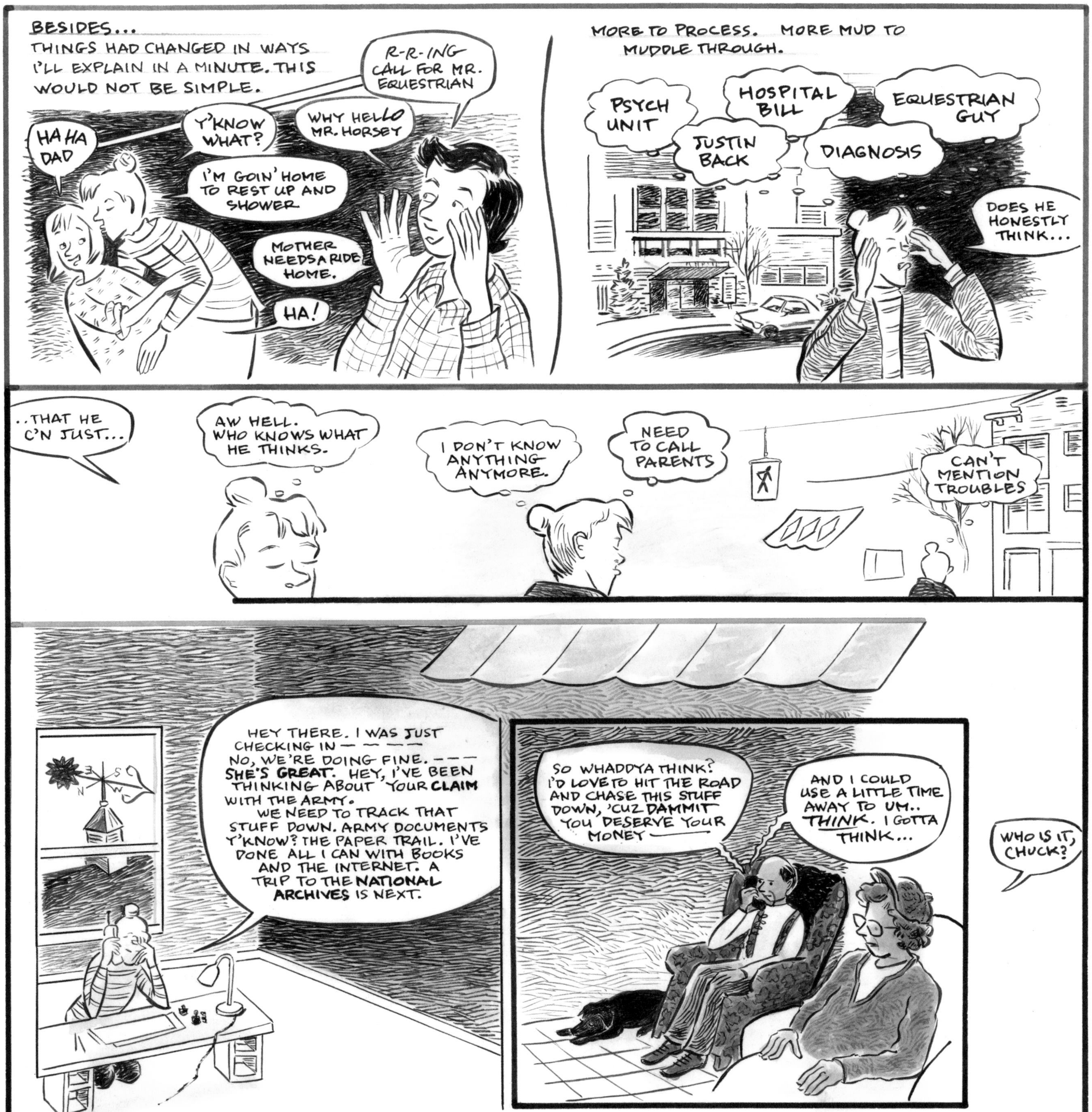
BESIDES...
THINGS HAD CHANGED IN WAYS I'LL EXPLAIN IN A MINUTE. THIS WOULD NOT BE SIMPLE.
R-R-ING CALL FOR MR. EQUESTRIAN
HA HA DAD
Y'KNOW WHAT?
WHY HELLO MR. HORSEY
I'M GOIN' HOME TO REST UP AND SHOWER
MOTHER NEEDS A RIDE HOME.
HA!
MORE TO PROCESS. MORE MUD TO MUDDLE THROUGH.
PSYCH UNIT
HOSPITAL BILL
EQUESTRIAN GUY
JUSTIN BACK
DIAGNOSIS
DOES HE HONESTLY THINK...
..THAT HE C'N JUST...
AW HELL. WHO KNOWS WHAT HE THINKS.
I DON'T KNOW ANYTHING ANYMORE.
NEED TO CALL PARENTS
CAN'T MENTION TROUBLES
HEY THERE. I WAS JUST CHECKING IN— — — — NO, WE'RE DOING FINE. — — — SHE'S GREAT. HEY, I'VE BEEN THINKING ABOUT YOUR CLAIM WITH THE ARMY. WE NEED TO TRACK THAT STUFF DOWN. ARMY DOCUMENTS Y'KNOW? THE PAPER TRAIL. I'VE DONE ALL I CAN WITH BOOKS AND THE INTERNET. A TRIP TO THE NATIONAL ARCHIVES IS NEXT.
SO WHADDYA THINK? I'D LOVE TO HIT THE ROAD AND CHASE THIS STUFF DOWN, 'CUZ DAMMIT YOU DESERVE YOUR MONEY
AND I COULD USE A LITTLE TIME AWAY TO UM.. THINK. I GOTTA THINK...
WHO IS IT, CHUCK?

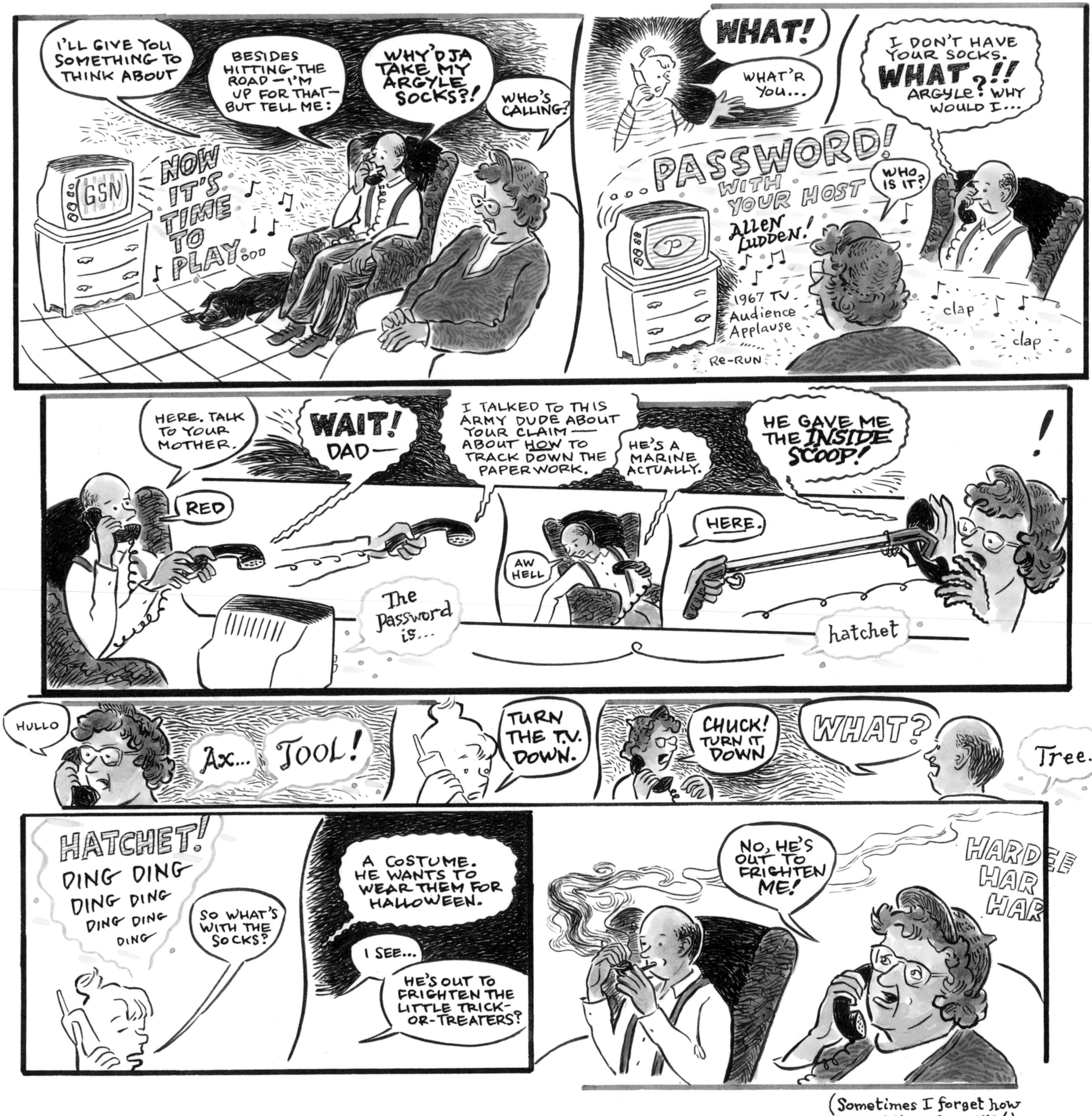
I'LL GIVE YOU SOMETHING TO THINK ABOUT
BESIDES HITTING THE ROAD — I'M UP FOR THAT — BUT TELL ME:
WHY'D JA TAKE MY ARGYLE SOCKS?!
WHO'S CALLING?
GSN
NOW IT'S TIME TO PLAY...
WHAT!
WHAT'R YOU...
I DON'T HAVE YOUR SOCKS. WHAT?!! ARGYLE? WHY WOULD I...
PASSWORD! WITH YOUR HOST ALLEN LUDDEN!
WHO IS IT?
1967 TV Audience Applause
Re-RUN
clap
clap
HERE. TALK TO YOUR MOTHER.
RED
WAIT! DAD—
I TALKED TO THIS ARMY DUDE ABOUT YOUR CLAIM — ABOUT HOW TO TRACK DOWN THE PAPERWORK.
HE'S A MARINE ACTUALLY.
AW HELL
The Password is...
HE GAVE ME THE INSIDE SCOOP!
!
HERE.
hatchet
HULLO
Ax...
TOOL!
TURN THE T.V. DOWN.
CHUCK! TURN IT DOWN
WHAT?
Tree...
HATCHET!
DING DING DING DING DING DING DING
SO WHAT'S WITH THE SOCKS?
A COSTUME. HE WANTS TO WEAR THEM FOR HALLOWEEN.
I SEE...
HE'S OUT TO FRIGHTEN THE LITTLE TRICK-OR-TREATERS?
NO, HE'S OUT TO FRIGHTEN ME!
HARDEE HAR HAR
(Sometimes I forget how NUTTY these two are!)

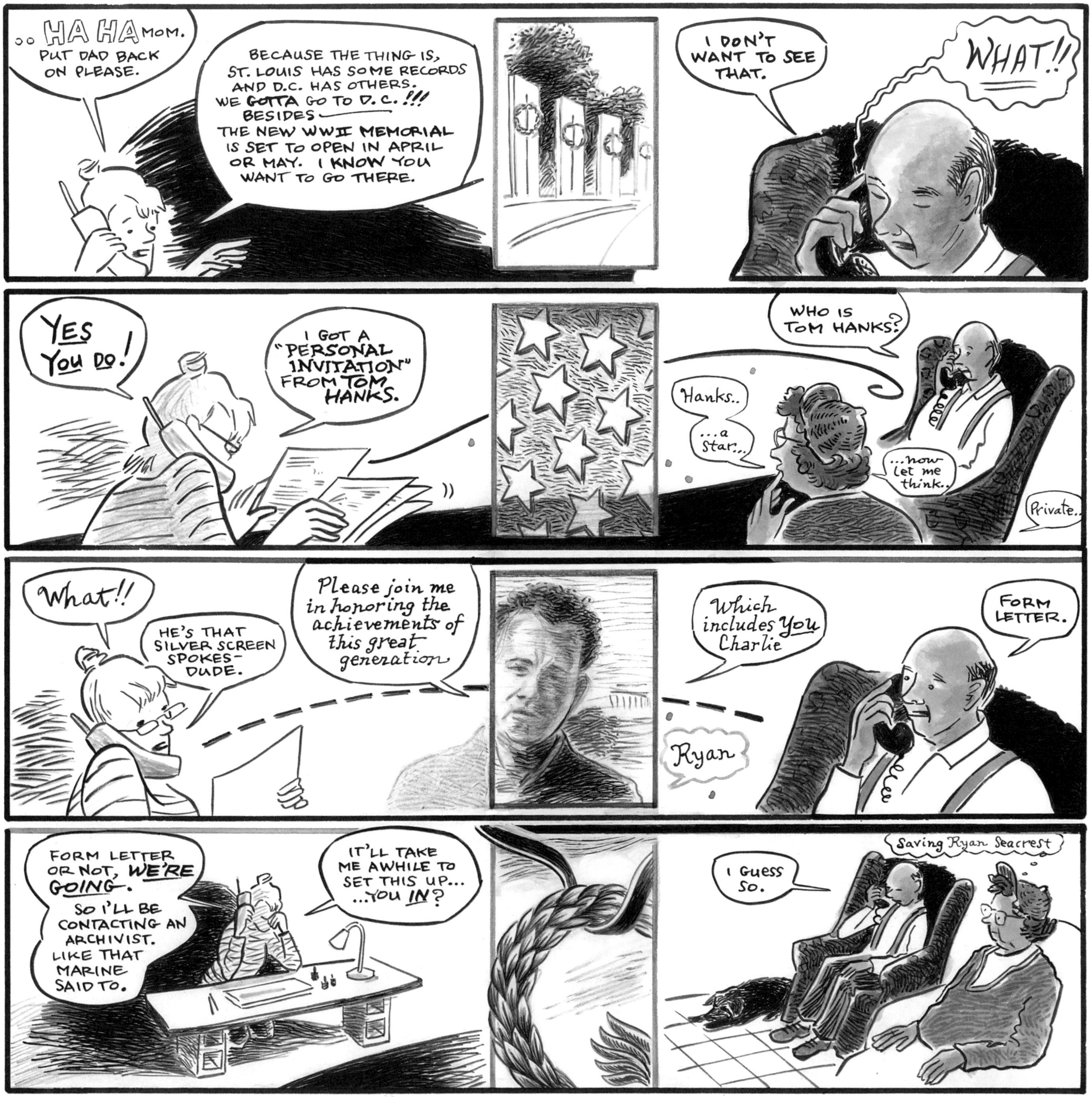
..HA HA MOM. PUT DAD BACK ON PLEASE.
BECAUSE THE THING IS, ST. LOUIS HAS SOME RECORDS AND D.C. HAS OTHERS. WE GOTTA GO TO D.C.!!! BESIDES — THE NEW WWII MEMORIAL IS SET TO OPEN IN APRIL OR MAY. I KNOW YOU WANT TO GO THERE.
I DON'T WANT TO SEE THAT.
WHAT!!
YES YOU DO!
I GOT A "PERSONAL INVITATION" FROM TOM HANKS.
WHO IS TOM HANKS?
Hanks..
...a Star...
...now let me think..
Private..
What!!
HE'S THAT SILVER SCREEN SPOKES-DUDE.
Please join me in honoring the achievements of this great generation
Which includes You Charlie
FORM LETTER.
Ryan
FORM LETTER OR NOT, WE'RE GOING. SO I'LL BE CONTACTING AN ARCHIVIST. LIKE THAT MARINE SAID TO.
IT'LL TAKE ME AWHILE TO SET THIS UP... ...YOU IN?
I GUESS SO.
Saving Ryan Seacrest

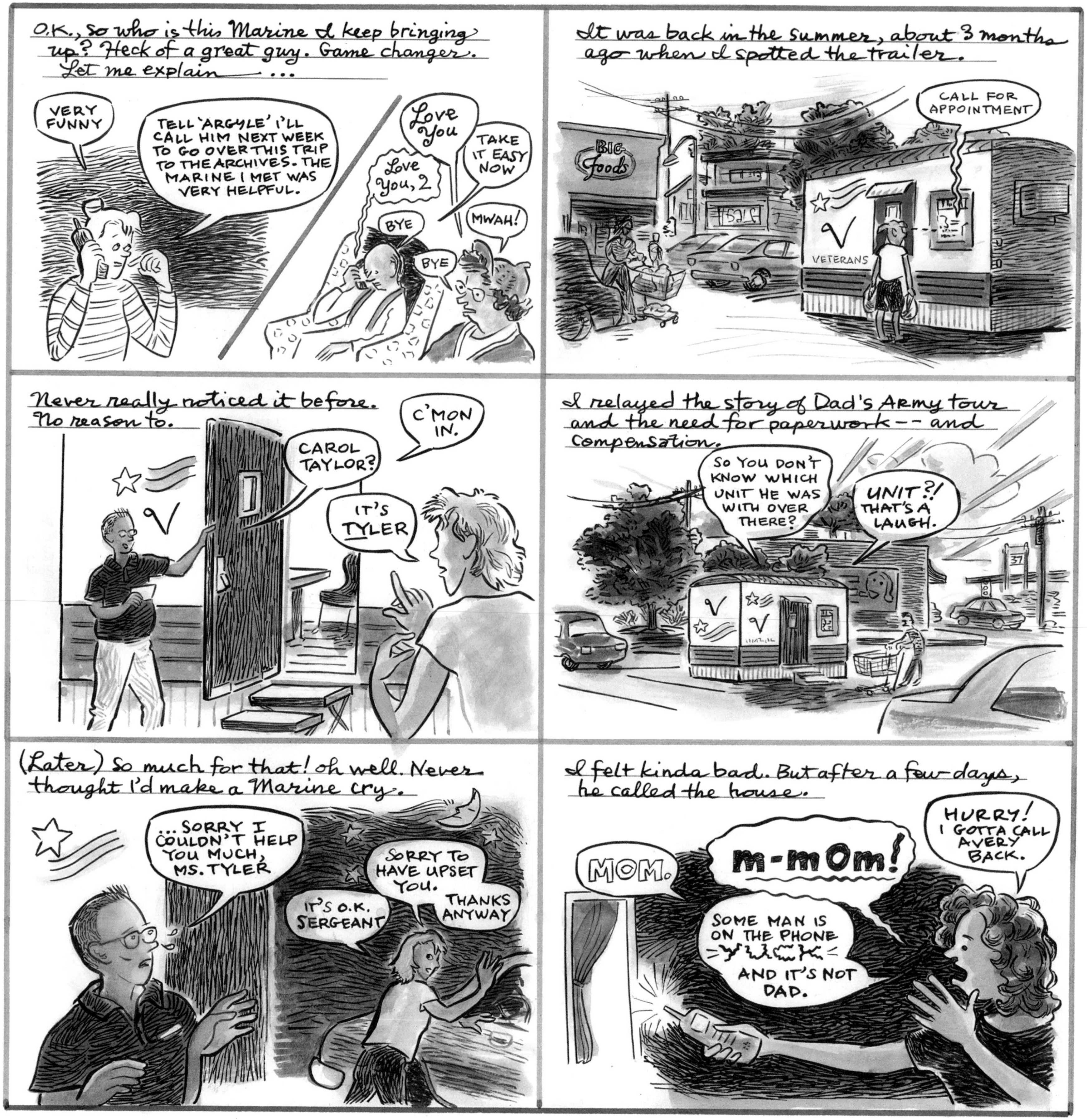
O.K., so who is this Marine I keep bringing up? Heck of a great guy. Game changer. Let me explain — ...
VERY FUNNY
TELL 'ARGYLE' I'LL CALL HIM NEXT WEEK TO GO OVER THIS TRIP TO THE ARCHIVES. THE MARINE I MET WAS VERY HELPFUL.
Love you
Love you, 2
TAKE IT EASY NOW
BYE
MWAH!
BYE
It was back in the summer, about 3 months ago when I spotted the trailer.
CALL FOR APPOINTMENT
BIG Foods
VETERANS
Never really noticed it before. No reason to.
C'MON IN.
CAROL TAYLOR?
IT'S TYLER
I relayed the story of Dad's Army tour and the need for paperwork -- and compensation.
SO YOU DON'T KNOW WHICH UNIT HE WAS WITH OVER THERE?
UNIT?! THAT'S A LAUGH.
(Later) So much for that! oh well. Never thought I'd make a Marine cry.
...SORRY I COULDN'T HELP YOU MUCH, MS. TYLER
SORRY TO HAVE UPSET YOU.
IT'S O.K. SERGEANT
THANKS ANYWAY
I felt kinda bad. But after a few days, he called the house.
MOM.
m-mOm!
HURRY! I GOTTA CALL AVERY BACK.
SOME MAN IS ON THE PHONE AND IT'S NOT DAD.

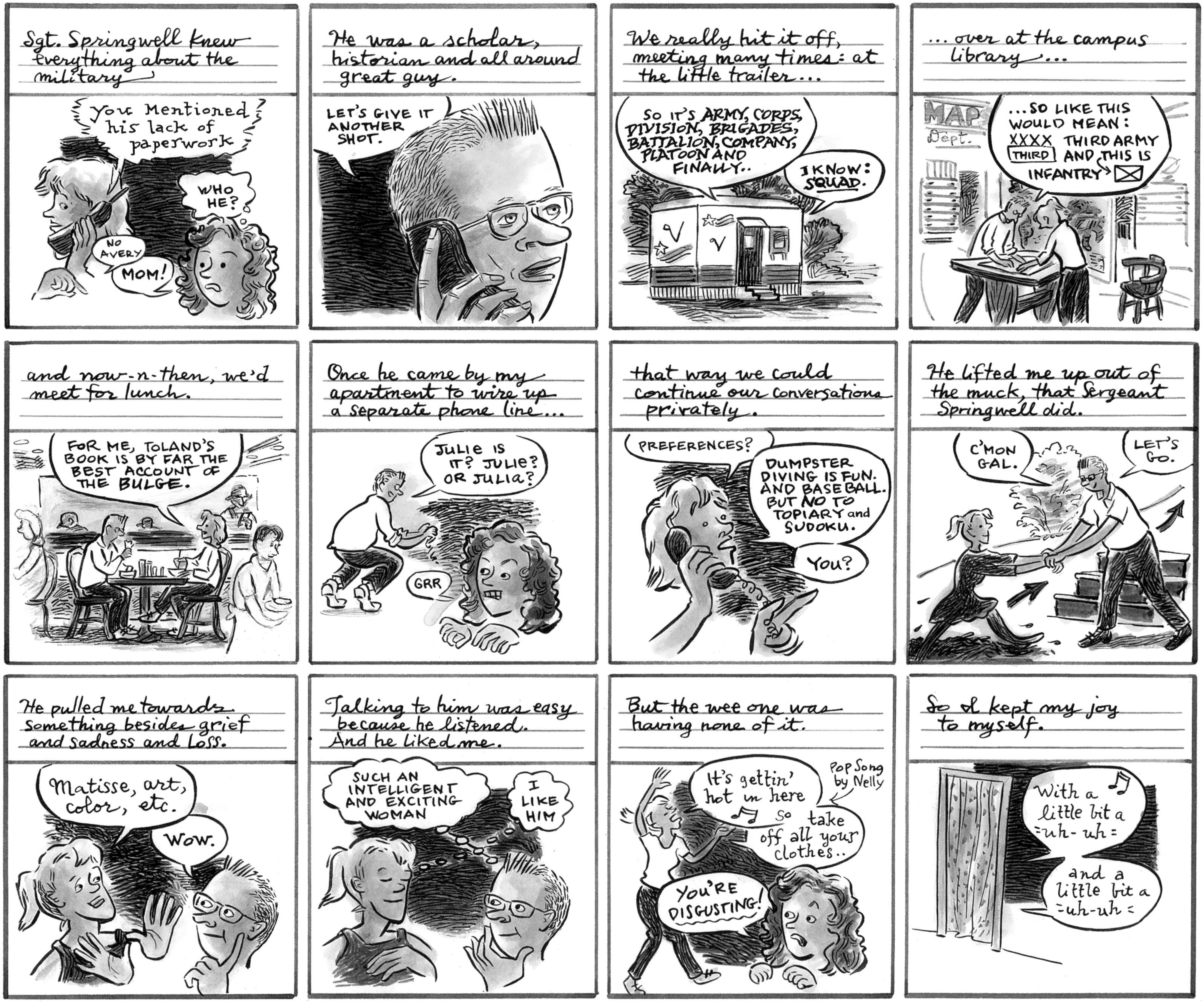
Sgt. Springwell knew everything about the military
You mentioned his lack of paperwork
Who he?
No Avery
Mom!
He was a scholar, historian and all around great guy.
Let's give it another shot.
We really hit it off, meeting many times: at the little trailer...
So it's army, corps, division, brigades, battalion, company, platoon and finally..
I know: squad.
... over at the campus library...
Map Dept.
...So like this would mean: XXXX Third Army THIRD and this is infantry
and now-n-then, we'd meet for lunch.
For me, Toland's book is by far the best account of the Bulge.
Once he came by my apartment to wire up a separate phone line...
Julie is it? Julie? or Julia?
GRR
that way we could continue our conversations privately.
Preferences?
Dumpster diving is fun. And baseball. But no to topiary and sudoku.
You?
He lifted me up out of the muck, that Sergeant Springwell did.
C'mon gal.
Let's go.
He pulled me towards something besides grief and sadness and loss.
Matisse, art, color, etc.
Wow.
Talking to him was easy because he listened. And he liked me.
Such an intelligent and exciting woman
I like him
But the wee one was having none of it.
It's gettin' hot in here so take off all your clothes..
Pop Song by Nelly
You're disgusting!
So I kept my joy to myself.
With a little bit a =uh-uh=
and a little bit a =uh-uh=

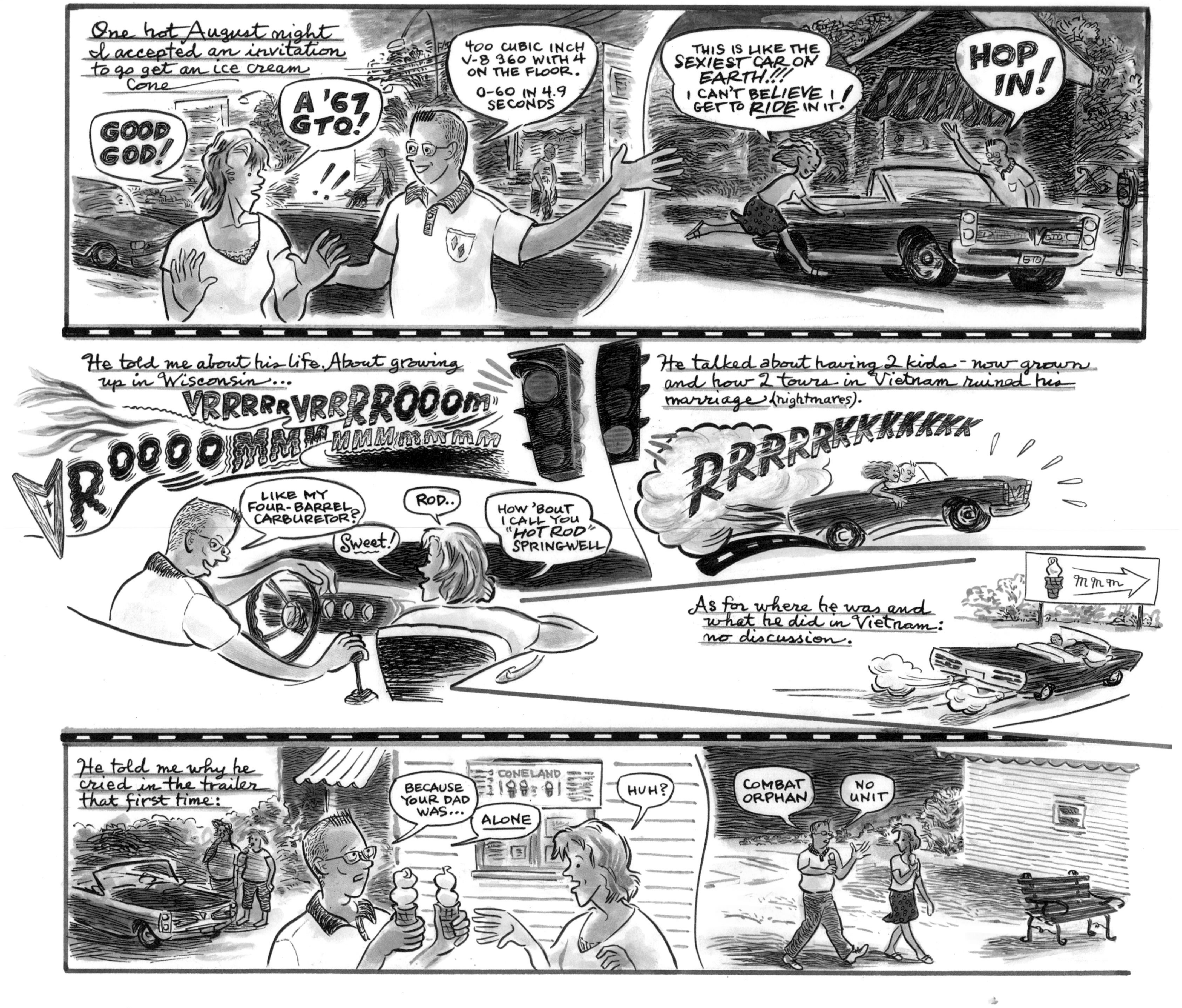
One hot August night I accepted an invitation to go get an ice cream cone
GOOD GOD!
A '67 GTO!
400 CUBIC INCH V-8 360 WITH 4 ON THE FLOOR. 0-60 IN 4.9 SECONDS
THIS IS LIKE THE SEXIEST CAR ON EARTH!!! I CAN'T BELIEVE I GET TO RIDE IN IT!
HOP IN!
He told me about his life. About growing up in Wisconsin...
VRRRRRVRRRROOOm
RrOOOOOMMMMMMMmmmm
LIKE MY FOUR-BARREL CARBURETOR?
Sweet!
ROD..
HOW 'BOUT I CALL YOU "HOT ROD" SPRINGWELL
He talked about having 2 kids - now grown and how 2 tours in Vietnam ruined his marriage (nightmares).
RRRRRKKKKKK
mmm
As for where he was and what he did in Vietnam: no discussion.
He told me why he cried in the trailer that first time:
CONELAND
BECAUSE YOUR DAD WAS...
ALONE
HUH?
COMBAT ORPHAN
NO UNIT

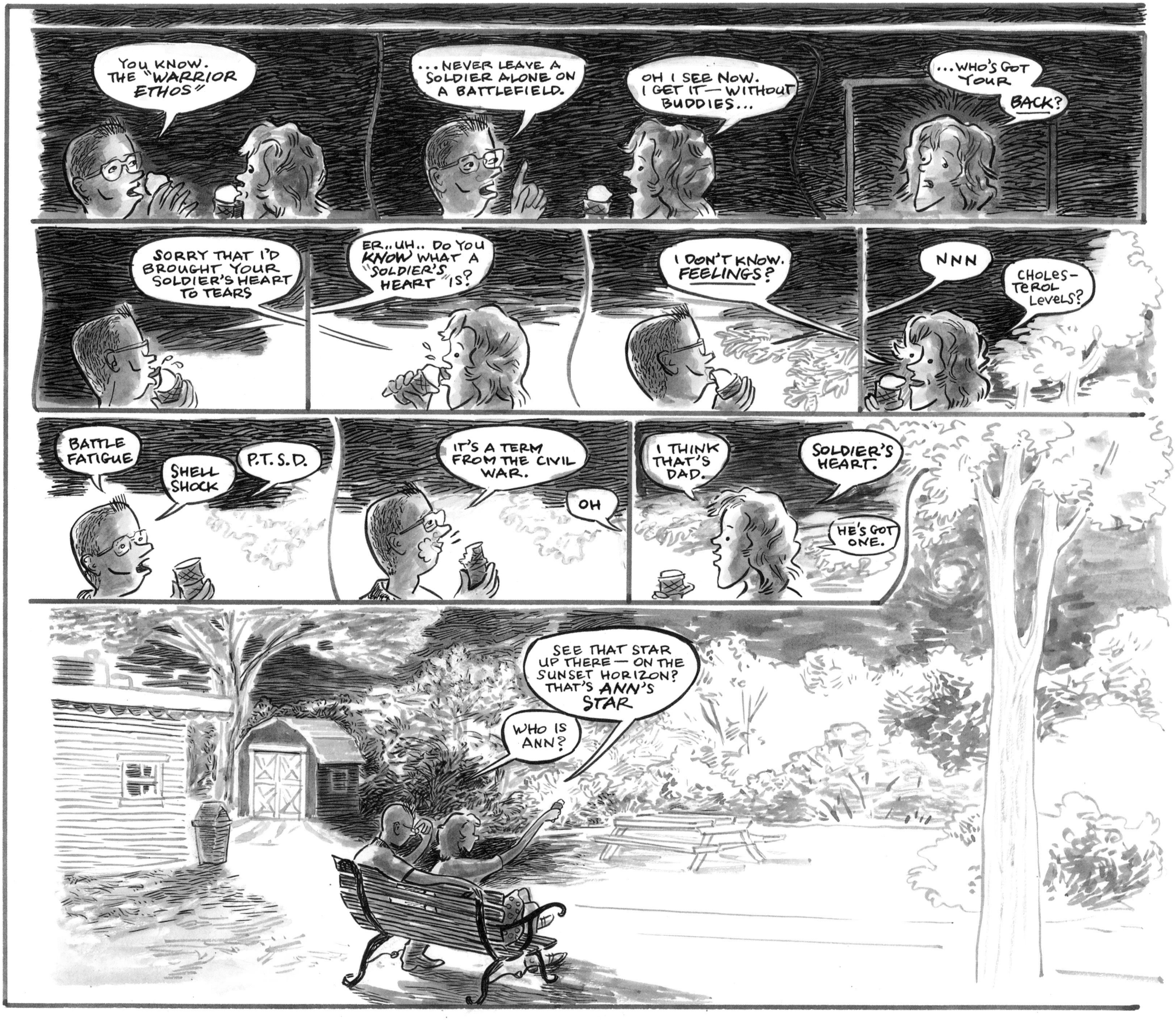
YOU KNOW. THE "WARRIOR ETHOS"
...NEVER LEAVE A SOLDIER ALONE ON A BATTLEFIELD.
OH I SEE NOW. I GET IT— WITHOUT BUDDIES...
...WHO'S GOT YOUR BACK?
SORRY THAT I'D BROUGHT YOUR SOLDIER'S HEART TO TEARS
ER.. UH.. DO YOU KNOW WHAT A "SOLDIER'S HEART" IS?
I DON'T KNOW. FEELINGS?
NNN
CHOLES-TEROL LEVELS?
BATTLE FATIGUE
SHELL SHOCK
P.T.S.D.
IT'S A TERM FROM THE CIVIL WAR.
OH
I THINK THAT'S DAD.
SOLDIER'S HEART.
HE'S GOT ONE.
SEE THAT STAR UP THERE — ON THE SUNSET HORIZON? THAT'S ANN'S STAR
WHO IS ANN?

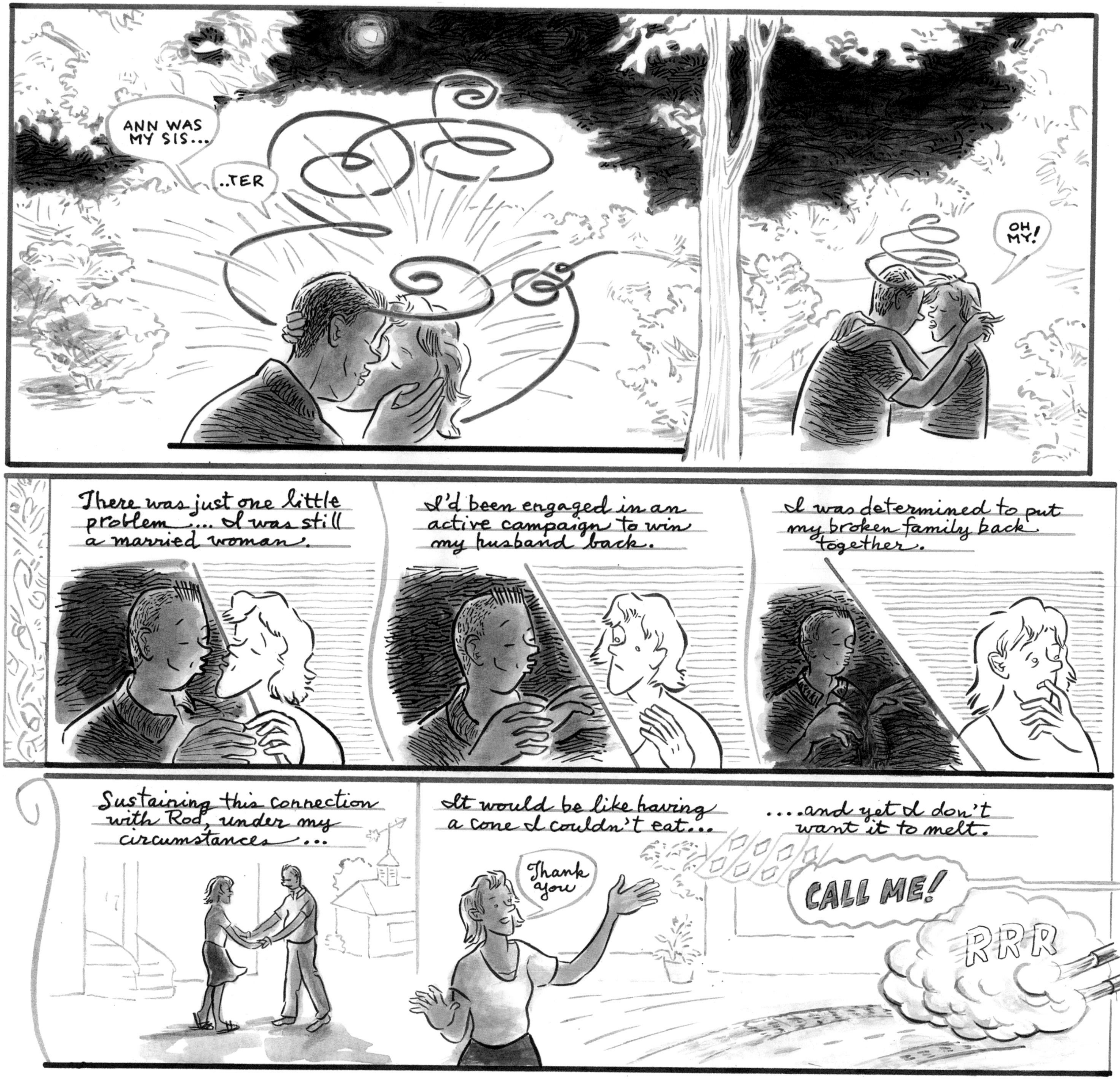
ANN WAS MY SIS...
..TER
OH MY!
There was just one little problem ... I was still a married woman.
I'd been engaged in an active campaign to win my husband back.
I was determined to put my broken family back together.
Sustaining this connection with Rod, under my circumstances...
It would be like having a cone I couldn't eat...
Thank you
...and yet I don't want it to melt.
CALL ME!
RRR

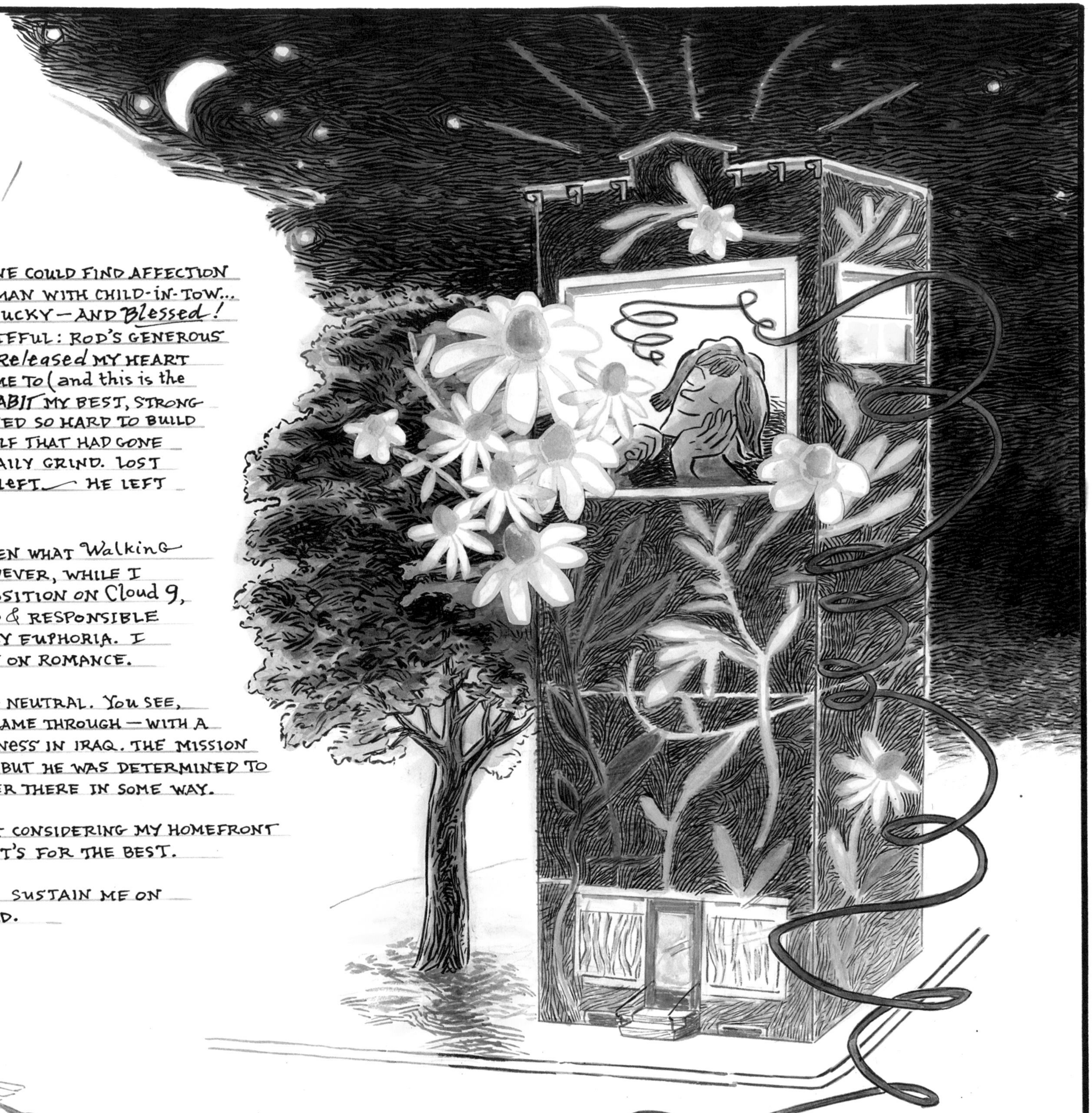

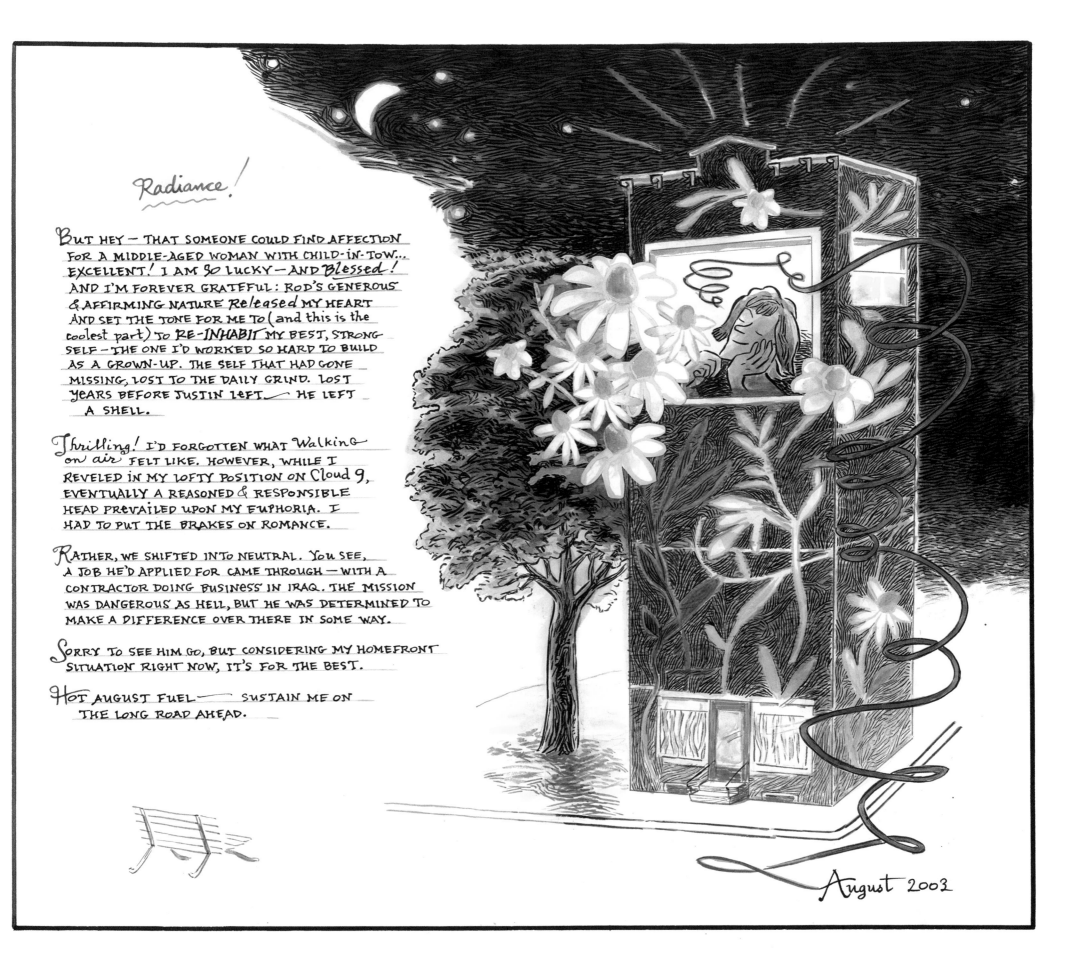

Radiance!

BUT HEY — THAT SOMEONE COULD FIND AFFECTION FOR A MIDDLE-AGED WOMAN WITH CHILD-IN-TOW… EXCELLENT! I AM SO LUCKY — AND *Blessed*! AND I'M FOREVER GRATEFUL: ROD'S GENEROUS & AFFIRMING NATURE *Released* MY HEART AND SET THE TONE FOR ME TO (and this is the coolest part) TO RE-INHABIT MY BEST, STRONG SELF — THE ONE I'D WORKED SO HARD TO BUILD AS A GROWN-UP. THE SELF THAT HAD GONE MISSING, LOST TO THE DAILY GRIND. LOST YEARS BEFORE JUSTIN LEFT — HE LEFT A SHELL.

Thrilling! I'D FORGOTTEN WHAT *Walking on air* FELT LIKE. HOWEVER, WHILE I REVELED IN MY LOFTY POSITION ON Cloud 9, EVENTUALLY A REASONED & RESPONSIBLE HEAD PREVAILED UPON MY EUPHORIA. I HAD TO PUT THE BRAKES ON ROMANCE.

RATHER, WE SHIFTED INTO NEUTRAL. YOU SEE, A JOB HE'D APPLIED FOR CAME THROUGH — WITH A CONTRACTOR DOING BUSINESS IN IRAQ. THE MISSION WAS DANGEROUS AS HELL, BUT HE WAS DETERMINED TO MAKE A DIFFERENCE OVER THERE IN SOME WAY.

SORRY TO SEE HIM GO, BUT CONSIDERING MY HOMEFRONT SITUATION RIGHT NOW, IT'S FOR THE BEST.

HOT AUGUST FUEL — SUSTAIN ME ON THE LONG ROAD AHEAD.

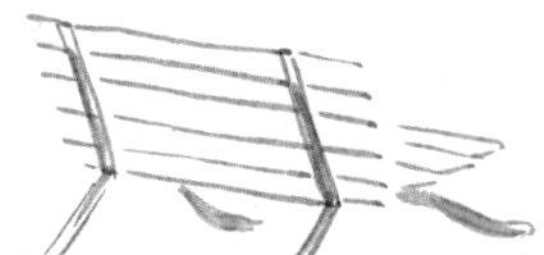

August 2003

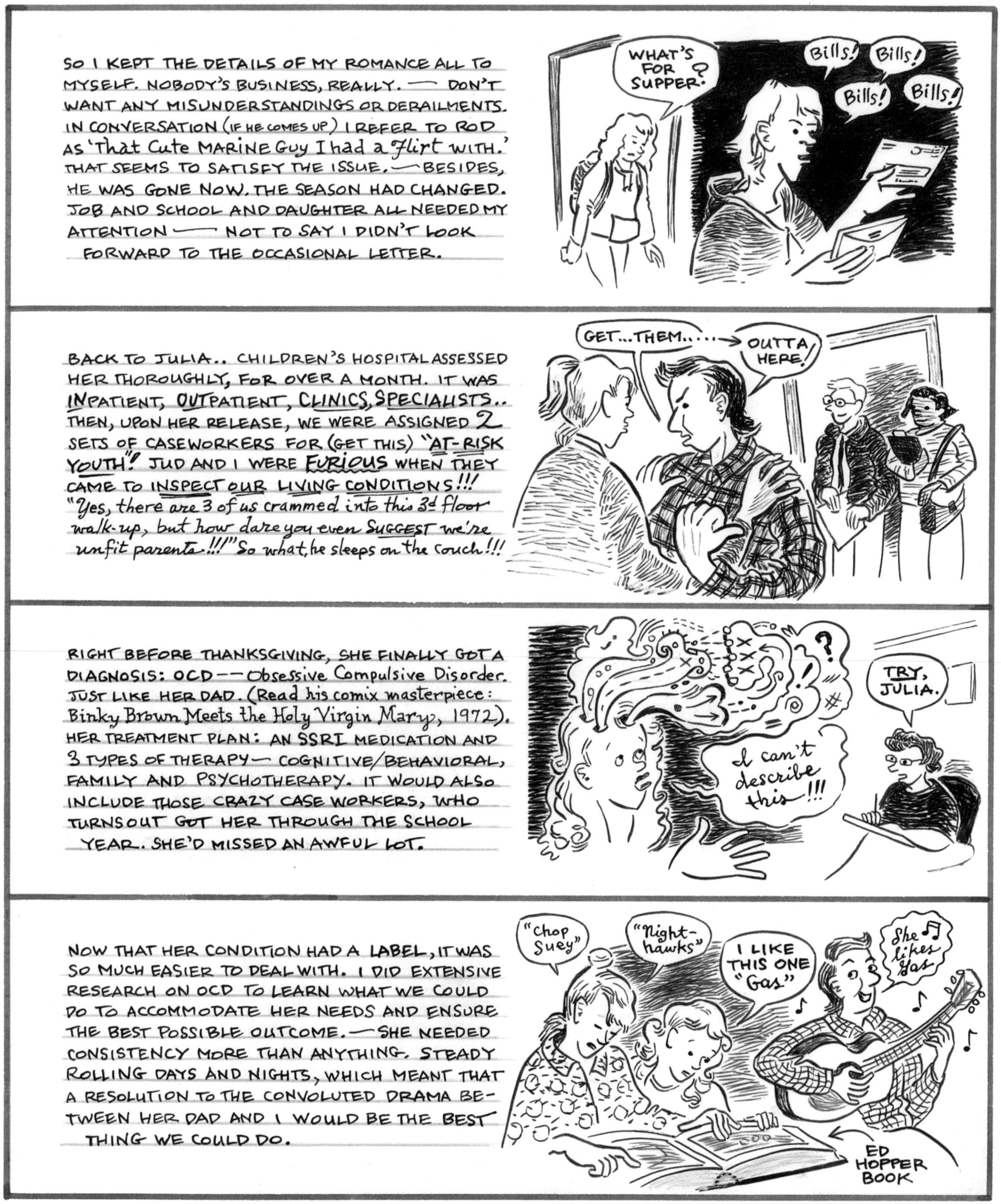
SO I KEPT THE DETAILS OF MY ROMANCE ALL TO MYSELF. NOBODY'S BUSINESS, REALLY. — DON'T WANT ANY MISUNDERSTANDINGS OR DERAILMENTS. IN CONVERSATION (IF HE COMES UP) I REFER TO ROD AS 'That Cute MARINE Guy I had a Flirt WITH.' THAT SEEMS TO SATISFY THE ISSUE. — BESIDES, HE WAS GONE NOW. THE SEASON HAD CHANGED. JOB AND SCHOOL AND DAUGHTER ALL NEEDED MY ATTENTION — NOT TO SAY I DIDN'T LOOK FORWARD TO THE OCCASIONAL LETTER.
WHAT'S FOR SUPPER?
Bills!
Bills!
Bills!
Bills!
BACK TO JULIA.. CHILDREN'S HOSPITAL ASSESSED HER THOROUGHLY, FOR OVER A MONTH. IT WAS INPATIENT, OUTPATIENT, CLINICS, SPECIALISTS.. THEN, UPON HER RELEASE, WE WERE ASSIGNED 2 SETS OF CASEWORKERS FOR (GET THIS) "AT-RISK YOUTH"! JUD AND I WERE FURIOUS WHEN THEY CAME TO INSPECT OUR LIVING CONDITIONS!!! "Yes, there are 3 of us crammed into this 3d floor walk-up, but how dare you even SUGGEST we're unfit parents!!!" So what, he sleeps on the couch!!!
GET...THEM.....→
OUTTA HERE!
RIGHT BEFORE THANKSGIVING, SHE FINALLY GOT A DIAGNOSIS: OCD — Obsessive Compulsive Disorder. JUST LIKE HER DAD. (Read his comix masterpiece: Binky Brown Meets the Holy Virgin Mary, 1972). HER TREATMENT PLAN: AN SSRI MEDICATION AND 3 TYPES OF THERAPY — COGNITIVE/BEHAVIORAL, FAMILY AND PSYCHOTHERAPY. IT WOULD ALSO INCLUDE THOSE CRAZY CASE WORKERS, WHO TURNS OUT GOT HER THROUGH THE SCHOOL YEAR. SHE'D MISSED AN AWFUL LOT.
I can't describe this!!!
TRY, JULIA.
NOW THAT HER CONDITION HAD A LABEL, IT WAS SO MUCH EASIER TO DEAL WITH. I DID EXTENSIVE RESEARCH ON OCD TO LEARN WHAT WE COULD DO TO ACCOMMODATE HER NEEDS AND ENSURE THE BEST POSSIBLE OUTCOME. — SHE NEEDED CONSISTENCY MORE THAN ANYTHING. STEADY ROLLING DAYS AND NIGHTS, WHICH MEANT THAT A RESOLUTION TO THE CONVOLUTED DRAMA BETWEEN HER DAD AND I WOULD BE THE BEST THING WE COULD DO.
"Chop Suey"
"Night-hawks"
I LIKE THIS ONE "Gas."
She likes Gas
ED HOPPER BOOK

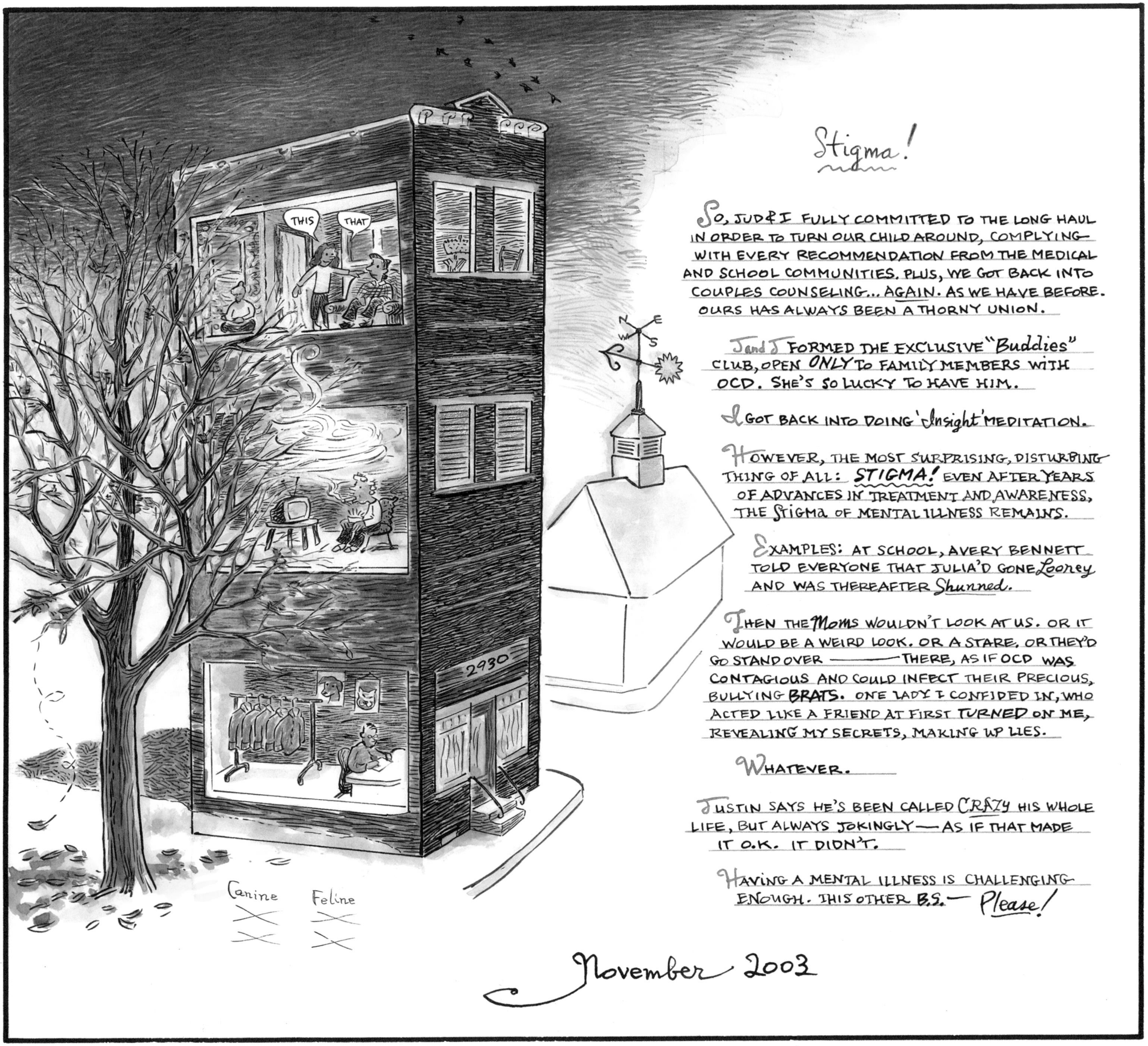

THIS
THAT
2930
Stigma!
So, Jud & I fully committed to the long haul in order to turn our child around, complying with every recommendation from the medical and school communities. Plus, we got back into couples counseling... again. As we have before. Ours has always been a thorny union.
J and J formed the exclusive "Buddies" club, open ONLY to family members with OCD. She's so lucky to have him.
I got back into doing 'Insight' meditation.
However, the most surprising, disturbing thing of all: STIGMA! Even after years of advances in treatment and awareness, the Stigma of mental illness remains.
Examples: At school, Avery Bennett told everyone that Julia'd gone Looney and was thereafter Shunned.
Then the Moms wouldn't look at us. Or it would be a weird look. Or a stare. Or they'd go stand over ——— there, as if OCD was contagious and could infect their precious, bullying BRATS. One lady I confided in, who acted like a friend at first TURNED on me, revealing my secrets, making up lies.
Whatever.
Justin says he's been called CRAZY his whole life, but always jokingly — as if that made it O.K. It didn't.
Having a mental illness is challenging enough. This other B.S. — Please!
Canine
Feline
November 2003

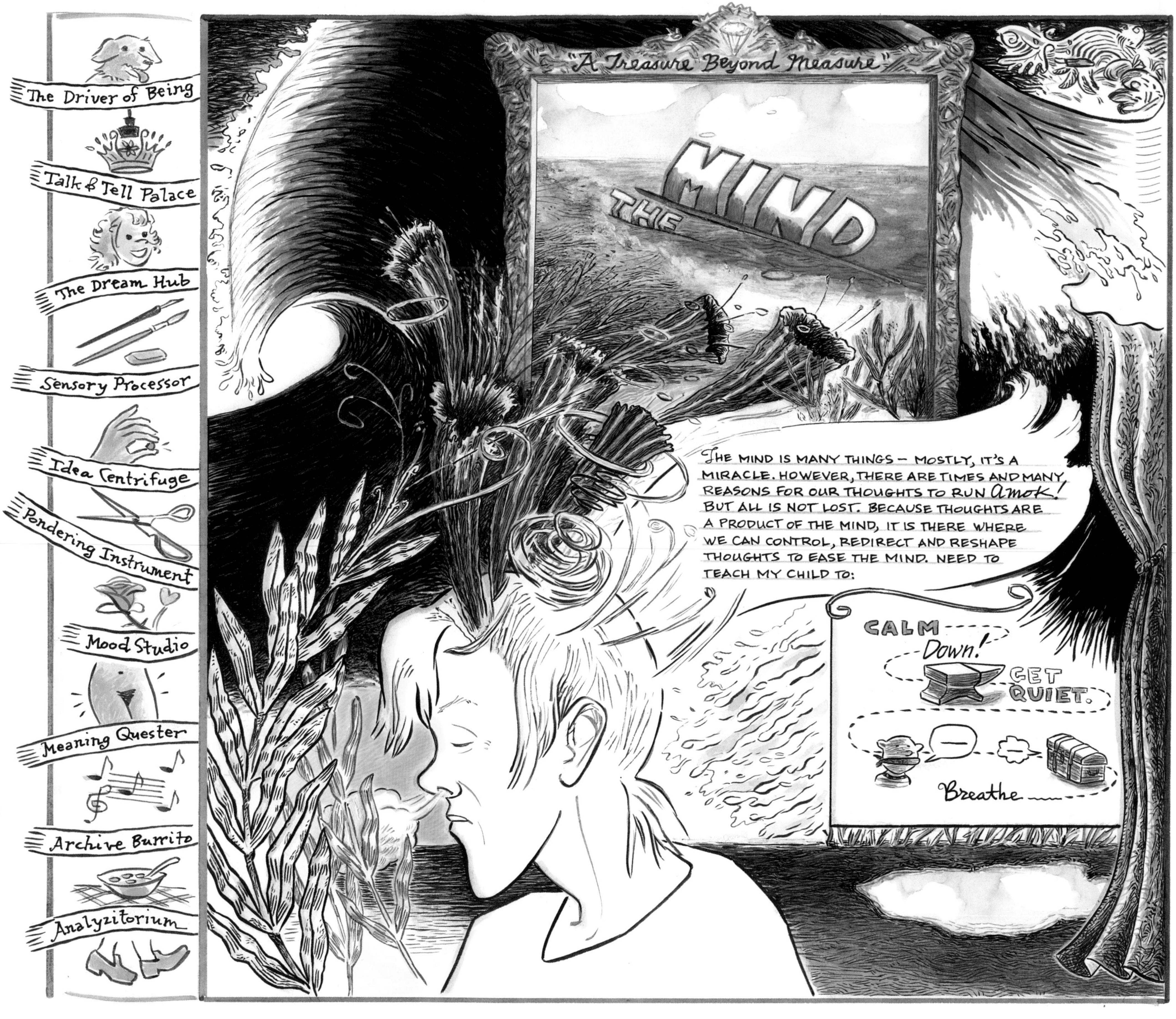

The Driver of Being
Talk & Tell Palace
The Dream Hub
Sensory Processor
Idea Centrifuge
Pondering Instrument
Mood Studio
Meaning Quester
Archive Burrito
Analyzitorium
"A Treasure Beyond Measure"
THE MIND
THE MIND IS MANY THINGS — MOSTLY, IT'S A MIRACLE. HOWEVER, THERE ARE TIMES AND MANY REASONS FOR OUR THOUGHTS TO RUN amok! BUT ALL IS NOT LOST. BECAUSE THOUGHTS ARE A PRODUCT OF THE MIND, IT IS THERE WHERE WE CAN CONTROL, REDIRECT AND RESHAPE THOUGHTS TO EASE THE MIND. NEED TO TEACH MY CHILD TO:
CALM Down!
GET QUIET.
Breathe......

HEY DAD!

THINK FAST!

HEY.

LET'S CALL MOM IN HERE

NO. LET MOTHER REST.

HUP!

MAKE ME PANCAKES FOR BREAKFAST

PAN-CAKES IT IS.

HE'S TERRIFIC WITH HER...
AND HE'S BEEN KIND AND GENEROUS TO ME.
SOULFULLY CLASSIC JUSTIN HAS TRULY RETURNED.

DESPITE THE GENTLE SHIFT OF MY HEART, (ROD), I STILL VALUE JUSTIN TREMENDOUSLY.

HE'S ONE OF THOSE ESSENTIALS. JUSTIN'S ABOUT *FIRE*. HE'S BROUGHT WARMTH TO MY LIFE AND NOURISHMENT. HIS *HEAT* HAS INSPIRED ME.

A BRILLIANT ILLUMINATION JUSTIN'S BROUGHT TO MY JOURNEY.

But...

Nite!

BUT I'M TRYING REALLY HARD TO FORGET THAT HE ALSO BURNED ME.

JEZ'S GAD! I CAN'T STAND THE SIGHT OF HIM.

I KNOW WHY HE'S HERE BUT WHY IS HE HERE!

THOUGHTS ARE A FACTOR. MEMORIES

BRAIN CIRCUITS, GOTTA REWIRE. NEED TO. FIND. SOLUTIONS

POSITIVE THOUGHTS. Positive thoughts.

Loving Kindness... COMPASSION... etc...

Sleepy

So Sleepy

ZZZZZ

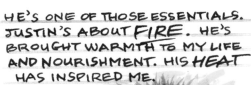

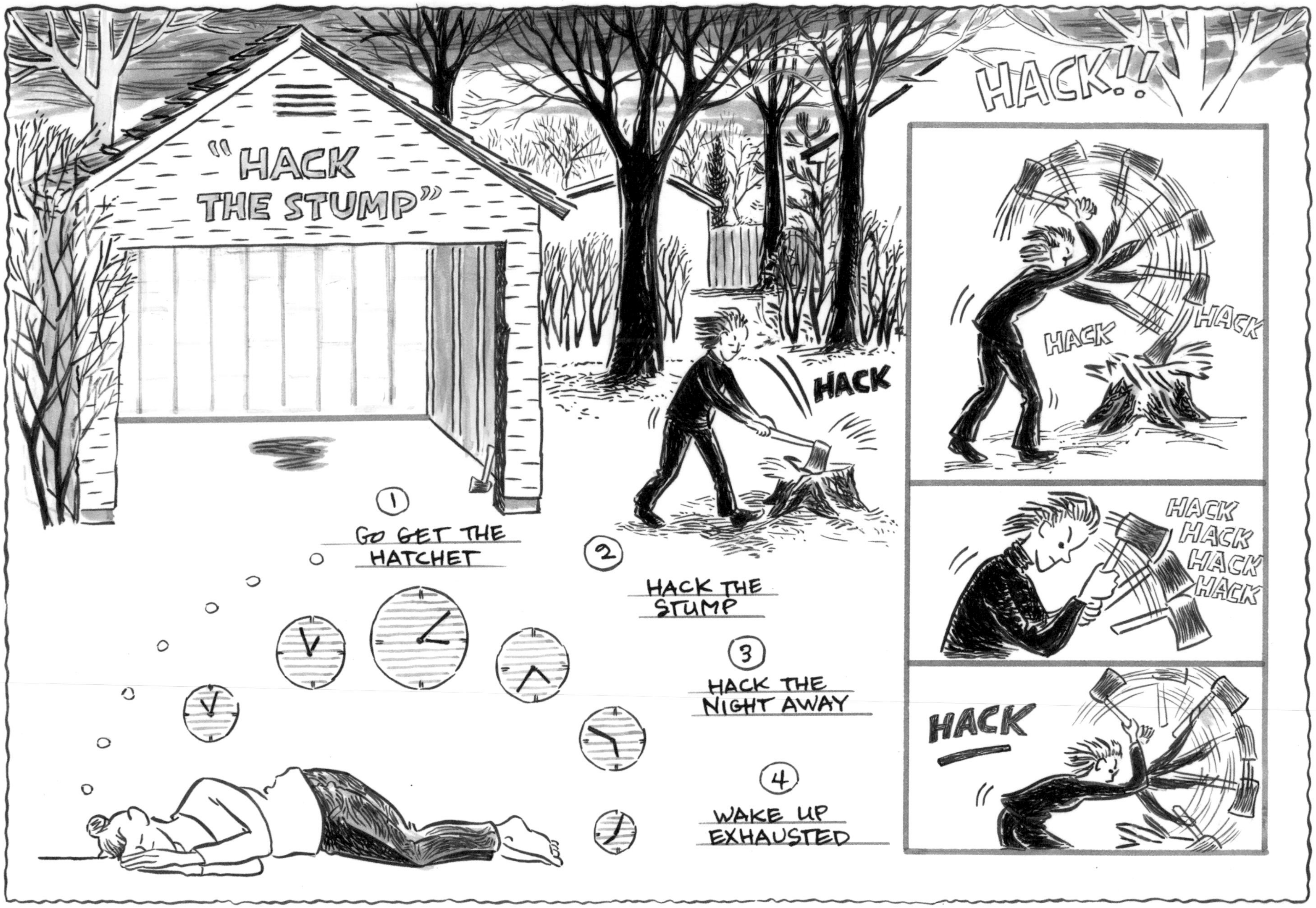
"HACK THE STUMP"
HACK!!
HACK
HACK
HACK
1 GO GET THE HATCHET
2 HACK THE STUMP
3 HACK THE NIGHT AWAY
4 WAKE UP EXHAUSTED
HACK HACK HACK HACK
HACK

BORN OUT OF THE FRUSTRATIONS I FELT WHEN JUSTIN LEFT, THIS REOCCURRING RAGE DREAM CAME NIGHTLY. MY UNRELENTING ATTACK ON THE POOR, BENIGN STUMP WAS NOT INTENDED TO OBLITERATE IT, BUT TO PROVIDE AN OUTLET FOR MY WEARY-WORN PSYCHE. — IT TAPERED OFF SOMEWHAT DURING DAD'S PROJECT AND STOPPED ALTOGETHER WHEN I MET ROD. NOW JUSTIN WAS BACK AND SO WAS THE DREAM. BUT TONIGHT, THE OUTCOME WOULD BE DIFFERENT.

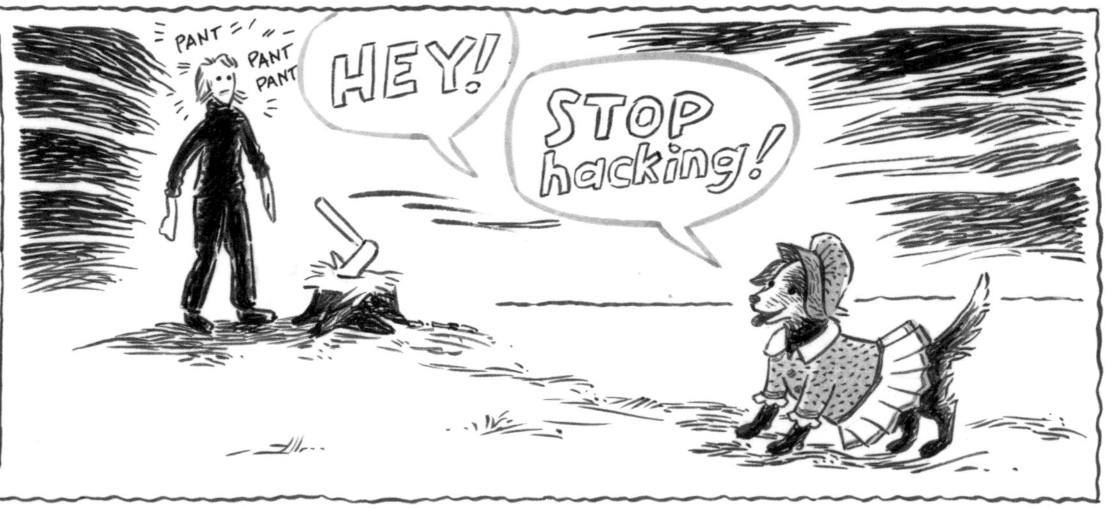
PANT
PANT PANT
HEY!
STOP hacking!

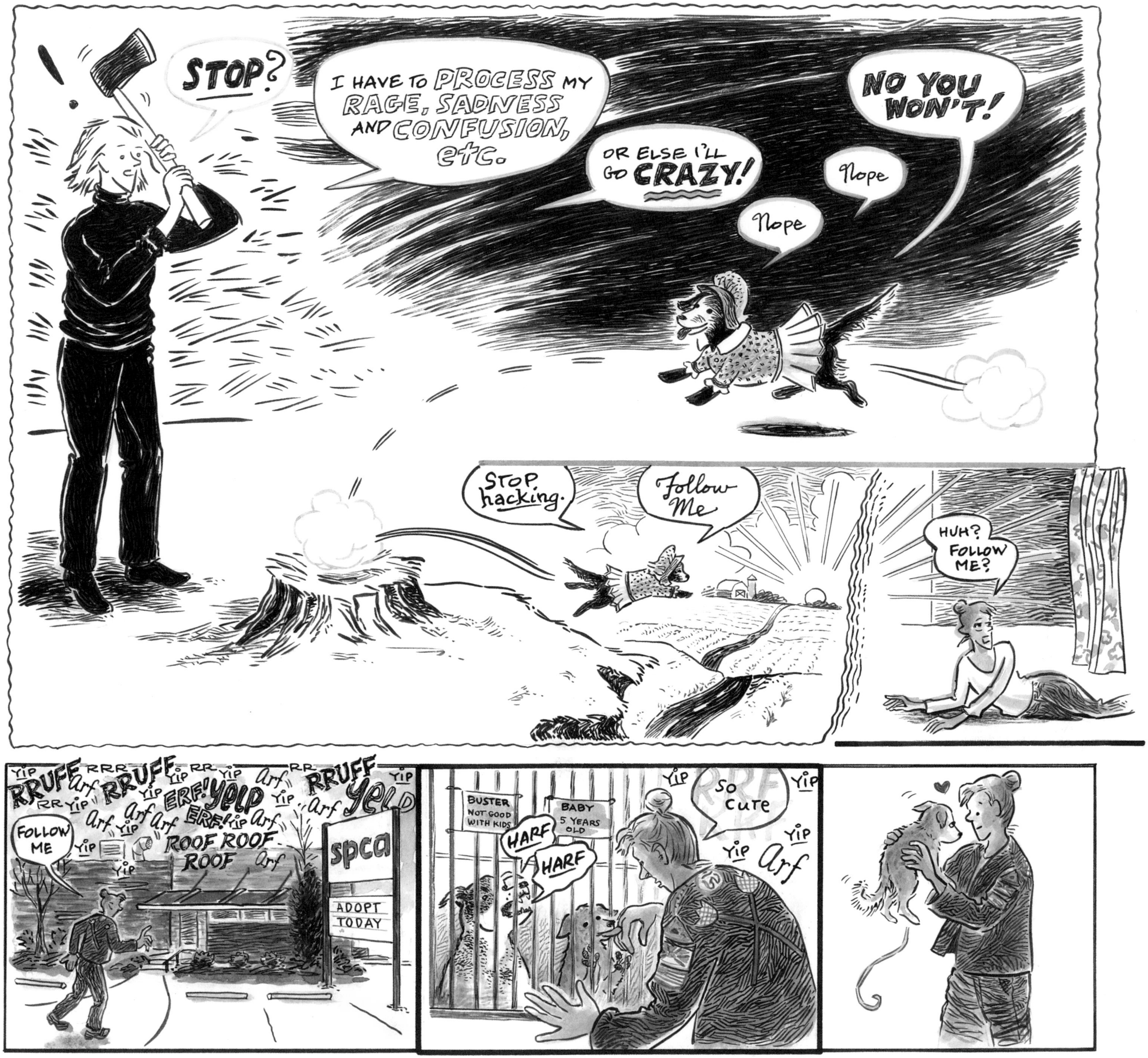

STOP?
I HAVE TO PROCESS MY RAGE, SADNESS AND CONFUSION, etc.
OR ELSE I'LL GO CRAZY!
NO YOU WON'T!
Nope
Nope
STOP hacking.
Follow Me
HUH? FOLLOW ME?
YIP RRUFF RRR arf RRUFF YIP RR RR RRUFF YIP
RR YIP ERF! YELP arf YIP YELP
FOLLOW ME
ROOF ROOF ROOF
spca
ADOPT TODAY
BUSTER NOT GOOD WITH KIDS
BABY 5 YEARS OLD
HARF
HARF
SO CUTE
YIP
arf

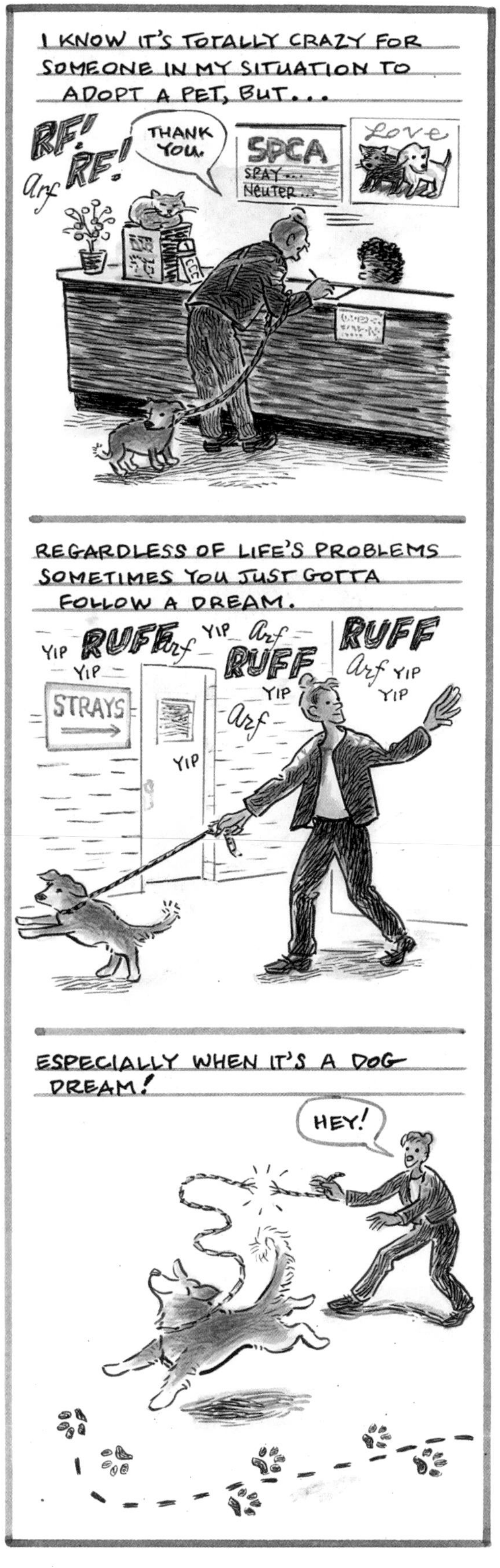
I KNOW IT'S TOTALLY CRAZY FOR SOMEONE IN MY SITUATION TO ADOPT A PET, BUT...
RF! RF!
Arf
THANK YOU.
SPCA
SPAY...
NEUTER...
Love
REGARDLESS OF LIFE'S PROBLEMS SOMETIMES YOU JUST GOTTA FOLLOW A DREAM.
YIP RUFF Arf YIP Arf RUFF RUFF
YIP
Arf YIP YIP
YIP
STRAYS
Arf
YIP
ESPECIALLY WHEN IT'S A DOG DREAM!
HEY!

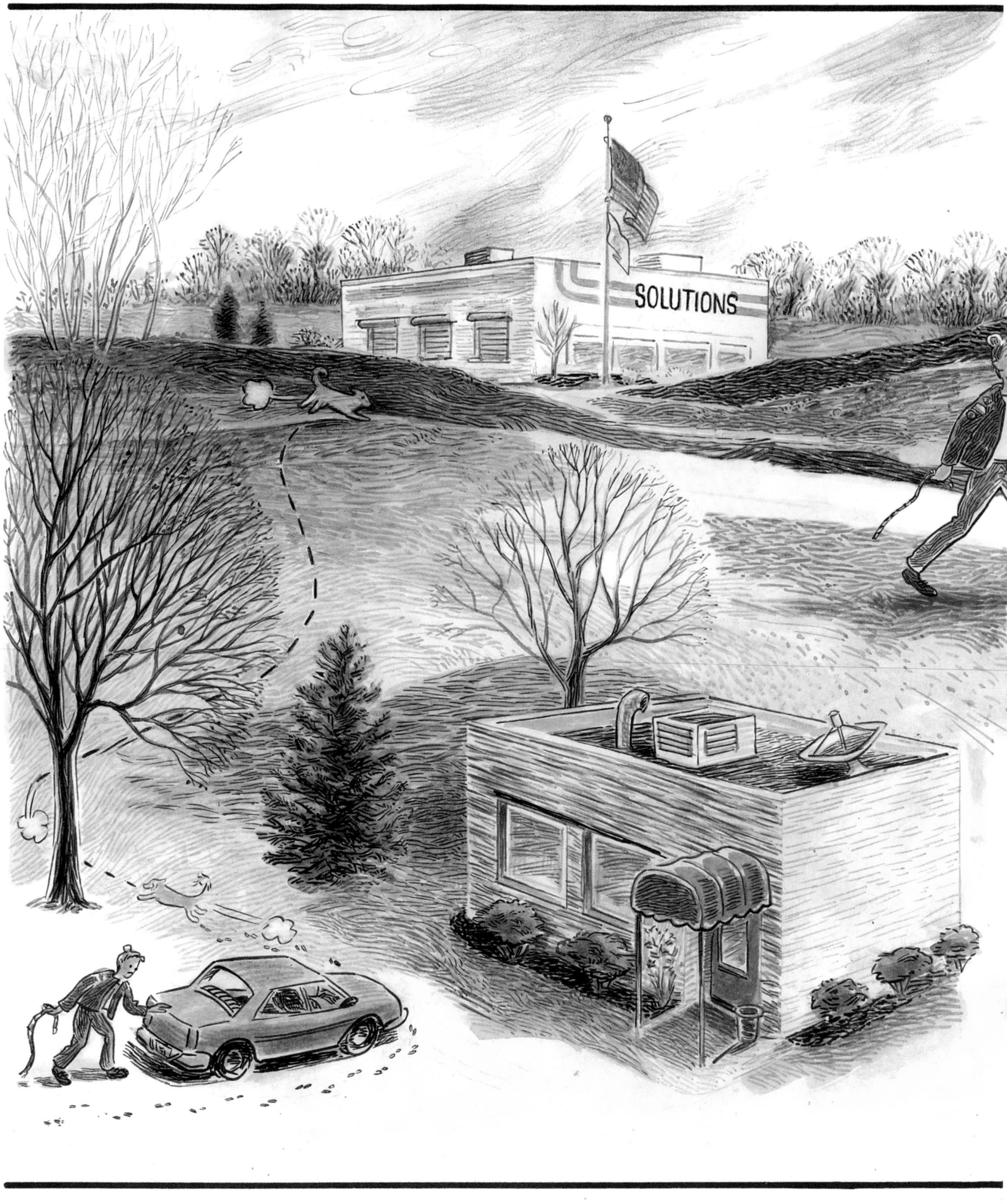
SOLUTIONS

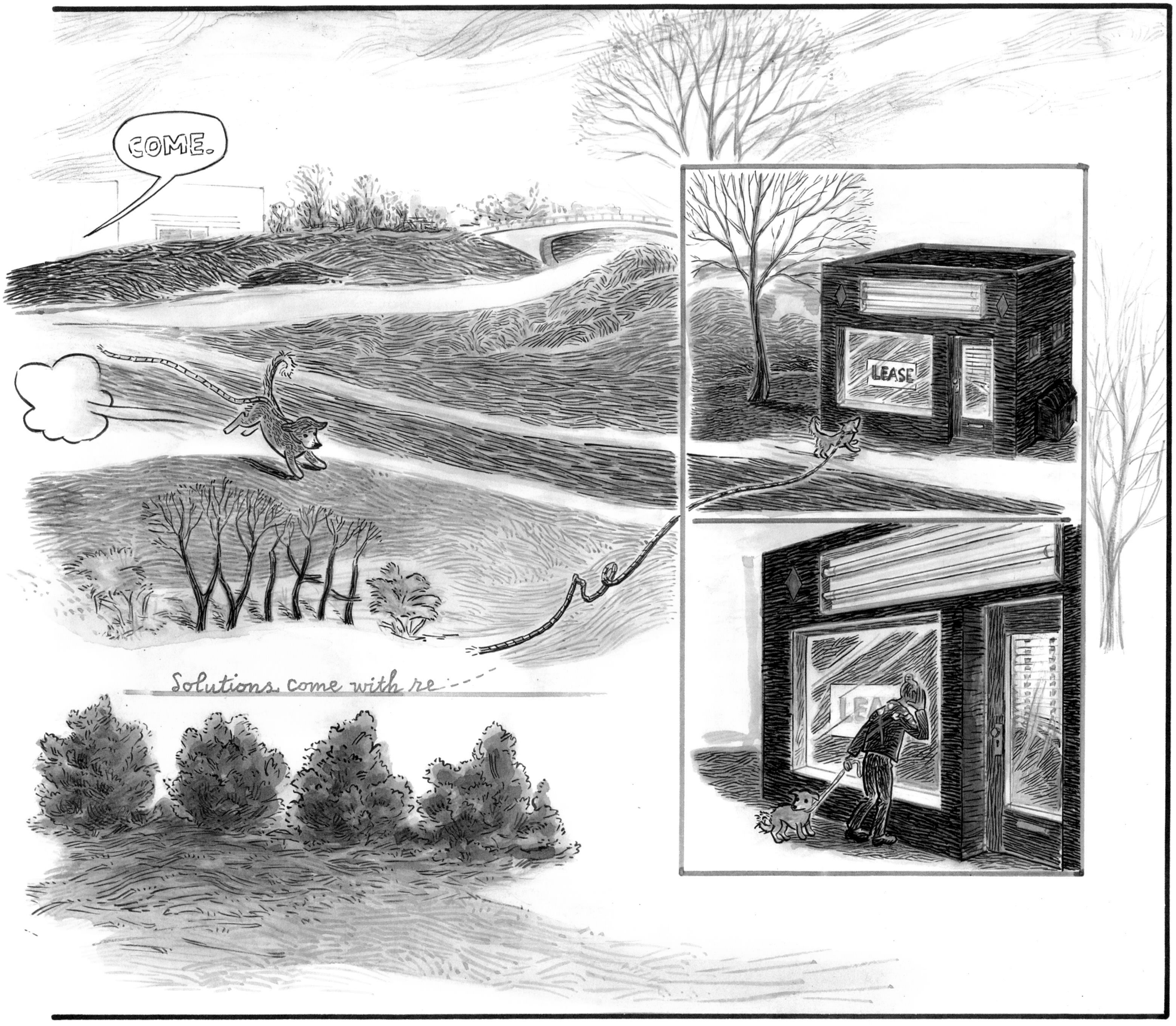
COME.
LEASE
Solutions come with re

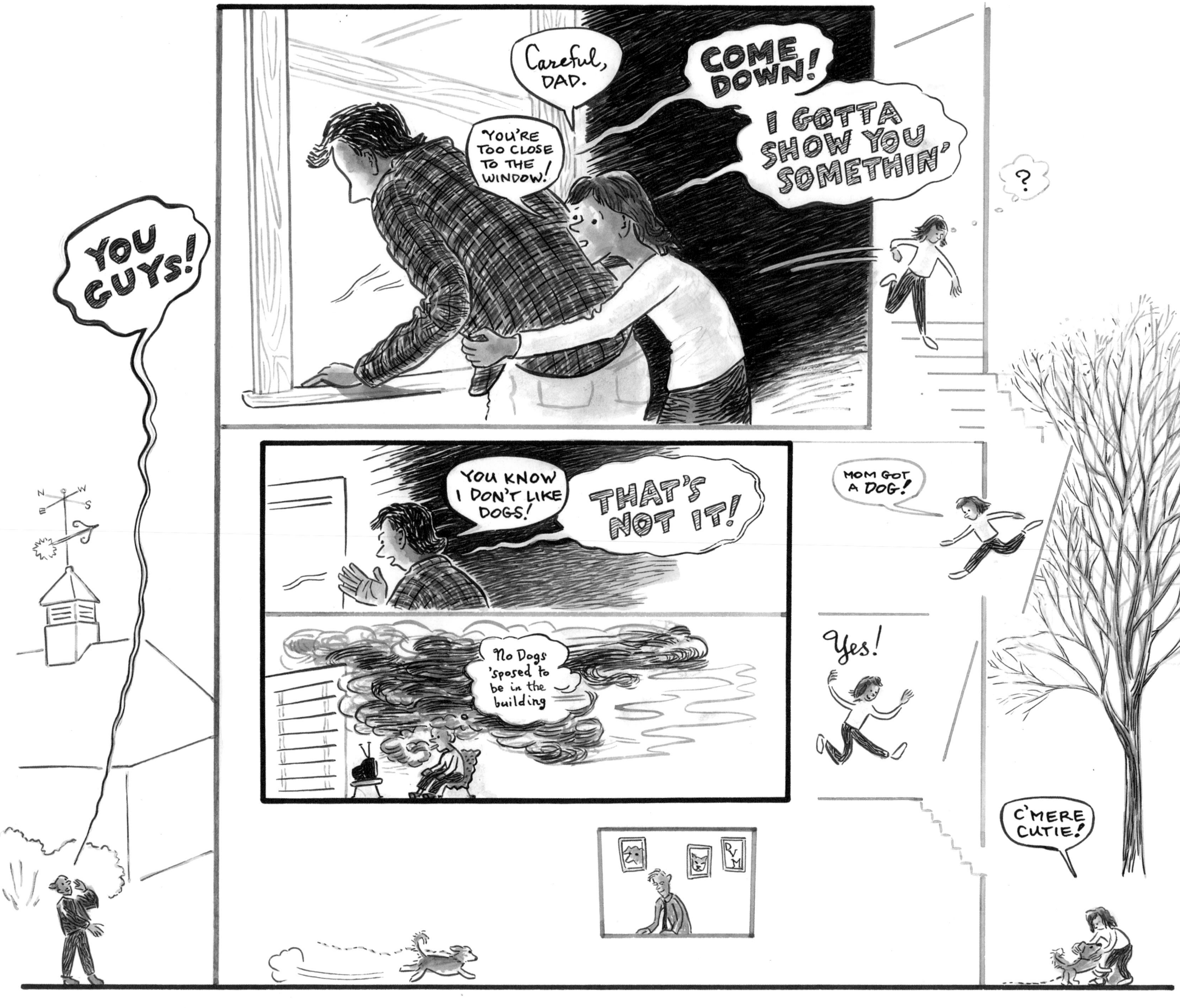
Careful, DAD.
YOU'RE TOO CLOSE TO THE WINDOW!
COME DOWN!
I GOTTA SHOW YOU SOMETHIN'
?
YOU GUYS!
YOU KNOW I DON'T LIKE DOGS!
THAT'S NOT IT!
MOM GOT A DOG!
No Dogs 'sposed to be in the building
Yes!
C'MERE CUTIE!
N
W
E
S
D.V.M.

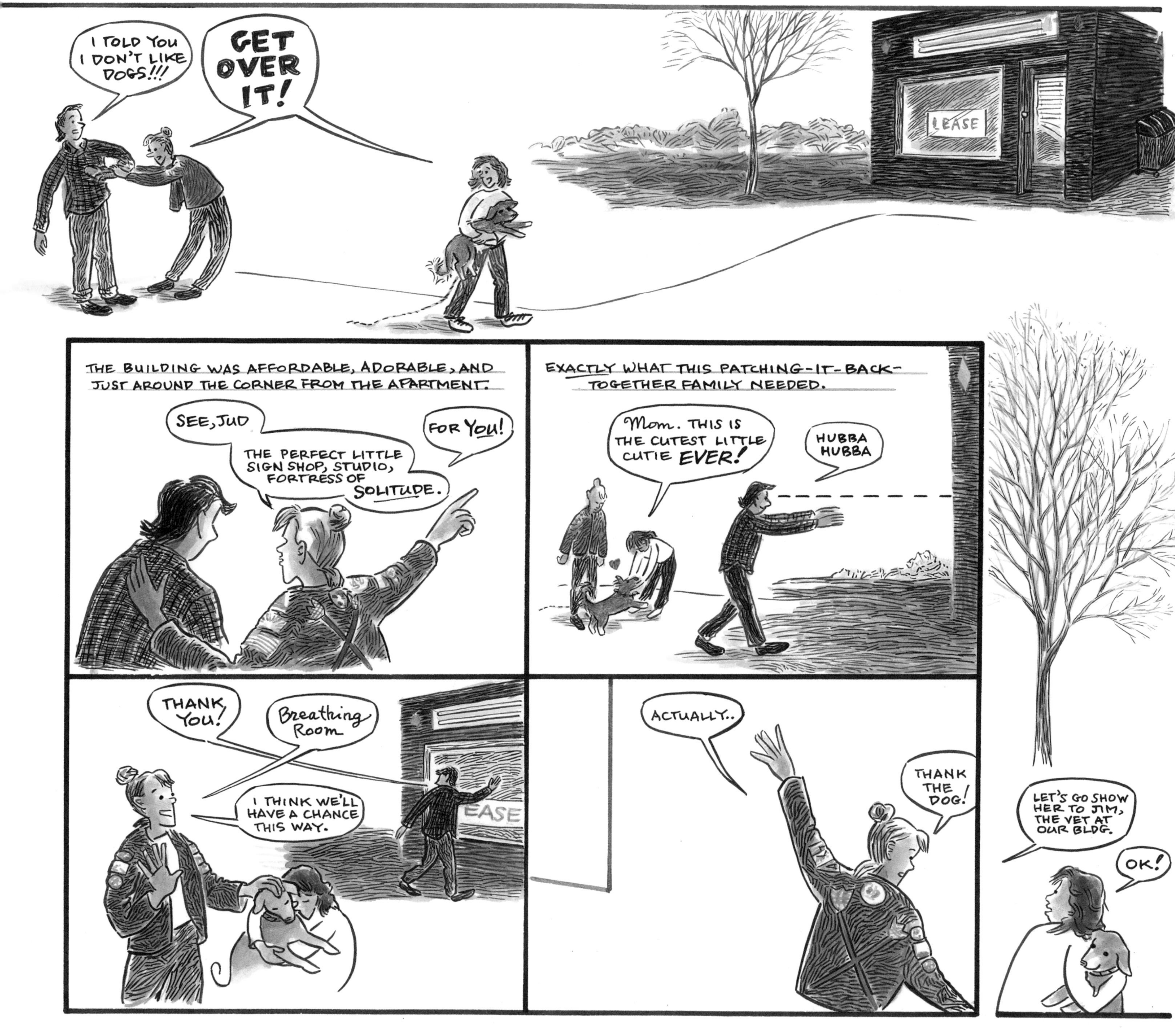
I TOLD YOU I DON'T LIKE DOGS!!!
GET OVER IT!
LEASE
THE BUILDING WAS AFFORDABLE, ADORABLE, AND JUST AROUND THE CORNER FROM THE APARTMENT.
SEE, JUD
THE PERFECT LITTLE SIGN SHOP, STUDIO, FORTRESS OF SOLITUDE.
FOR YOU!
EXACTLY WHAT THIS PATCHING-IT-BACK-TOGETHER FAMILY NEEDED.
Mom. THIS IS THE CUTEST LITTLE CUTIE EVER!
HUBBA HUBBA
THANK YOU!
Breathing Room
I THINK WE'LL HAVE A CHANCE THIS WAY.
EASE
ACTUALLY..
THANK THE DOG!
LET'S GO SHOW HER TO JIM, THE VET AT OUR BLDG.
OK!

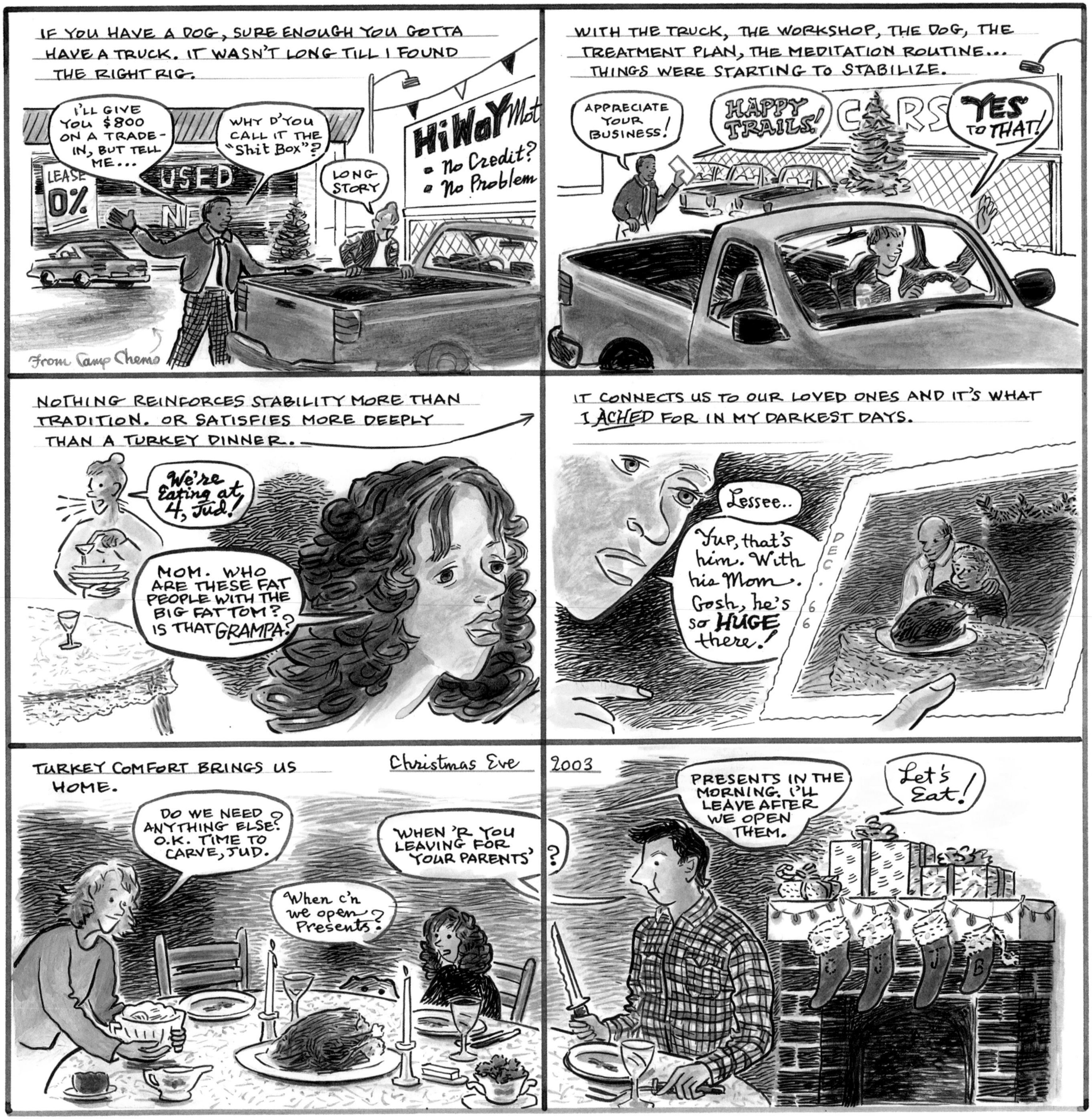
IF YOU HAVE A DOG, SURE ENOUGH YOU GOTTA HAVE A TRUCK. IT WASN'T LONG TILL I FOUND THE RIGHT RIG.
I'LL GIVE YOU $800 ON A TRADE-IN, BUT TELL ME...
WHY D'YOU CALL IT THE "Shit Box"?
LONG STORY
LEASE 0%
USED
HiWaY Mot
No Credit?
No Problem
From Camp Chemo
WITH THE TRUCK, THE WORKSHOP, THE DOG, THE TREATMENT PLAN, THE MEDITATION ROUTINE... THINGS WERE STARTING TO STABILIZE.
APPRECIATE YOUR BUSINESS!
HAPPY TRAILS!
CARS
YES TO THAT!
NOTHING REINFORCES STABILITY MORE THAN TRADITION. OR SATISFIES MORE DEEPLY THAN A TURKEY DINNER.
We're Eating at 4, Jud!
MOM. WHO ARE THESE FAT PEOPLE WITH THE BIG FAT TOM? IS THAT GRAMPA?
IT CONNECTS US TO OUR LOVED ONES AND IT'S WHAT I ACHED FOR IN MY DARKEST DAYS.
Lessee..
Yup, that's him. With his Mom. Gosh, he's so HUGE there!
DEC. 66
TURKEY COMFORT BRINGS US HOME.
Christmas Eve 2003
DO WE NEED ANYTHING ELSE? O.K. TIME TO CARVE, JUD.
WHEN 'R YOU LEAVING FOR YOUR PARENTS'?
When c'n we open Presents?
PRESENTS IN THE MORNING. I'LL LEAVE AFTER WE OPEN THEM.
Let's Eat!

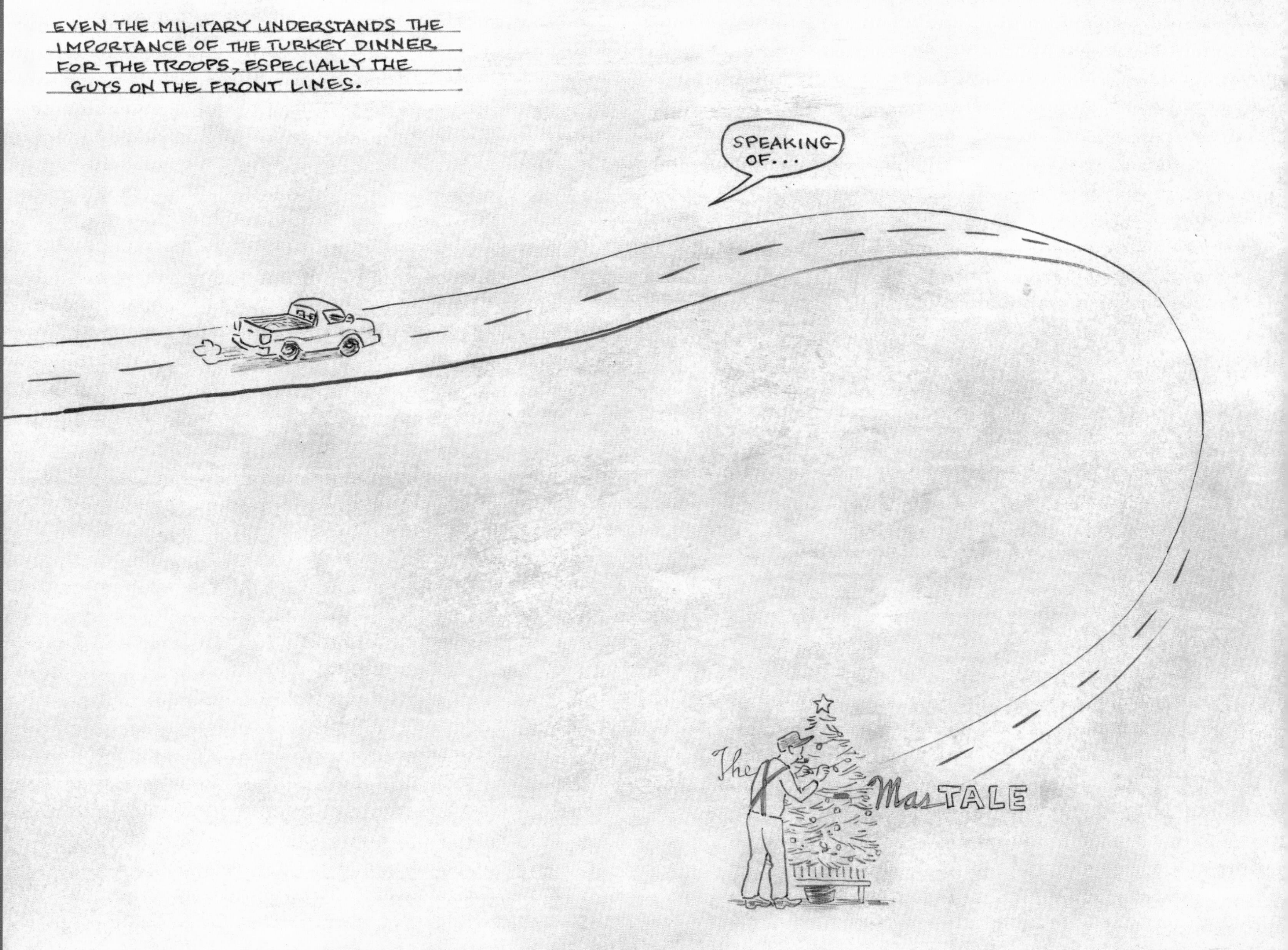
EVEN THE MILITARY UNDERSTANDS THE IMPORTANCE OF THE TURKEY DINNER FOR THE TROOPS, ESPECIALLY THE GUYS ON THE FRONT LINES.
SPEAKING OF...
The
MasTALE

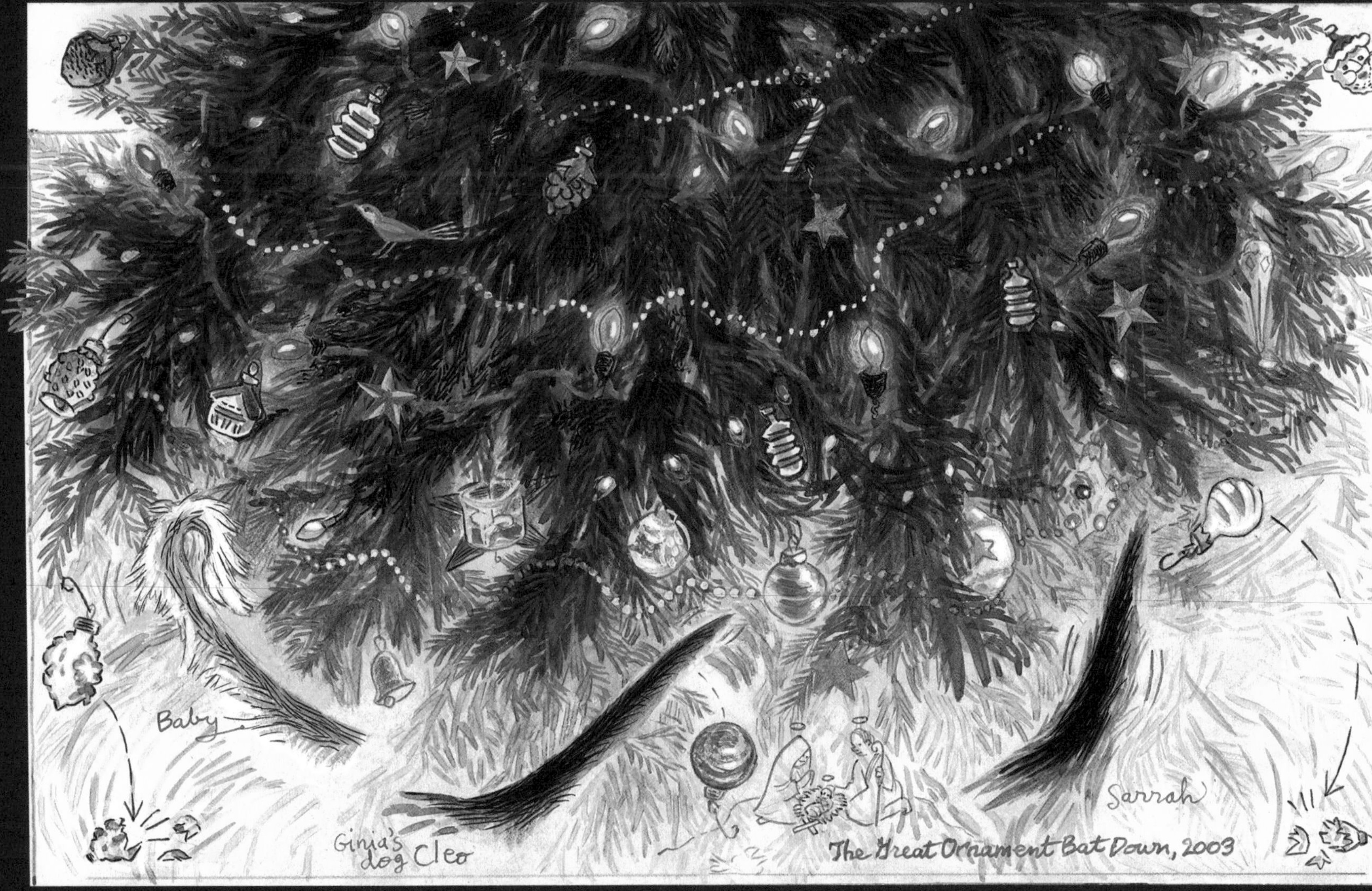
Baby
Ginia's dog Cleo
Sarrah
The Great Ornament Bat Down, 2003

O Tannenbaum! O Tannenbaum! Wie treu sind deine Blätter! Your ornaments are dazzle-ing, 'til dog tails almost chaos bring! — Oh Christmas tree, oh Christmas tree — How loyal are your branches!

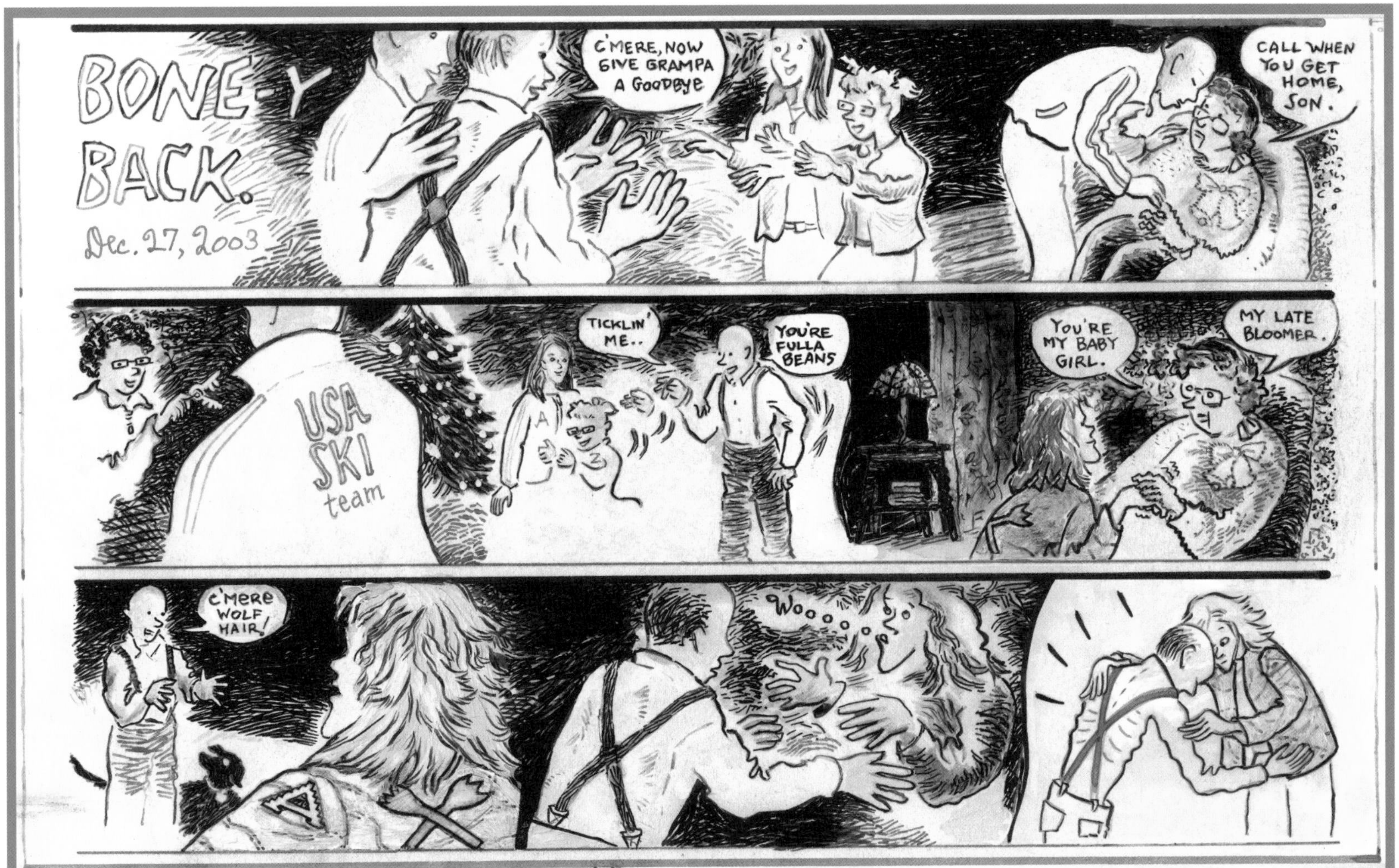
BONE-Y BACK.
Dec. 27, 2003
C'MERE, NOW GIVE GRAMPA A GOODBYE
CALL WHEN YOU GET HOME, SON.
USA SKI team
TICKLIN' ME..
YOU'RE FULLA BEANS
YOU'RE MY BABY GIRL.
MY LATE BLOOMER.
C'MERE WOLF HAIR!
Woooooo

DAD TRIES. HE REALLY DOES. BUT WHY IN THE HECK WOULD ANYONE PUT DELICATE HAND-BLOWN DANGLERS LOW ENOUGH FOR DOG TAILS TO **LOFT** THEM ACROSS THE ROOM LIKE **MISSILES**? STILL, YOU GOTTA GIVE IT TO CHUCK BECAUSE THE TREE TRIMMING TORCH HAD RATHER ABRUPTLY BEEN PASSED TO HIM UPON **CHRISTMAS LOVIN' MOM'S** INCAPACITATION. HIS CONTRIBUTION TO THE YULETIDE TRADITION: CUSS DECORATING.

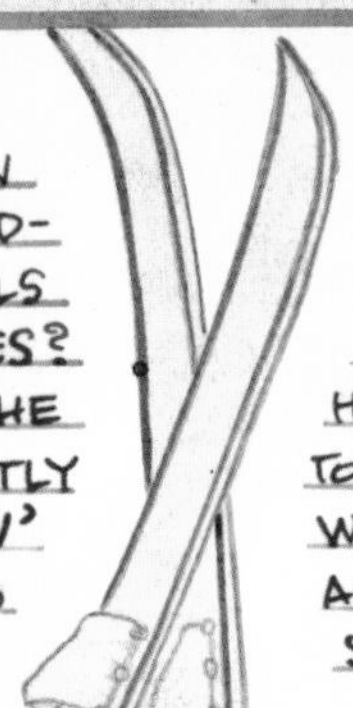

TODAY IS DEC. 27. MY BROTHER JIM AND HIS FAMILY ARE HEADED BACK UP TO N.Y. I WAS OUT THE DOOR, TOO, HAVING DRIVEN OVER FROM CINCI ON X-MAS MORNING. CHRISTMAS EVE WAS SPENT WITH **JUSTIN** and **JULIA** HAVING A NICE MEAL. JIM AND I WOULD GO IN TANDEM TO INDY, STOP FOR A MILKSHAKE, THEN GO OUR SEPARATE WAYS— OH YEAH. SOMETHING TO NOTE: WHILE LOOKING AROUND FOR BLEACH TO CLEAN UP DOG VOMIT (BABY GOT INTO SOME GARBAGE) JIM CAME ACROSS A **HUGE** MOUSE HOLE.

How loyal I am to the winter landscape! Graphically exquisite like an expensive Tiffany lamp. I especially like it on the cusp between 'all that's been known in daylight' and 'yield to sobering dusk.' Fall in.

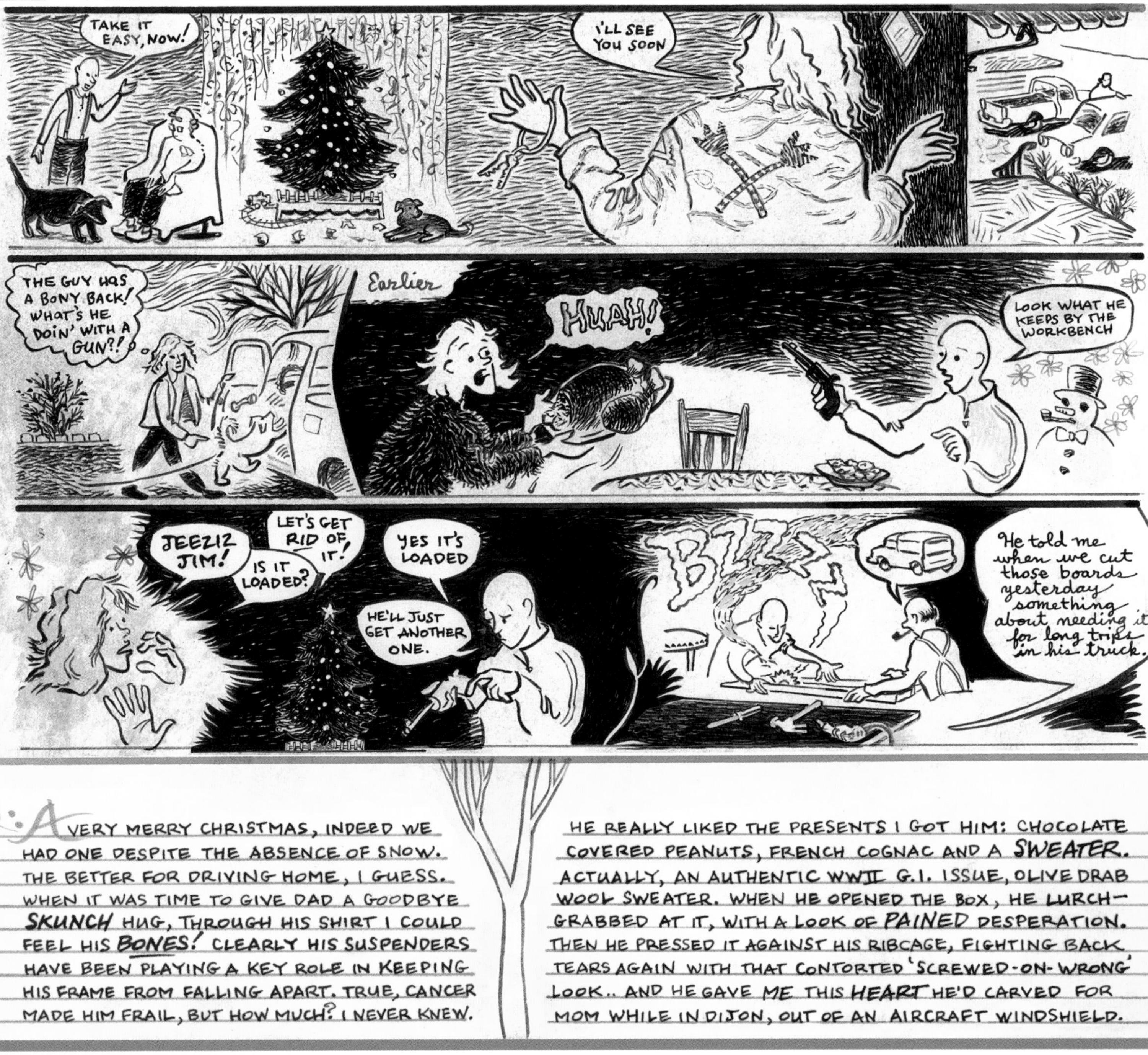
TAKE IT EASY, NOW!
I'LL SEE YOU SOON
THE GUY HAS A BONY BACK! WHAT'S HE DOIN' WITH A GUN?!
Earlier
HUAH!
LOOK WHAT HE KEEPS BY THE WORKBENCH
JEEZIZ JIM!
LET'S GET RID OF IT!
IS IT LOADED?
YES IT'S LOADED
HE'LL JUST GET ANOTHER ONE.
He told me when we cut those boards yesterday something about needing it for long trips in his truck.

A VERY MERRY CHRISTMAS, INDEED WE HAD ONE DESPITE THE ABSENCE OF SNOW. THE BETTER FOR DRIVING HOME, I GUESS. WHEN IT WAS TIME TO GIVE DAD A GOODBYE *SKUNCH* HUG, THROUGH HIS SHIRT I COULD FEEL HIS *BONES!* CLEARLY HIS SUSPENDERS HAVE BEEN PLAYING A KEY ROLE IN KEEPING HIS FRAME FROM FALLING APART. TRUE, CANCER MADE HIM FRAIL, BUT HOW MUCH? I NEVER KNEW.

HE REALLY LIKED THE PRESENTS I GOT HIM: CHOCOLATE COVERED PEANUTS, FRENCH COGNAC AND A **SWEATER.** ACTUALLY, AN AUTHENTIC WWII G.I. ISSUE, OLIVE DRAB WOOL SWEATER. WHEN HE OPENED THE BOX, HE **LURCH**-GRABBED AT IT, WITH A LOOK OF *PAINED* DESPERATION. THEN HE PRESSED IT AGAINST HIS RIBCAGE, FIGHTING BACK TEARS AGAIN WITH THAT CONTORTED 'SCREWED-ON-WRONG' LOOK.. AND HE GAVE *ME* THIS ***HEART*** HE'D CARVED FOR MOM WHILE IN DIJON, OUT OF AN AIRCRAFT WINDSHIELD.

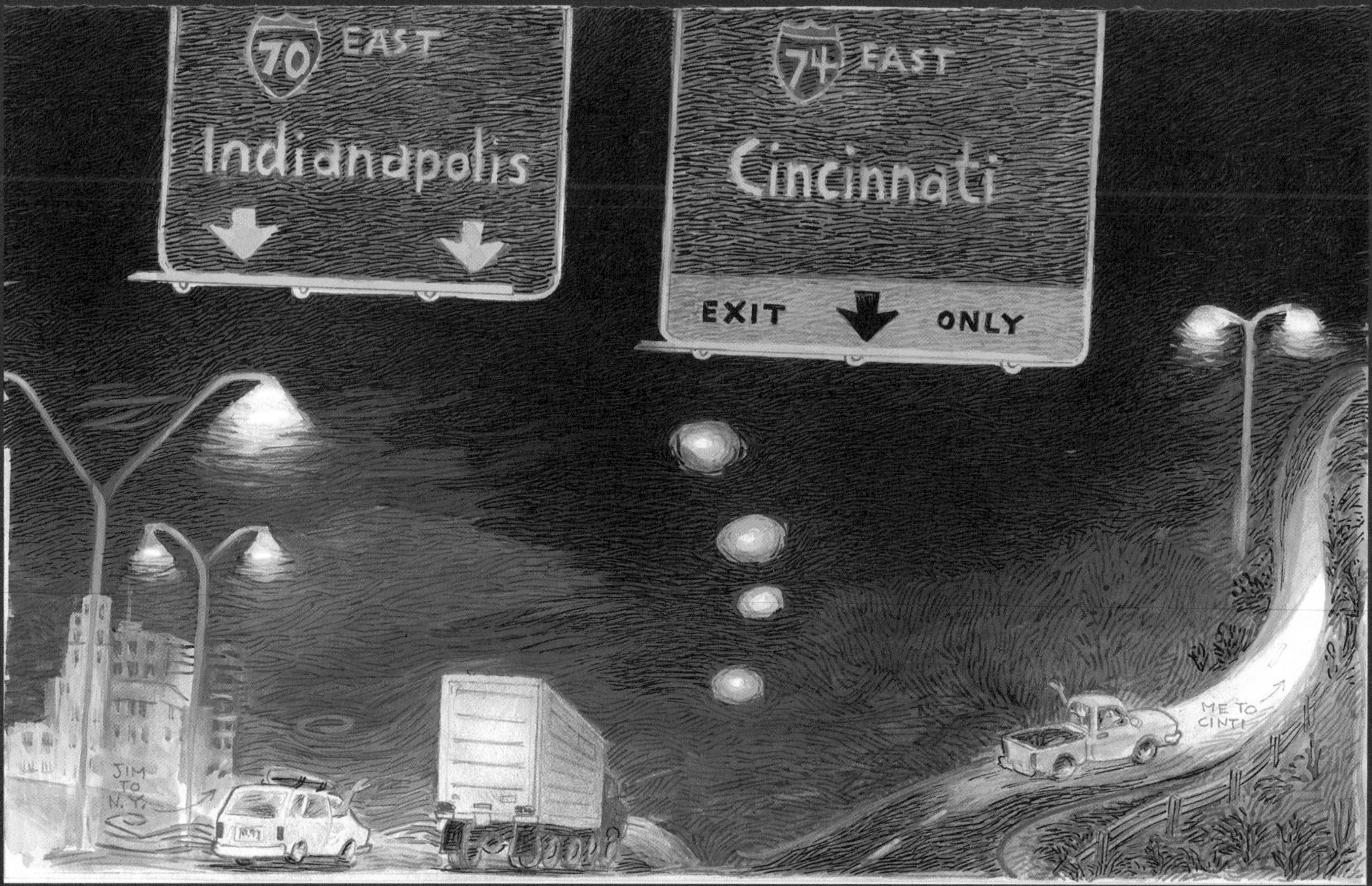
70 EAST
Indianapolis
74 EAST
Cincinnati
EXIT ONLY
JIM TO N.Y.
ME TO CINTI

*Yield to the municipal pink sky, its atmospheric opalescence,
its favorable, cost-saving glow. Are your bricks dissolving, fair city?
And how clever to challenge my assumption that 'black' top really is.*

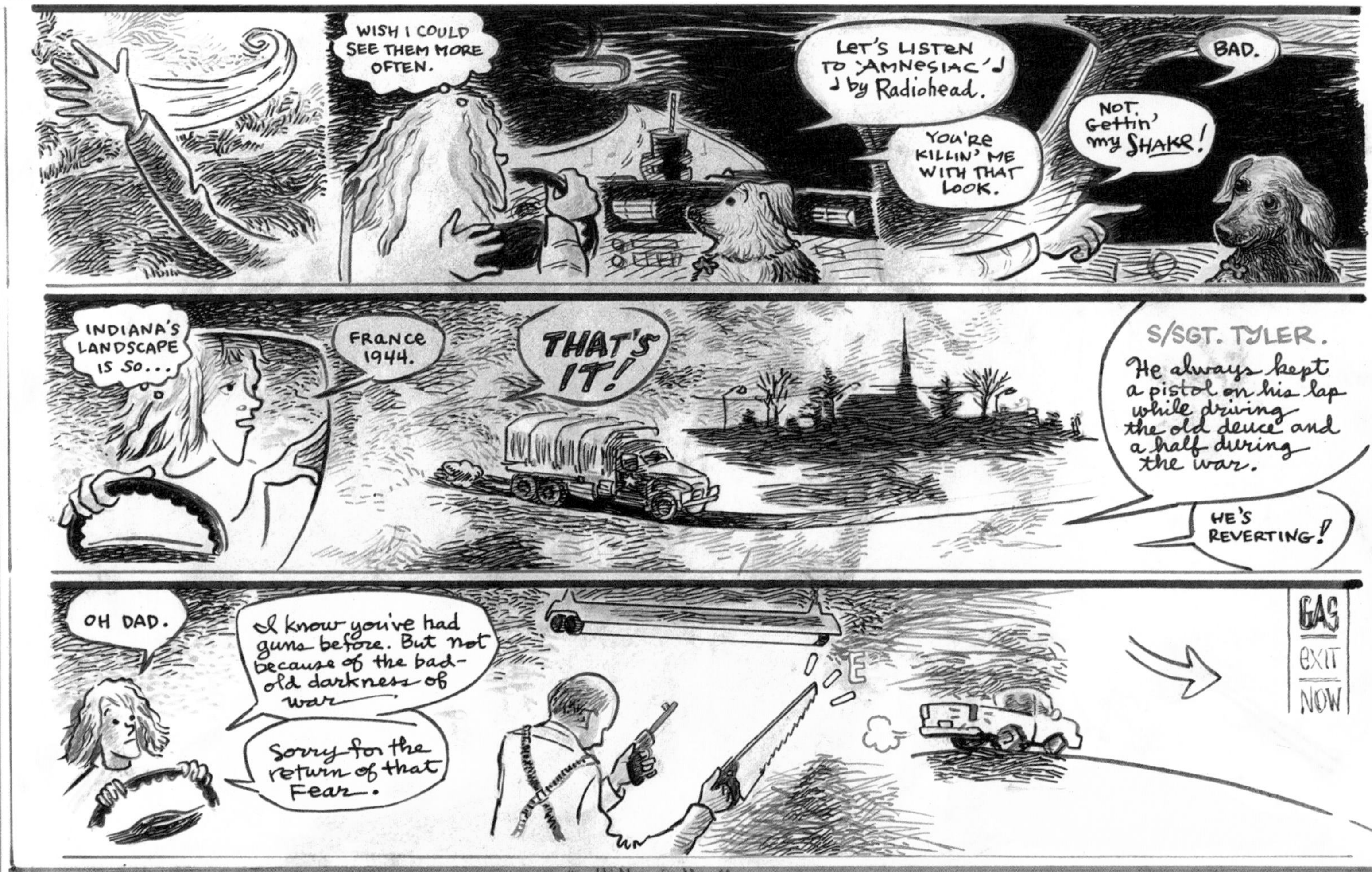

WISH I COULD SEE THEM MORE OFTEN.
LET'S LISTEN TO 'AMNESIAC' by Radiohead.
YOU'RE KILLIN' ME WITH THAT LOOK.
BAD.
NOT. Gettin' my SHAKE!
INDIANA'S LANDSCAPE IS SO...
FRANCE 1944.
THAT'S IT!
S/SGT. TYLER.
He always kept a pistol on his lap while driving the old deuce and a half during the war.
HE'S REVERTING!
OH DAD.
I know you've had guns before. But not because of the bad-old darkness of war.
Sorry for the return of that Fear.
GAS
EXIT
NOW

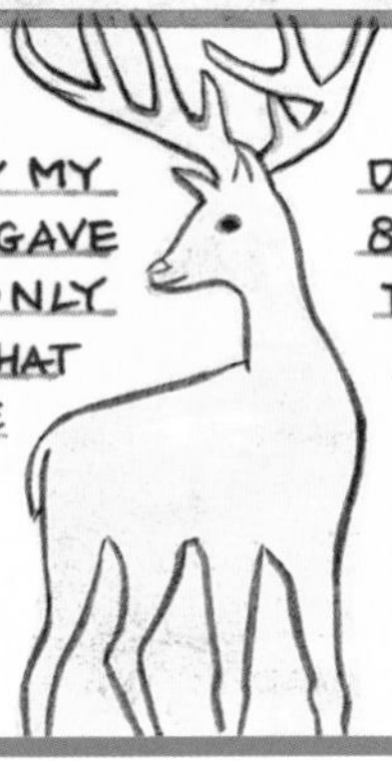

LAST SUMMER, CHUCK TOLD ME 'THE DAY MY DAD LAID DOWN HIS TOOLS WAS THE DAY HE GAVE UP ON LIFE.' SAME FOR HIM, I WOULD SAY. ONLY ADD **KEYS**. FOR DAD TO STOP DRIVING—THAT WOULD SURELY SIGNAL HIS DEMISE. A LOVE AFFAIR THAT BEGAN WITH THE *MODEL 'T'* IN THE 1920S. DRIVING HAS BEEN HIS LIFELONG SURE THING. I CAN RELATE. I ♡ DRIVING. REMEMBER THE '*SHIT BOX*' FROM CAMP CHEMO? DAD GOT RID OF IT BECAUSE ONE NIGHT, WHILE PUSHING 80 MPH, A DEER *DARTED* ACROSS. SO HE UPGRADED TO THIS ENORMOUS GMC SIERRA. SO BIG THAT LITTLE MR. PEANUT GUY HAD TO BUILD A *STEP-STOOL* TO GET UP INTO THE DAMN THING! THE SIERRA IS SIMILAR IN SIZE TO THE TRUCKS HE DROVE IN EUROPE. IT COULD HAVE TRIGGERED HIS DESIRE FOR A **GUN**. ALTHOUGH HE CLAIMS THAT WITH OIL AND GAS PRICES GOING UP THERE'S BOUND TO BE TROUBLE AT THE FILLING STATION.

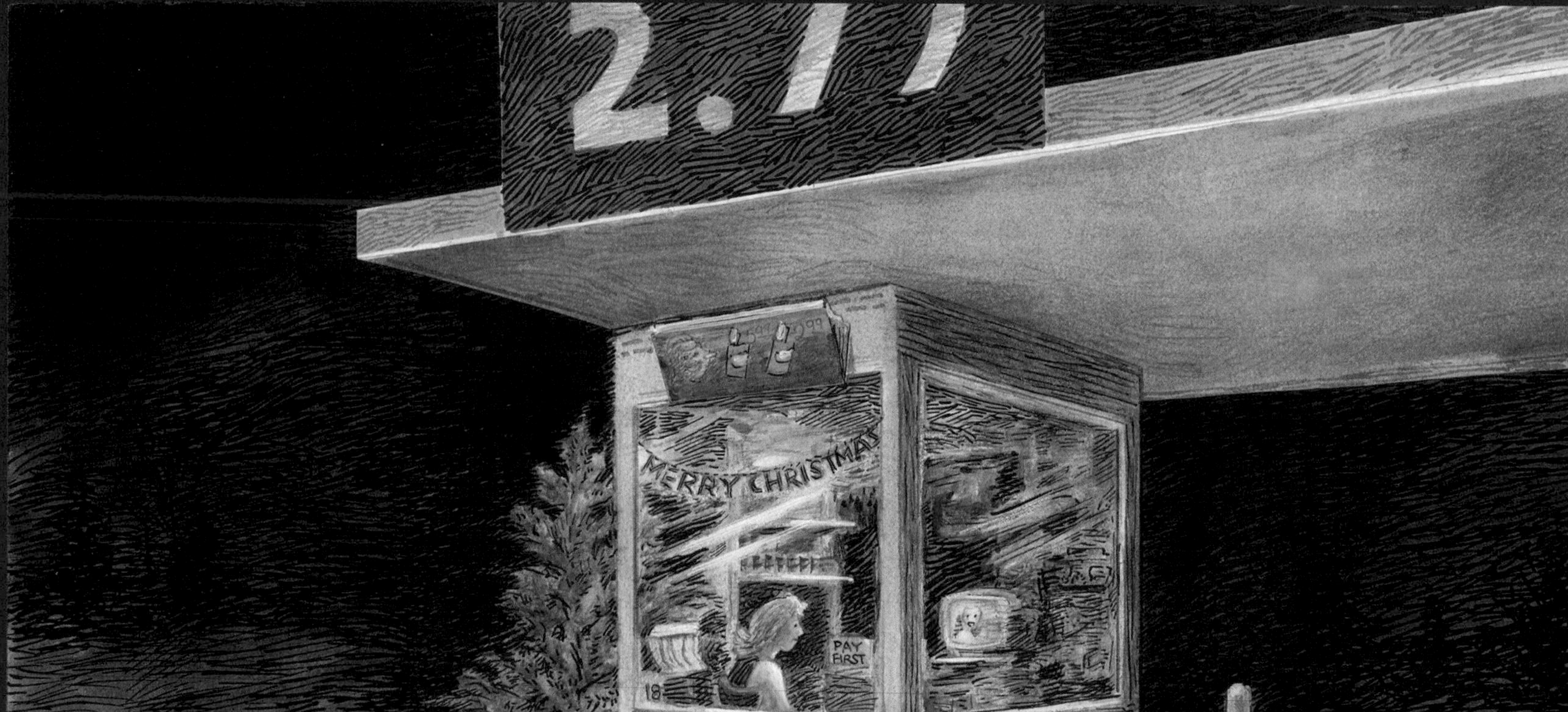
2.7?
MERRY CHRISTMAS
PAY FIRST
18

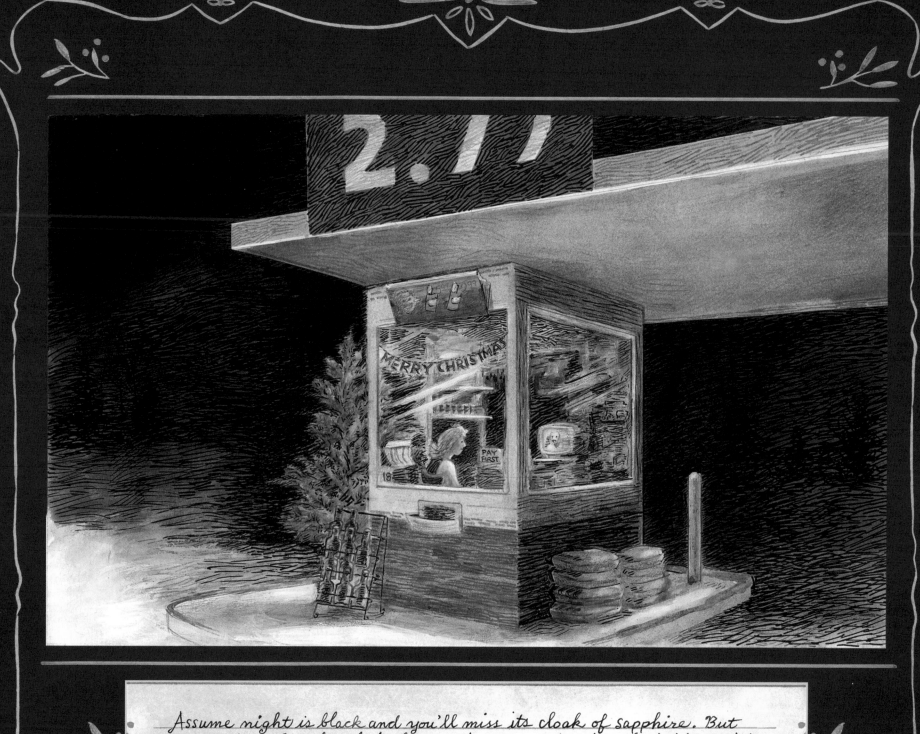

Assume night is black and you'll miss its cloak of sapphire. But no matter the color of darkness, there's no denying the bright prairie pop-ups that anchor freeway off-ramps like rivets on dungarees.

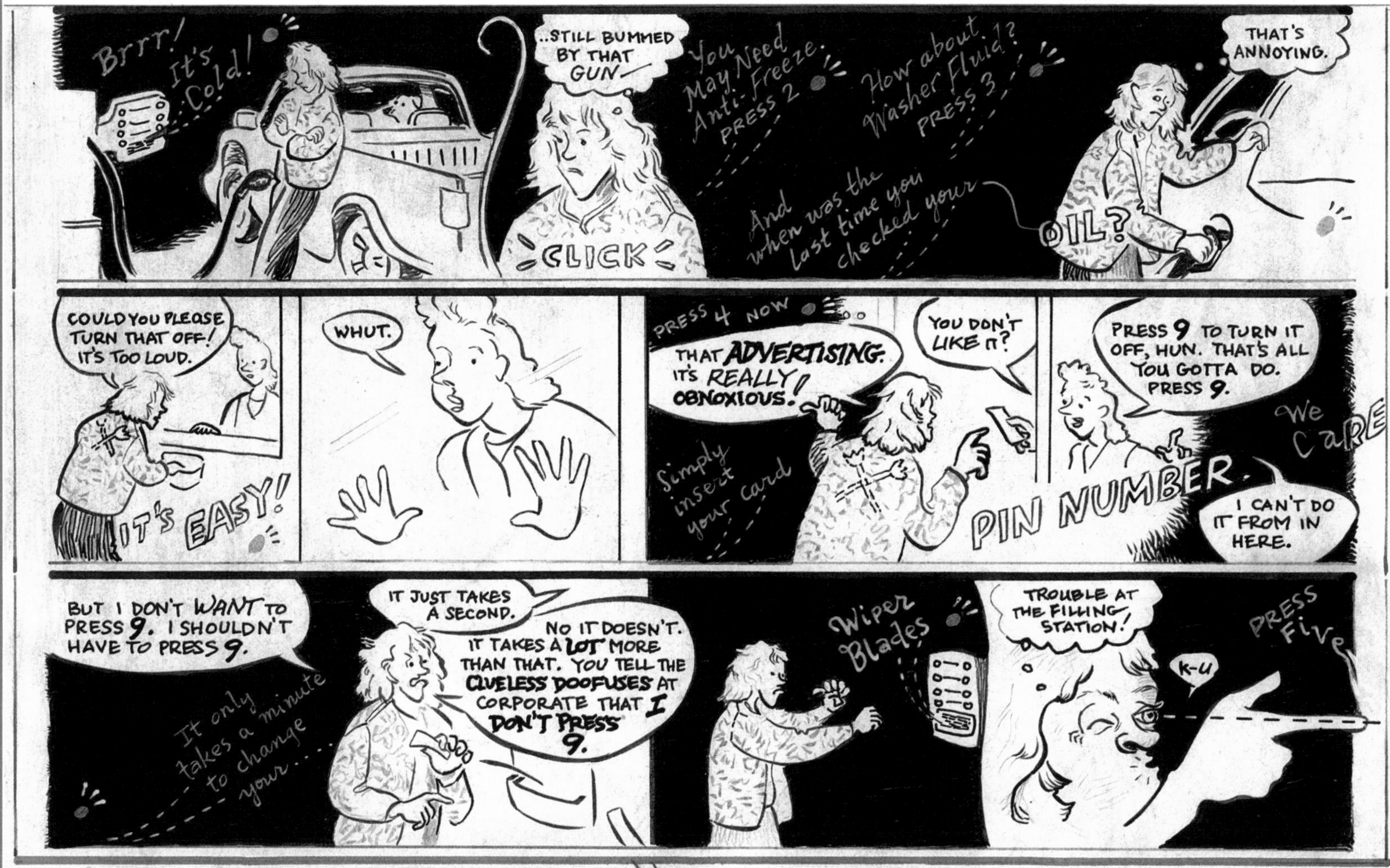
Brrr! It's Cold!
...STILL BUMMED BY THAT GUN.
CLICK!
You May Need Anti-Freeze. PRESS 2
How about Washer Fluid? PRESS 3
And when was the last time you checked your
OIL?
THAT'S ANNOYING.
COULD YOU PLEASE TURN THAT OFF! IT'S TOO LOUD.
IT'S EASY!
WHUT.
PRESS 4 NOW
THAT ADVERTISING. IT'S REALLY OBNOXIOUS!
YOU DON'T LIKE IT?
Simply insert your card
PRESS 9 TO TURN IT OFF, HUN. THAT'S ALL YOU GOTTA DO. PRESS 9.
We Care
PIN NUMBER
I CAN'T DO IT FROM IN HERE.
BUT I DON'T WANT TO PRESS 9. I SHOULDN'T HAVE TO PRESS 9.
It only takes a minute to change your...
IT JUST TAKES A SECOND.
NO IT DOESN'T. IT TAKES A LOT MORE THAN THAT. YOU TELL THE CLUELESS DOOFUSES AT CORPORATE THAT I DON'T PRESS 9.
Wiper Blades
TROUBLE AT THE FILLING STATION.
PRESS Five
K-U

A FEW WEEKS AGO, I WENT WITH DAD TO THE V.A. FOR HIS ANNUAL CHECK UP. MANAGED TO GET A PRIVATE CONSULTATION WITH HIS DOCTOR. THE DIAGNOSIS: DEGENERATIVE ARTHRITIS OF THE KNEES AND SPINE. (HE'S 5" SHORTER THAN HIS YOUNGER SELF). AND HIS CT SCAN SHOWED THAT HIS BRAIN WAS SHRINKING. AWAY FROM THE SKULL! MEANING IT'S THE BASAL GANGLIA CALLING FOR SURVIVAL. HENCE, THE GUN, SWEATER AND THE MONSTER TRUCK.

YET HE MUSTERED ENOUGH BRAIN POWER TO THINK OF THE PERFECT GIFT FOR ME: THAT CARVED HEART (GIVEN WITH MOM'S BLESSING). AND I AM SO GLAD HE LIKED THE SWEATER. FINALLY, FOR THE FIRST TIME IN POSSIBLY OUR WHOLE LIVES, WE HIT THE BULLSEYE ON GIFT EXCHANGE. WHO COULD ASK FOR ANYTHING MORE? WELL, I COULD. THERE IS ONE MORE ITEM ON MY X-MAS LIST: FOR MY BIG STRONG DADDY NOT TO HAVE A BONE-Y BACK!

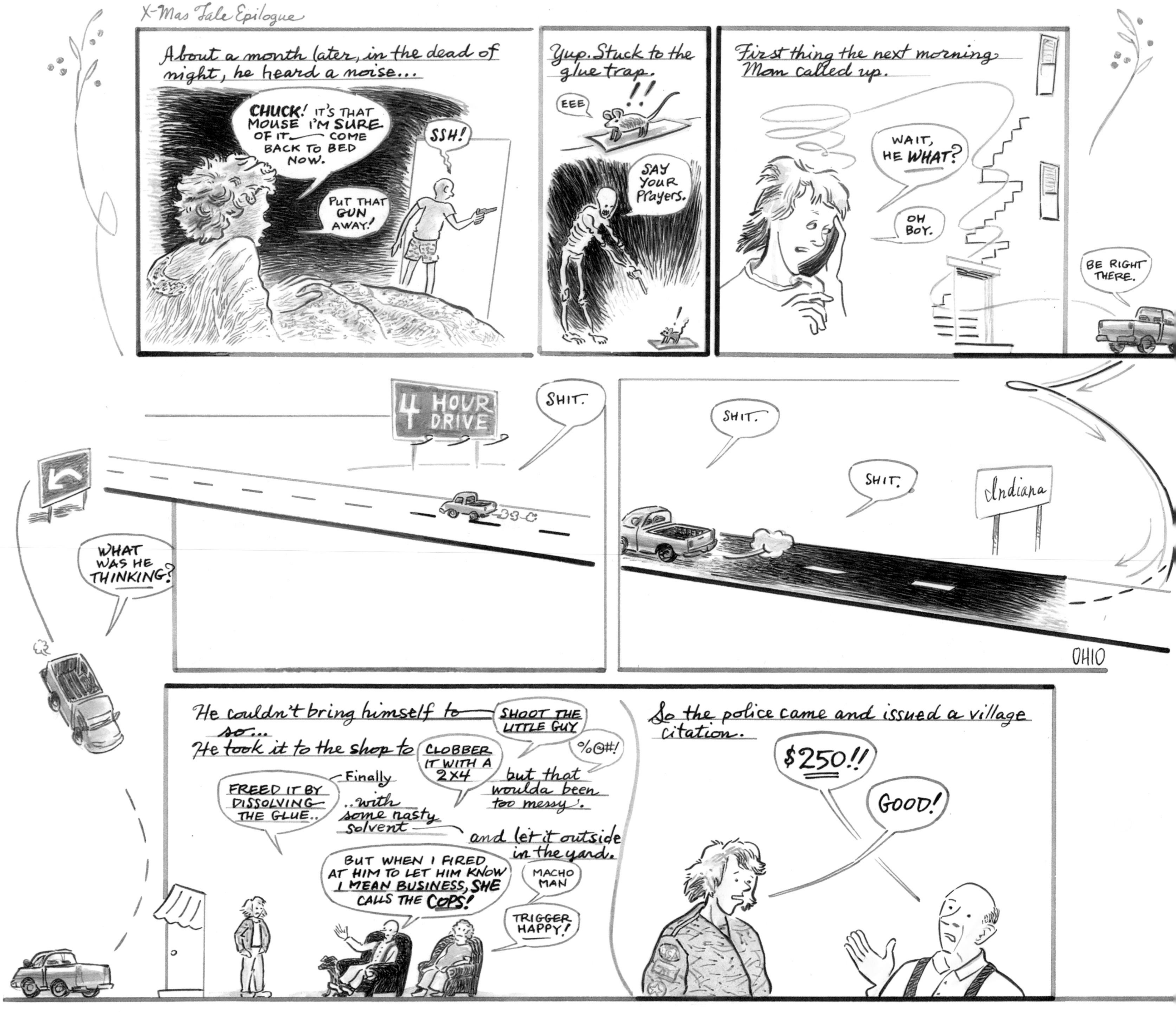
X-Mas Tale Epilogue
About a month later, in the dead of night, he heard a noise...
CHUCK! IT'S THAT MOUSE I'M SURE OF IT— COME BACK TO BED NOW.
SSH!
PUT THAT GUN AWAY!
Yup. Stuck to the glue trap.
EEE
!!
SAY YOUR Prayers.
First thing the next morning Mom called up.
WAIT, HE WHAT?
OH BOY.
BE RIGHT THERE.
4 HOUR DRIVE
SHIT.
WHAT WAS HE THINKING?
SHIT.
SHIT.
Indiana
OHIO
He couldn't bring himself to
SHOOT THE LITTLE GUY
so...
He took it to the shop to
CLOBBER IT WITH A 2X4
%@#!
but that woulda been too messy.
Finally
FREED IT BY DISSOLVING THE GLUE..
..with some nasty solvent
and let it outside in the yard.
BUT WHEN I FIRED AT HIM TO LET HIM KNOW I MEAN BUSINESS, SHE CALLS THE COPS!
MACHO MAN
TRIGGER HAPPY!
So the police came and issued a village citation.
$250!!
GOOD!

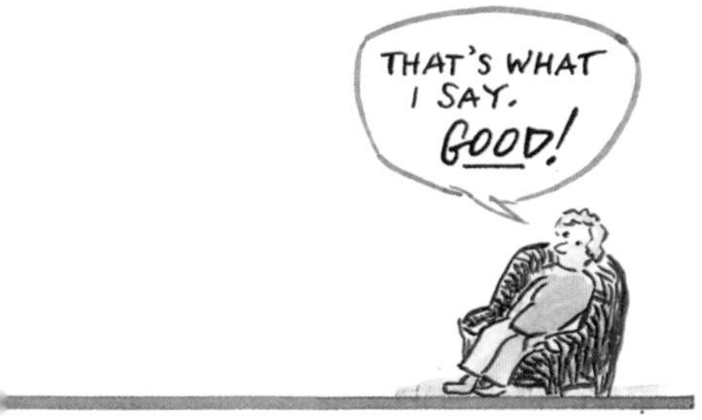
THAT'S WHAT I SAY. GOOD!

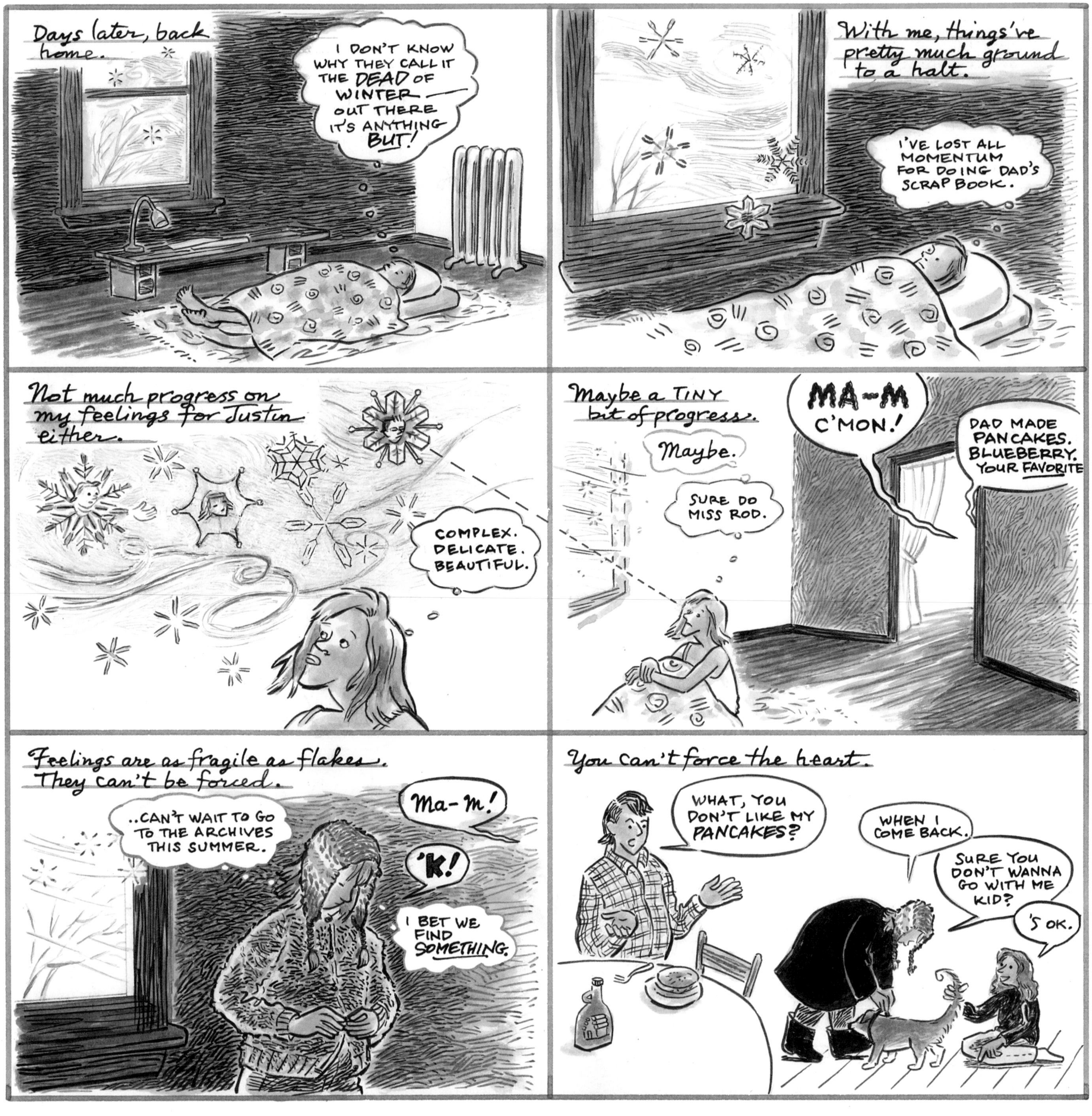

Days later, back home.
I DON'T KNOW WHY THEY CALL IT THE DEAD OF WINTER — OUT THERE IT'S ANYTHING BUT!
With me, things've pretty much ground to a halt.
I'VE LOST ALL MOMENTUM FOR DOING DAD'S SCRAP BOOK.
Not much progress on my feelings for Justin either.
COMPLEX. DELICATE. BEAUTIFUL.
Maybe a TINY bit of progress.
Maybe.
SURE DO MISS ROD.
MA-M C'MON!
DAD MADE PANCAKES. BLUEBERRY. YOUR FAVORITE
Feelings are as fragile as flakes. They can't be forced.
..CAN'T WAIT TO GO TO THE ARCHIVES THIS SUMMER.
Ma-m!
'K!
I BET WE FIND SOMETHING.
You can't force the heart.
WHAT, YOU DON'T LIKE MY PANCAKES?
WHEN I COME BACK.
SURE YOU DON'T WANNA GO WITH ME KID?
'S OK.

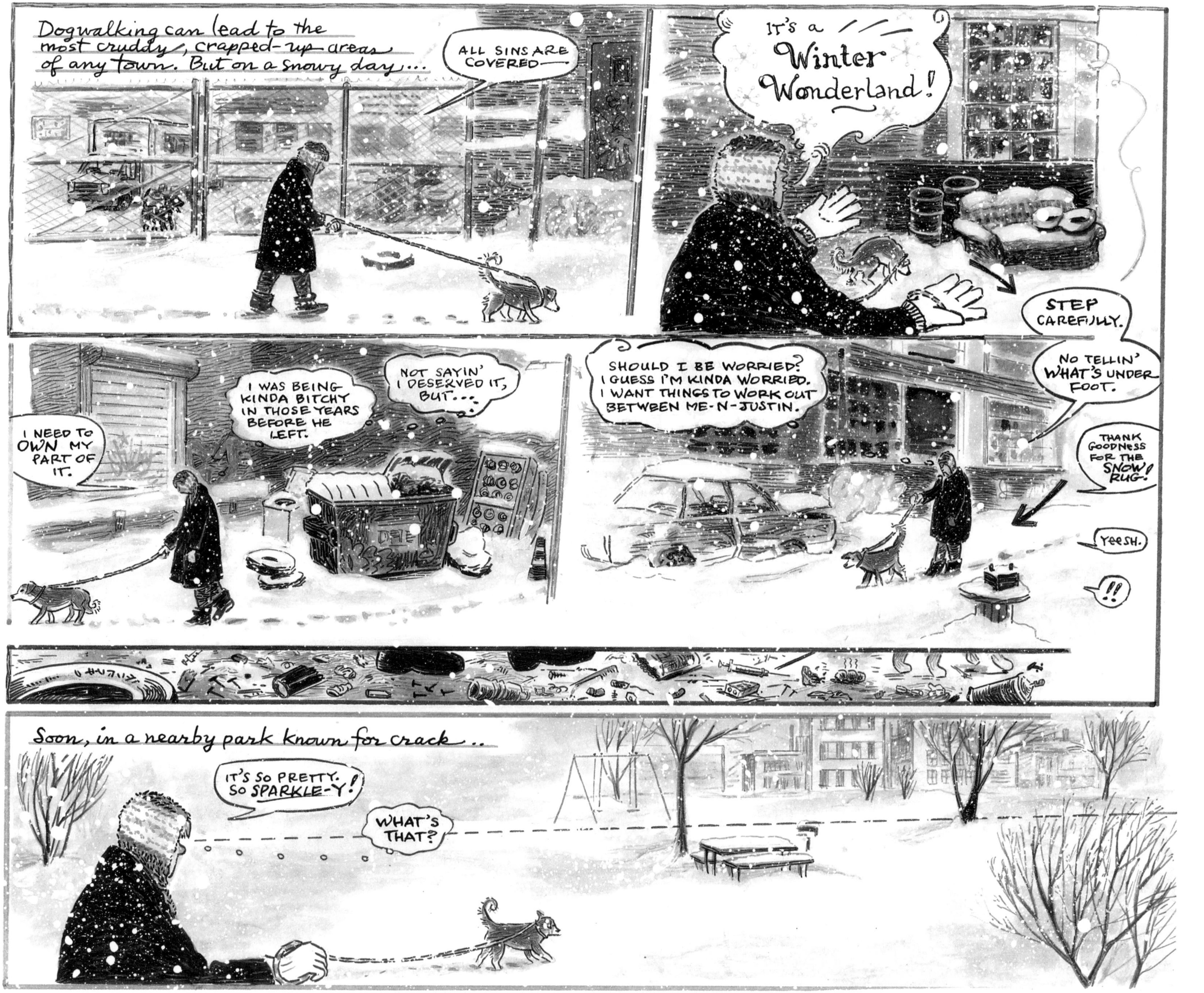
Dogwalking can lead to the most cruddy, crapped-up areas of any town. But on a snowy day...
ALL SINS ARE COVERED—
IT'S a Winter Wonderland!
STEP CAREFULLY.
I NEED TO OWN MY PART OF IT.
I WAS BEING KINDA BITCHY IN THOSE YEARS BEFORE HE LEFT.
NOT SAYIN' I DESERVED IT, BUT...
SHOULD I BE WORRIED? I GUESS I'M KINDA WORRIED. I WANT THINGS TO WORK OUT BETWEEN ME-N-JUSTIN.
NO TELLIN' WHAT'S UNDER FOOT.
THANK GOODNESS FOR THE SNOW RUG!
YEESH.
!!
Soon, in a nearby park known for crack..
IT'S SO PRETTY. SO SPARKLE-Y!
WHAT'S THAT?

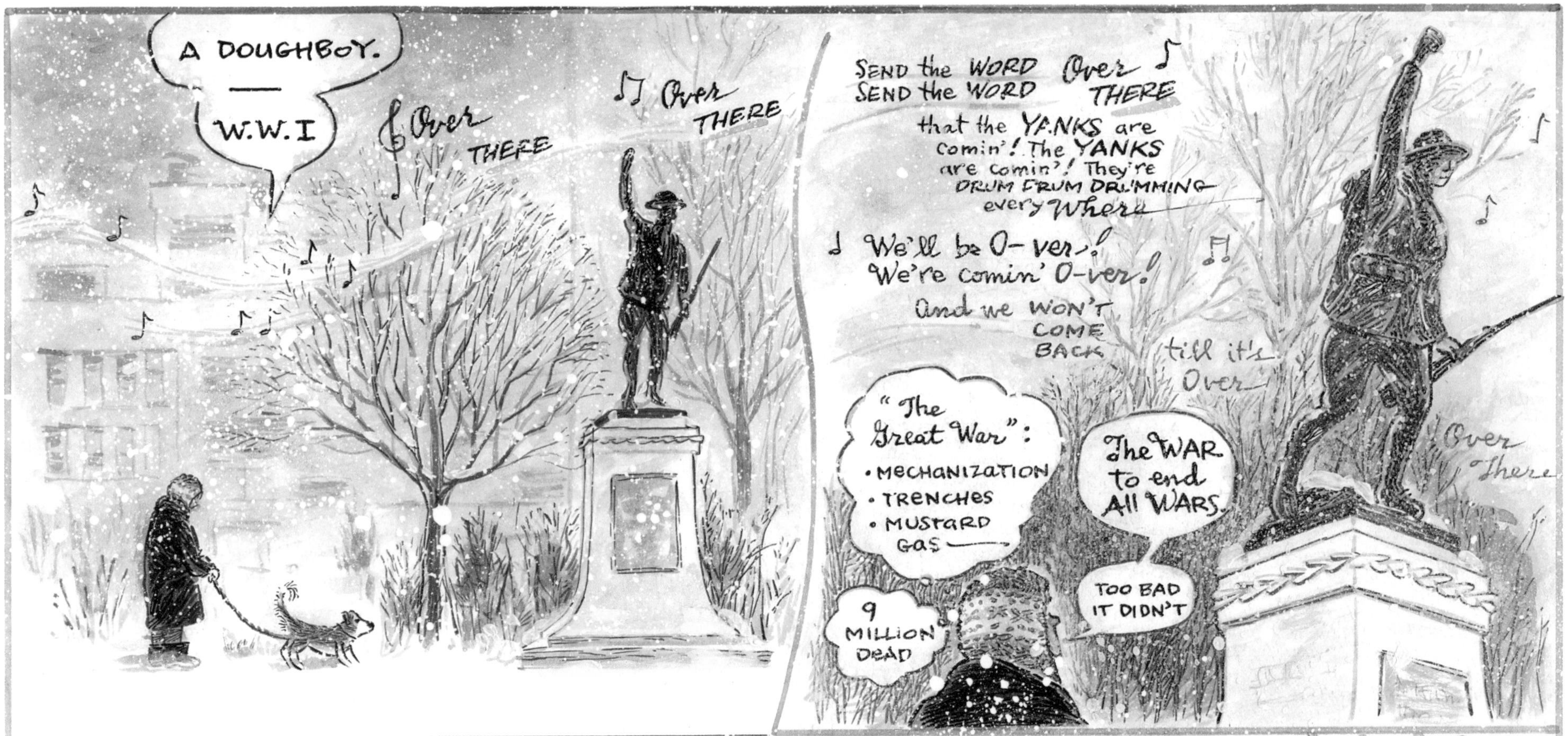
A DOUGHBOY.
W.W.I
Over THERE
Over THERE
SEND the WORD SEND the WORD Over THERE
that the YANKS are comin'! The YANKS are comin'! They're DRUM DRUM DRUMMING every Where
We'll be O-ver! We're comin' O-ver!
And we WON'T COME BACK till it's Over
Over There
"The Great War": • MECHANIZATION • TRENCHES • MUSTARD GAS
The WAR to end All WARS.
9 MILLION DEAD
TOO BAD IT DIDN'T

Dulce et Decorum est

REMEMBERING THIS POEM ABOUT WWI

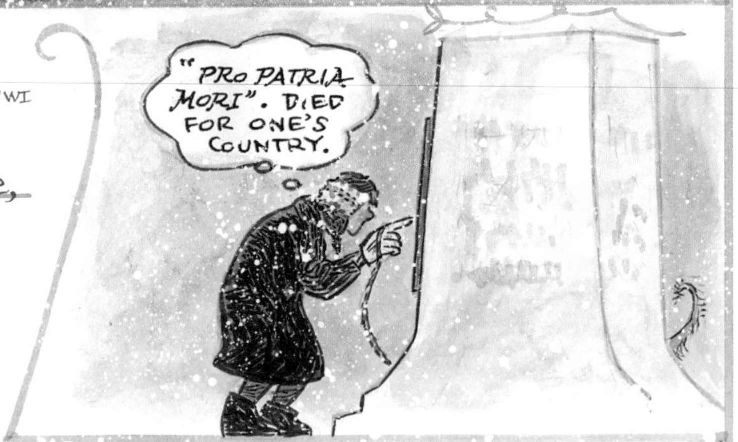
"PRO PATRIA MORI". DIED FOR ONE'S COUNTRY.

Bent double, like old beggars under sacks,
Knock-kneed, coughing like hags, we cursed through sludge,
Till on the haunting flares we turned our backs,
And towards our distant rest began to trudge.
Men marched asleep. Many had lost their boots
But limped on, blood-shod. All went lame, all blind;
Drunk with fatigue; deaf even to the hoots
Of gas-shells dropping softly behind.

Gas! GAS! Quick, boys!-- An ecstasy of fumbling
Fitting the clumsy helmets just in time,
But someone still was yelling out and stumbling
And flound'ring like a man in fire or lime.--
Dim through the misty panes and thick green light,
As under a green sea, I saw him drowning.

In all my dreams before my helpless sight
He plunges at me, guttering, choking, drowning.

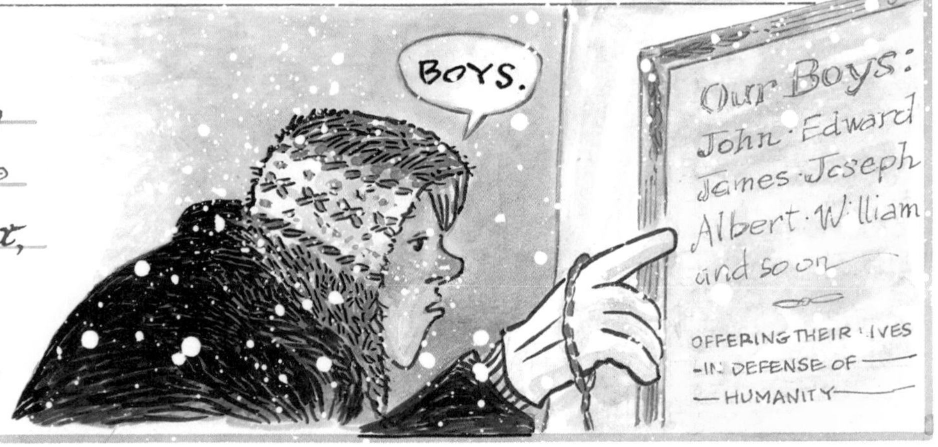
BOYS.
Our Boys:
John · Edward
James · Joseph
Albert · William
and so on
OFFERING THEIR LIVES
IN DEFENSE OF
HUMANITY

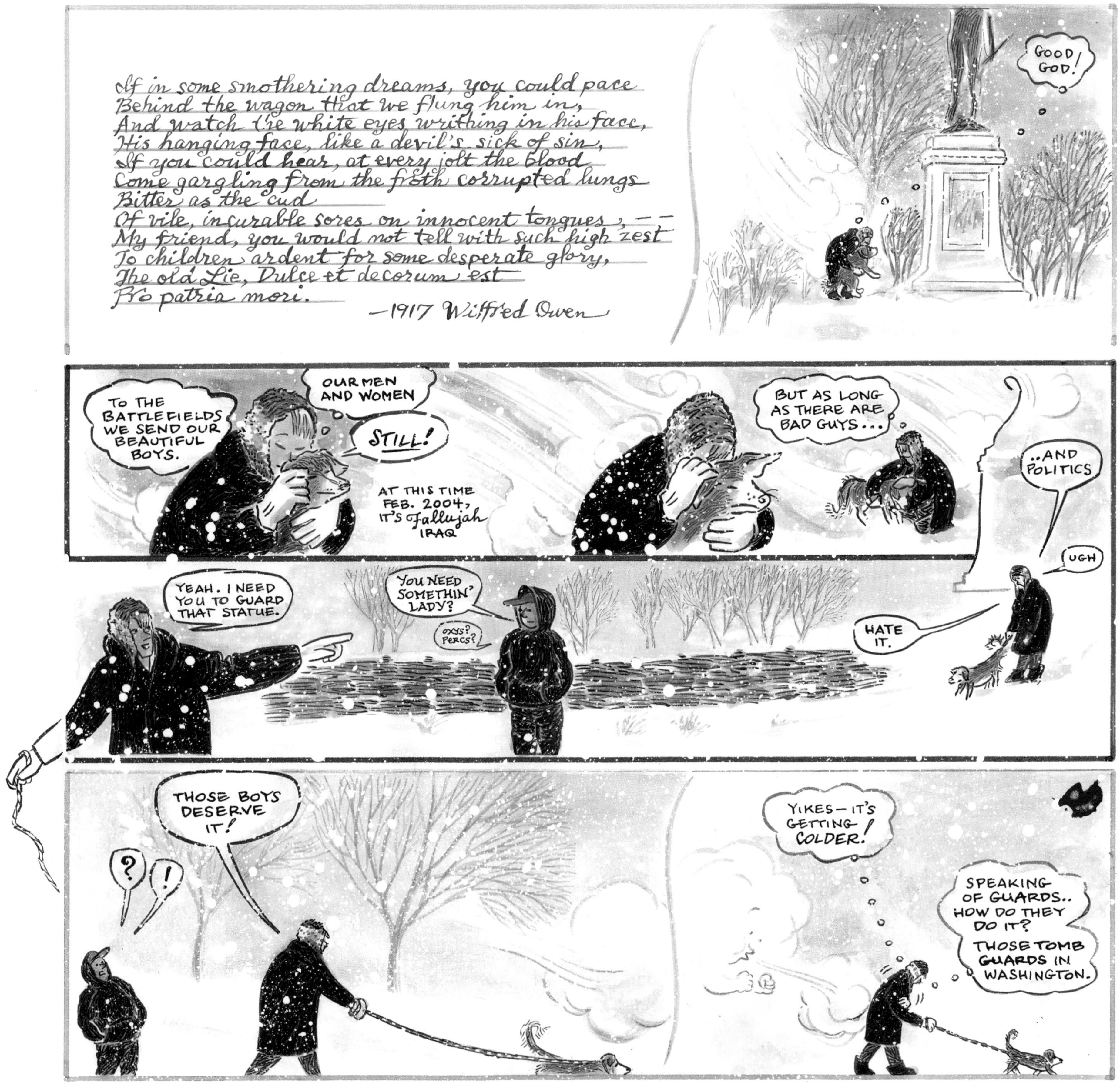
If in some smothering dreams, you could pace
Behind the wagon that we flung him in,
And watch the white eyes writhing in his face,
His hanging face, like a devil's sick of sin,
If you could hear, at every jolt the blood
Come gargling from the froth corrupted lungs
Bitter as the cud
Of vile, incurable sores on innocent tongues, --
My friend, you would not tell with such high zest
To children ardent for some desperate glory,
The old Lie, Dulce et decorum est
Pro patria mori.
—1917 Wilfred Owen
GOOD! GOD!
TO THE BATTLEFIELDS WE SEND OUR BEAUTIFUL BOYS.
OUR MEN AND WOMEN
STILL!
AT THIS TIME FEB. 2004, IT'S Fallujah IRAQ
BUT AS LONG AS THERE ARE BAD GUYS...
..AND POLITICS
YEAH. I NEED YOU TO GUARD THAT STATUE.
YOU NEED SOMETHIN' LADY?
OXYS? PERCS?
UGH
HATE IT.
?
!
THOSE BOYS DESERVE IT!
YIKES—IT'S GETTING COLDER!
SPEAKING OF GUARDS.. HOW DO THEY DO IT?
THOSE TOMB GUARDS IN WASHINGTON.

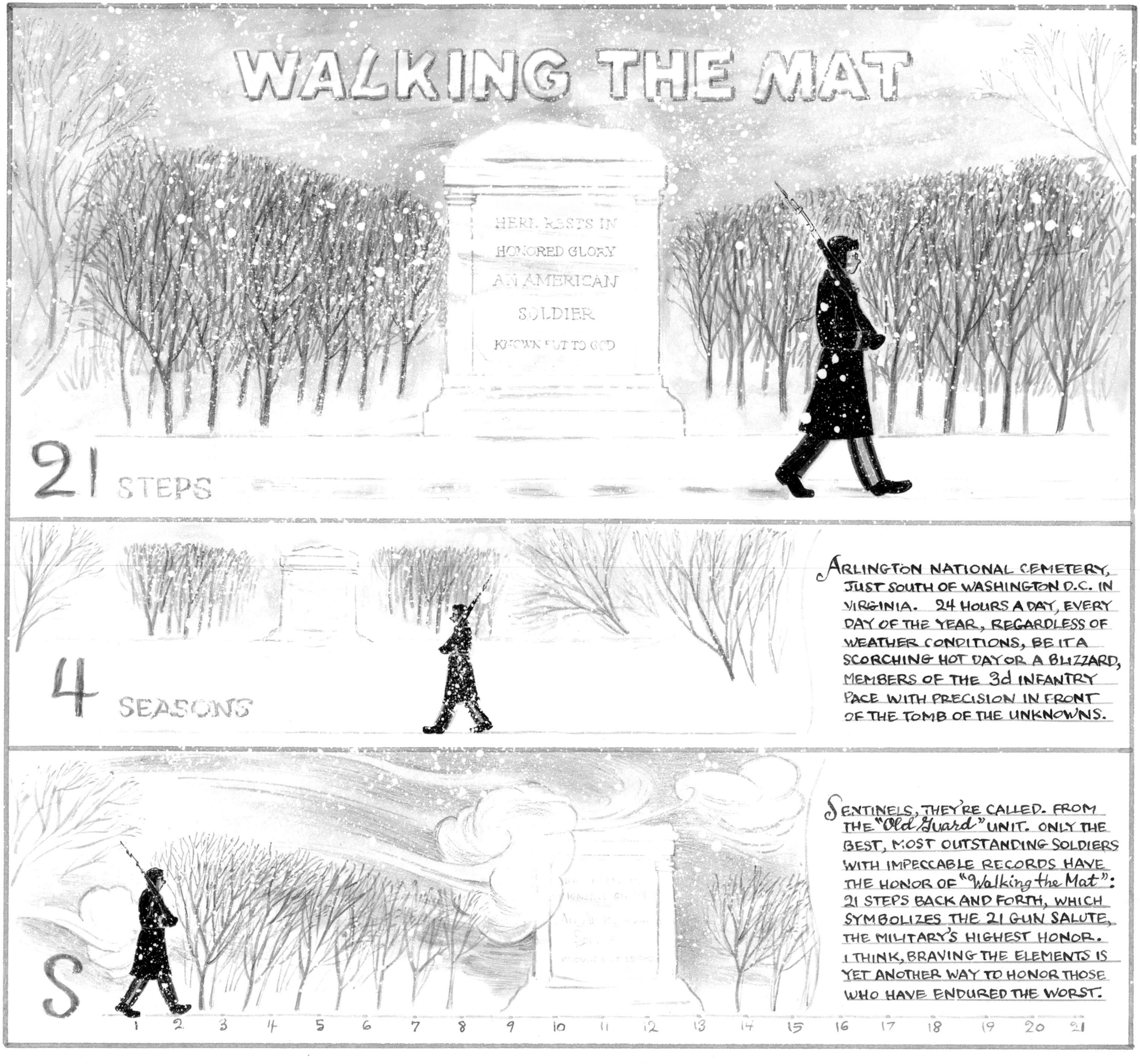

WALKING THE MAT
HERE RESTS IN
HONORED GLORY
AN AMERICAN
SOLDIER
KNOWN BUT TO GOD
21 STEPS
4 SEASONS
ARLINGTON NATIONAL CEMETERY, JUST SOUTH OF WASHINGTON D.C. IN VIRGINIA. 24 HOURS A DAY, EVERY DAY OF THE YEAR, REGARDLESS OF WEATHER CONDITIONS, BE IT A SCORCHING HOT DAY OR A BLIZZARD, MEMBERS OF THE 3d INFANTRY PACE WITH PRECISION IN FRONT OF THE TOMB OF THE UNKNOWNS.
S
SENTINELS, THEY'RE CALLED. FROM THE "Old Guard" UNIT. ONLY THE BEST, MOST OUTSTANDING SOLDIERS WITH IMPECCABLE RECORDS HAVE THE HONOR OF "Walking the Mat": 21 STEPS BACK AND FORTH, WHICH SYMBOLIZES THE 21 GUN SALUTE, THE MILITARY'S HIGHEST HONOR. I THINK, BRAVING THE ELEMENTS IS YET ANOTHER WAY TO HONOR THOSE WHO HAVE ENDURED THE WORST.
1 2 3 4 5 6 7 8 9 10 11 12 13 14 15 16 17 18 19 20 21

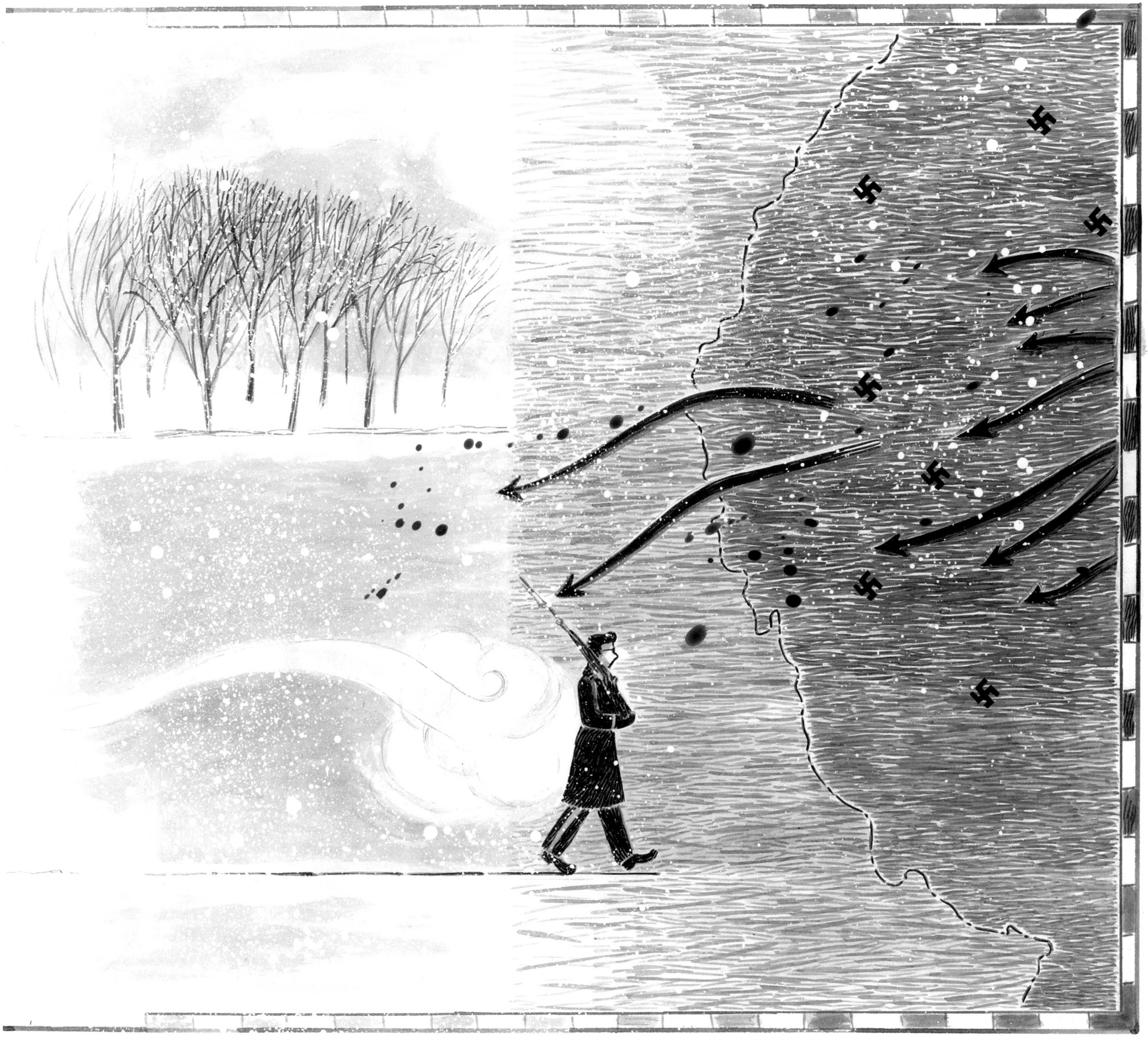

DAD'S ARMY SCRAPBOOK
AND
TOUR OF DUTY HIGHLIGHTS

PART V

RHINELAND

DEC. 1944 – MAR. 1945

67

It was Field Marshal von Rundstedt that used the phrase 'Es Geht Ums Ganze' as a way of firing-up what was left of Hitler's fighting elite before the Dec. 16 push to take back Europe. Rout the Allies and take no prisoners. 'Give all you've got.' Ultra fanatic Hitler youth also signed on for the campaign, although according to Chuck: "The Germans we fought against were starving. They were hurting. They didn't have nothing left except to fight for the Fatherland. So many of them were just kids."

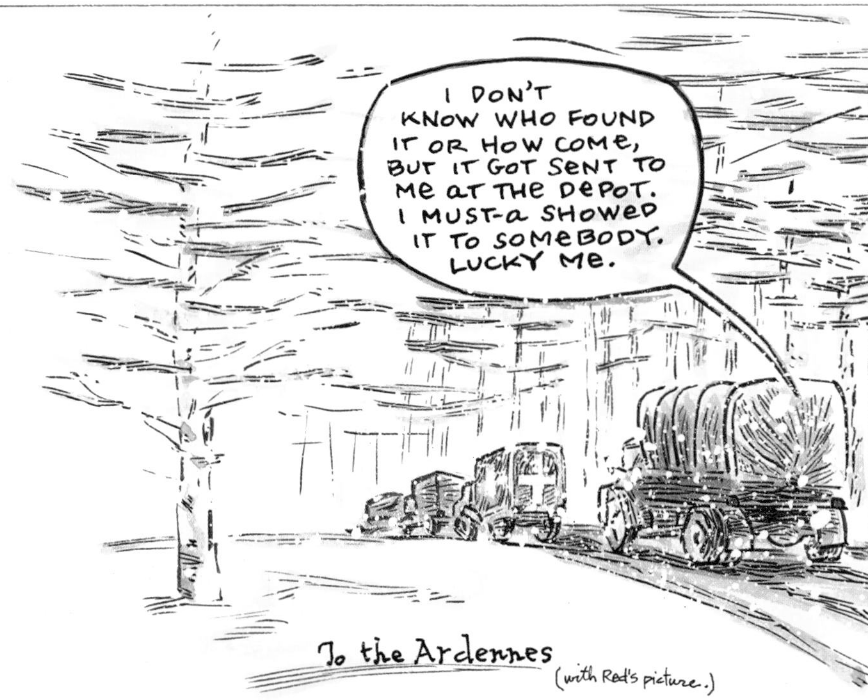
I DON'T KNOW WHO FOUND IT OR HOW COME, BUT IT GOT SENT TO ME AT THE DEPOT. I MUST-A SHOWED IT TO SOMEBODY. LUCKY ME.

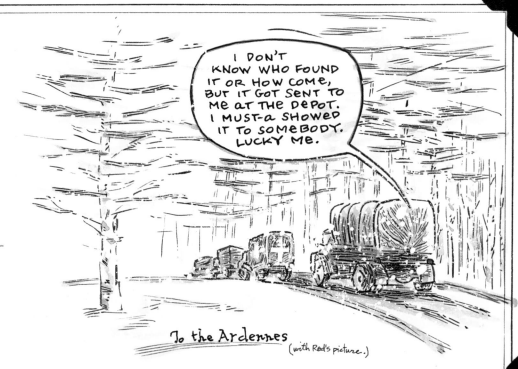

To the Ardennes (with Red's picture.)

68

"Then I got sent up there along with clerks and cooks— it didn't matter. Warm bodies with guns, that's what was needed most." So you've got a bunch of guys that had never been together, never trained together, scared to death and going into battle. Piled into troop trucks and driven up to the front.

"Everybody went to the Bulge because things were desperate. The people were hurting and there was that damn frost and cold. It was Christmastime, cold and snowy."

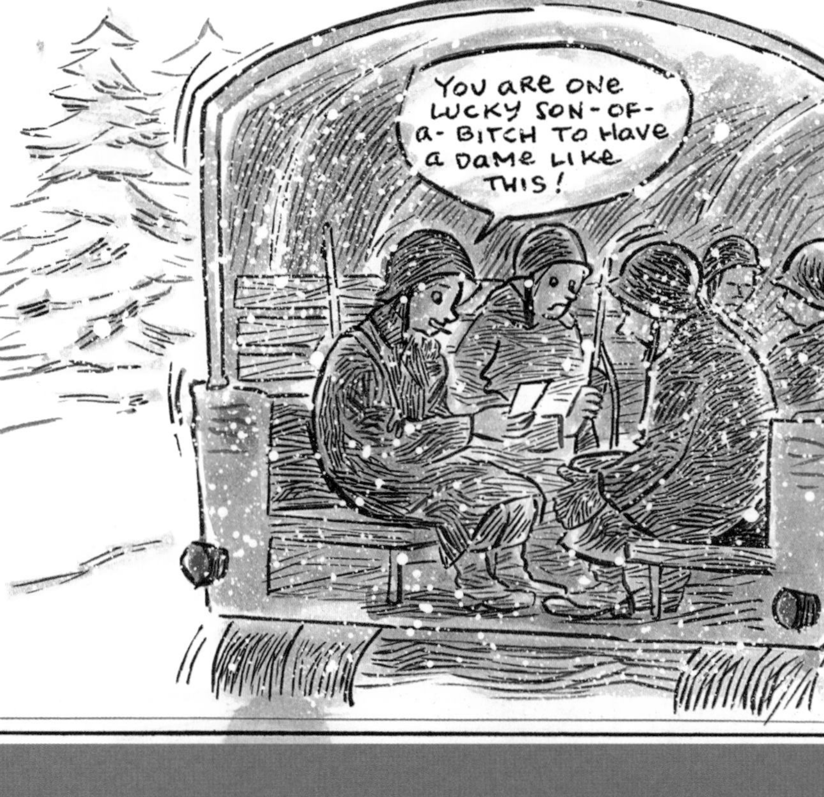
YOU ARE ONE LUCKY SON-OF-A-BITCH TO HAVE A DAME LIKE THIS!

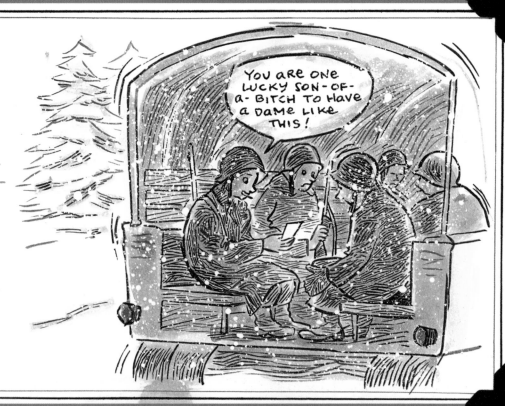

69

"They had our uniforms on! We never knew if they were them or us. We'd holler at them and if they didn't answer right back, we'd shoot 'em. Take no chances. Shoot anything that moves. We'd say 'This is it!'"

"We loaded airplanes, B-29s, NO with those gas drums. They ran low, 200 feet over the 101st Airborne at Bastogne. We let the drums roll out the back." Bastogne was surrounded. When given the option of, the mandate of surrender, General Anthony McAuliffe famously replied: 'Nuts'. "This made us bolder."

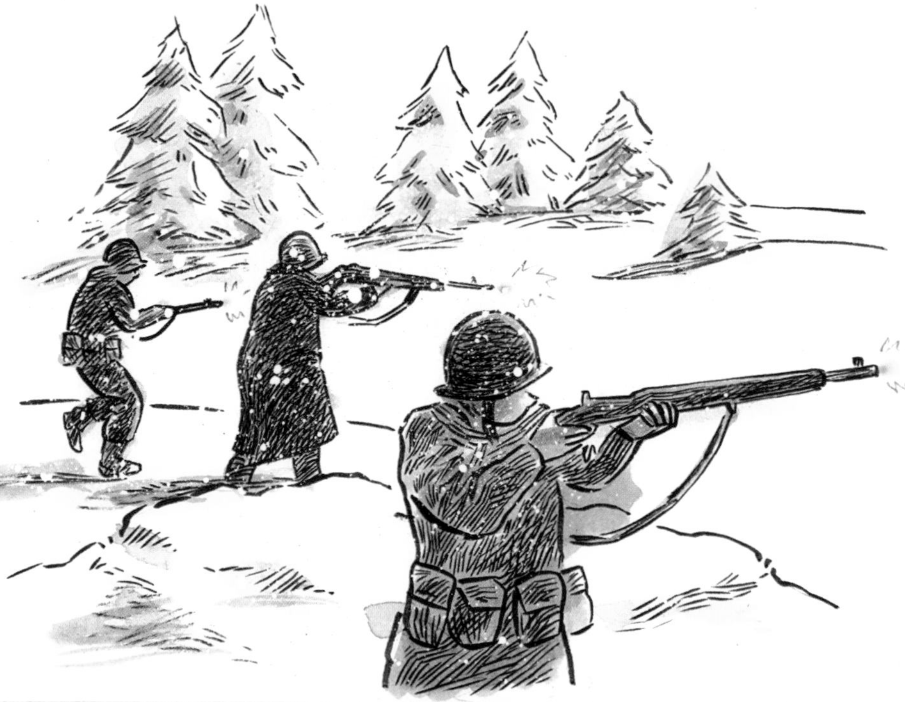

70

"No doubt about it. We were fighting an evil force bent on world domination, but up close to a German soldier, dead or alive, that idea didn't seem real. My Great-Grandparents came from Germany, which meant I could have been shootin' at my kin.

"The Germans I had as prisoners at the depot talked about the Jews and how the war was their fault. Then up there at the Bulge, we had heard rumors about large scale extermination camps But I never knew to what extent until after I got home and saw the pictures in LIFE magazine."

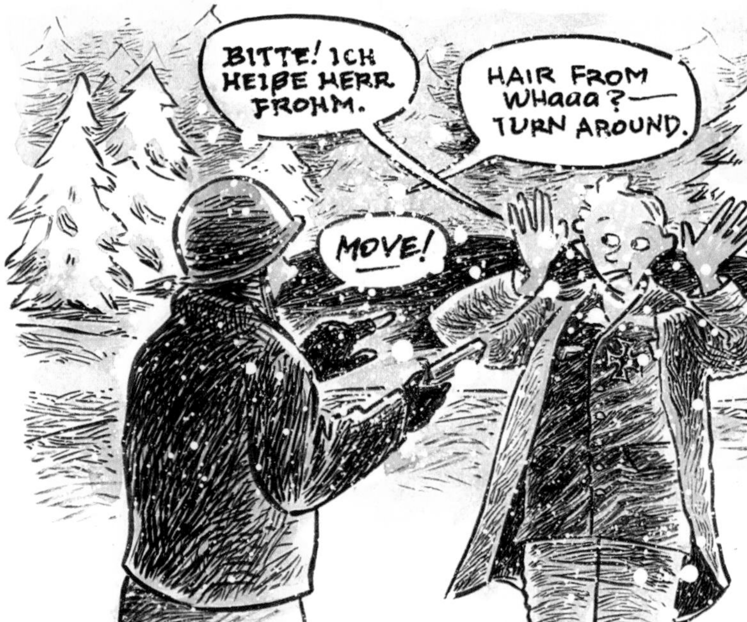
BITTE! ICH HEIßE HERR FROHM.
HAIR FROM WHaaa?— TURN AROUND.
MOVE!

71

"It was hard to think at all. Even about the littlest things. Everything I did functioned on automatic: eat, shit, load the gun.

"I have a lot of trouble remembering the details of that time or where I was even. I had no maps. The towns, roads, rivers and the countryside all frozen up — it all looked the same. There were no signs. They'd been blown to bits or had been changed to mix us up. I never knew where the hell I was or what day it was. France? Luxembourg? Belgium? Nobody knew."

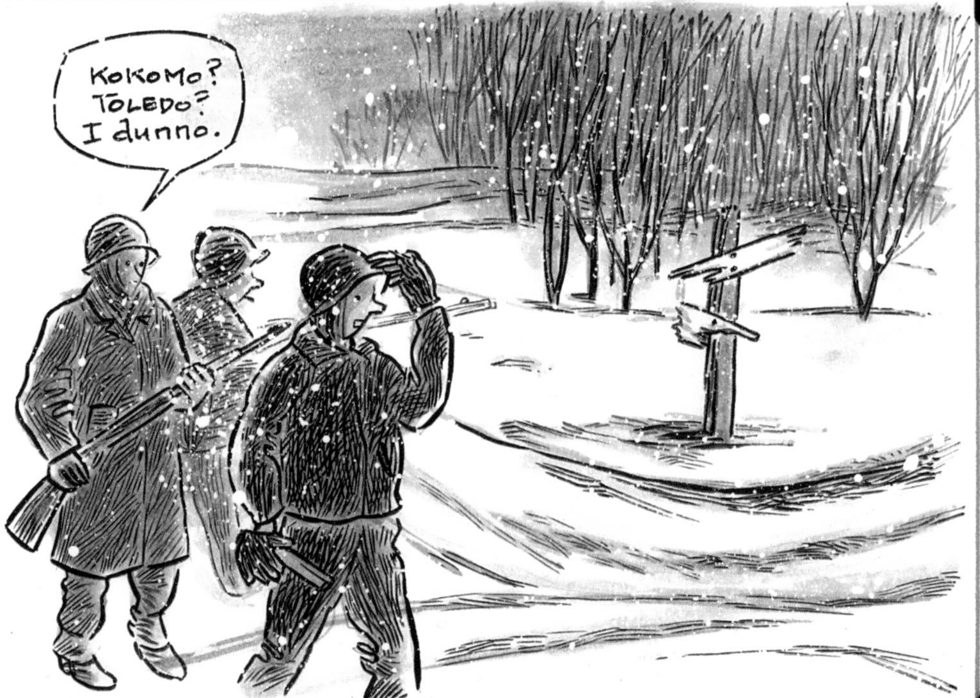
KOKOMO? TOLEDO? I dunno.

72

"The most important thing now was to survive. Hunker down, stay warm and try not to catch a bullet. Oh yeah, and pray. I couldn't sleep but maybe an hour or two here and there.

"I did pray whenever I could and tried to think of home, my parents and friends. I tried to remember anything — it was all so long ago and far away. I tried extra hard to bring that redhead to mind and imagine my new little girl, but then POOF. Gone."

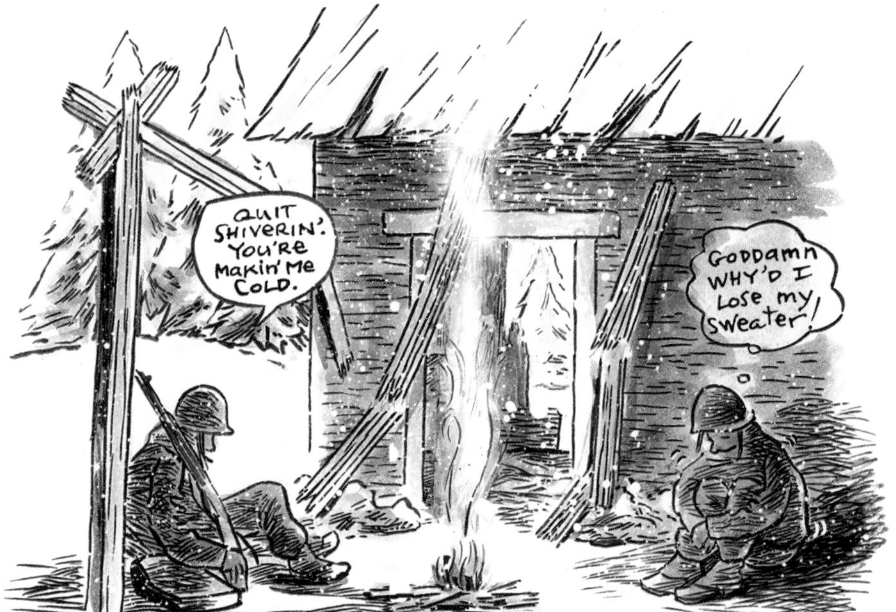
QUIT SHIVERIN'. YOU'RE MAKIN' ME COLD.
GODDAMN WHY'D I LOSE MY SWEATER!

73

Back on the Homefront, life may have been quieter and a little less harrowing but still rife with anxiety. It was difficult to know exactly what was going on with a loved one because of censored mail. You could read accounts of the war's progress or watch a newsreel. Life magazine brought the war home in a big way. Everyone read LIFE.

The most troublesome sight, however, was the humble Western Union telegram delivery boy bearing the awful news.

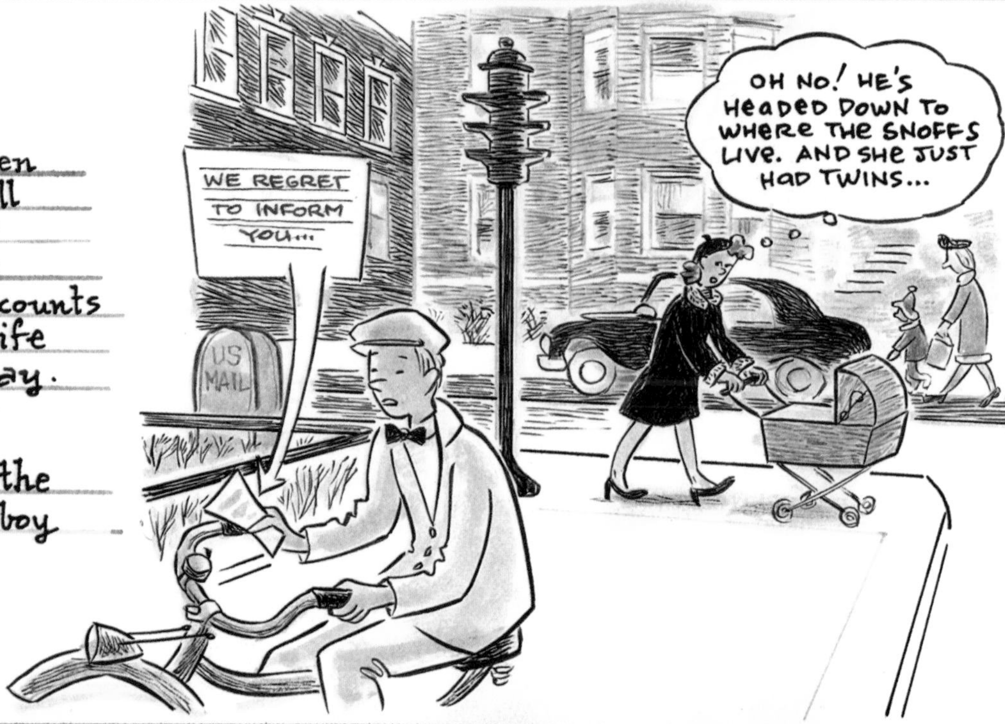
WE REGRET TO INFORM YOU...
US MAIL
OH NO! HE'S HEADED DOWN TO WHERE THE SNOFFS LIVE. AND SHE JUST HAD TWINS...

74

"The noise up there in the Bulge, all the loud shelling, gunfire and explosions, never ever stopped. Day and night. I don't know who captured it, my squad or one of 'em, but we had a German 88 that didn't blow the breech on us. That screaming mee-mee son-of-a-bitch — an eerie sound, you couldn't sleep. That thing would scream and scream. Run you *NUTS*! But if you couldn't hear it, that was your shell, 'cuz otherwise it was going by you.

"That's why I don't go to fireworks shows on the 4th. Too much noise."

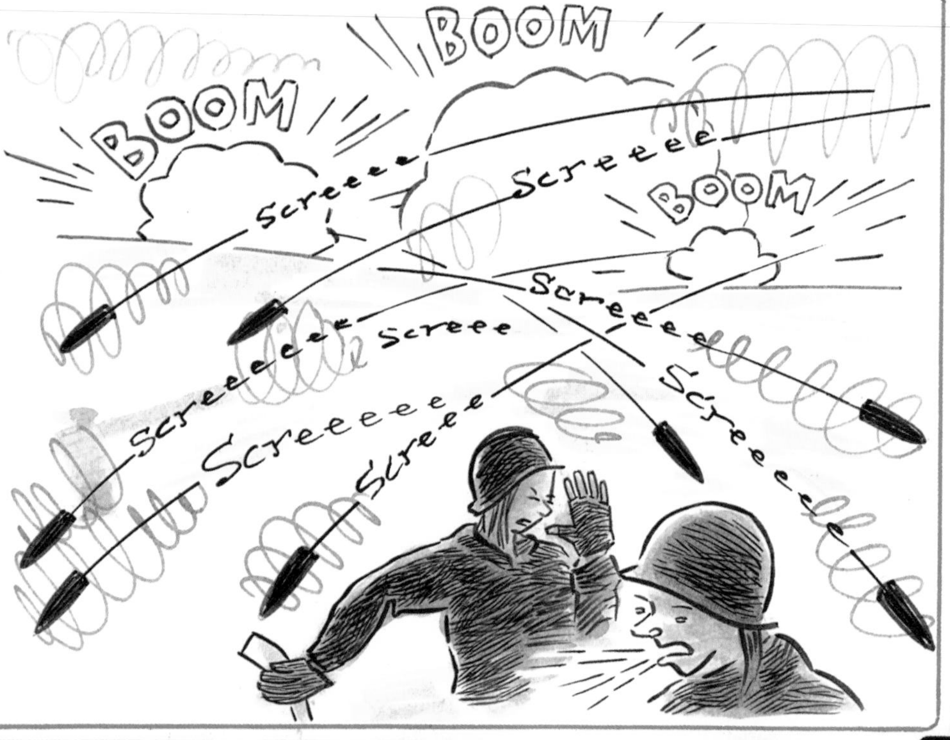
BOOM
BOOM
BOOM
Screeee
Screeeee
Screeee
Screeeeee
Screeee
Screeeeee
Screeeeee
Screee
Screeeee

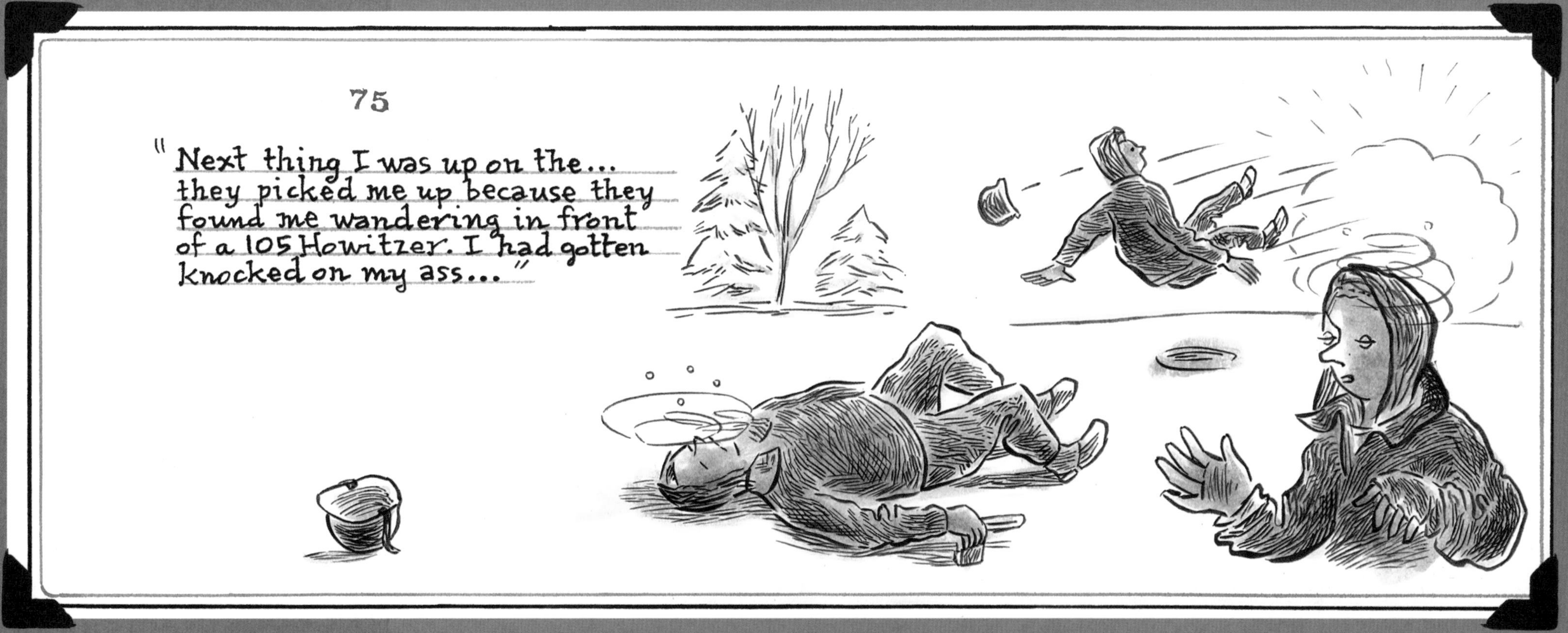
75
"Next thing I was up on the... they picked me up because they found me wandering in front of a 105 Howitzer. I had gotten knocked on my ass..."

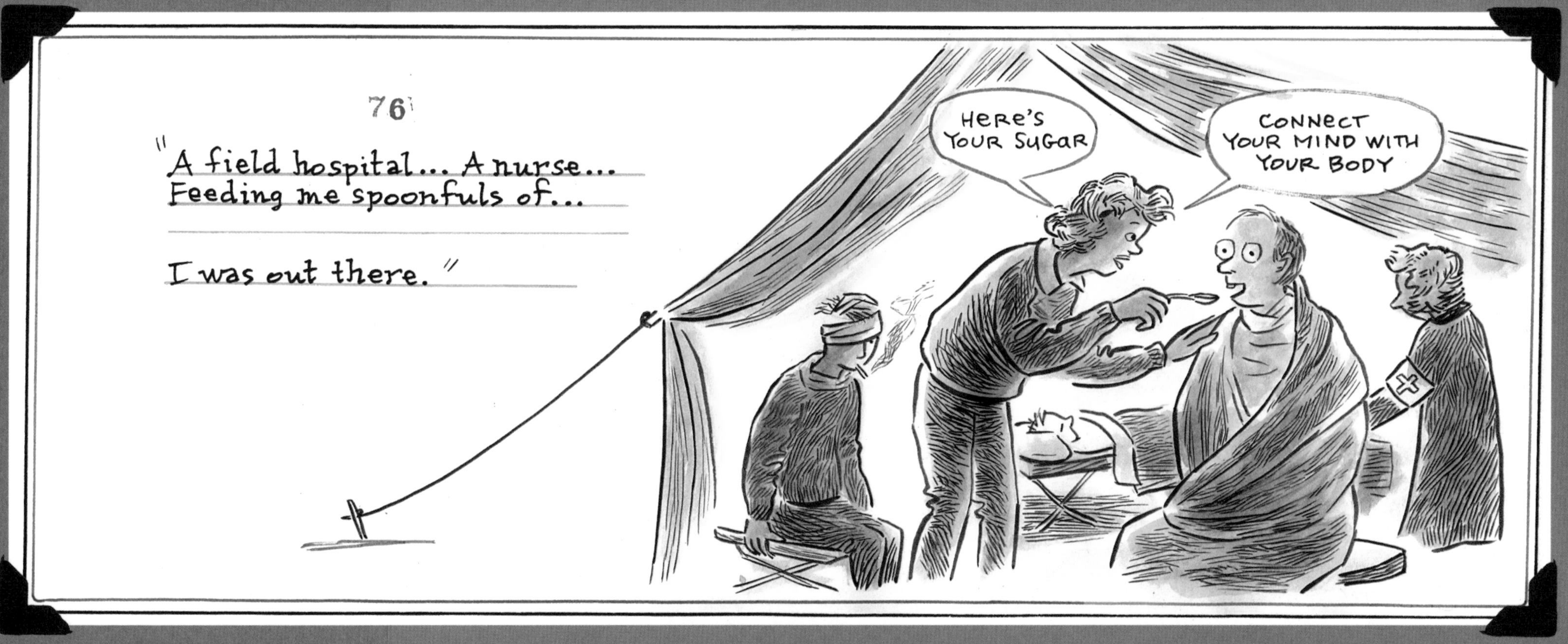
76
"A field hospital... A nurse... Feeding me spoonfuls of...
I was out there."
HERE'S YOUR SUGAR
CONNECT YOUR MIND WITH YOUR BODY

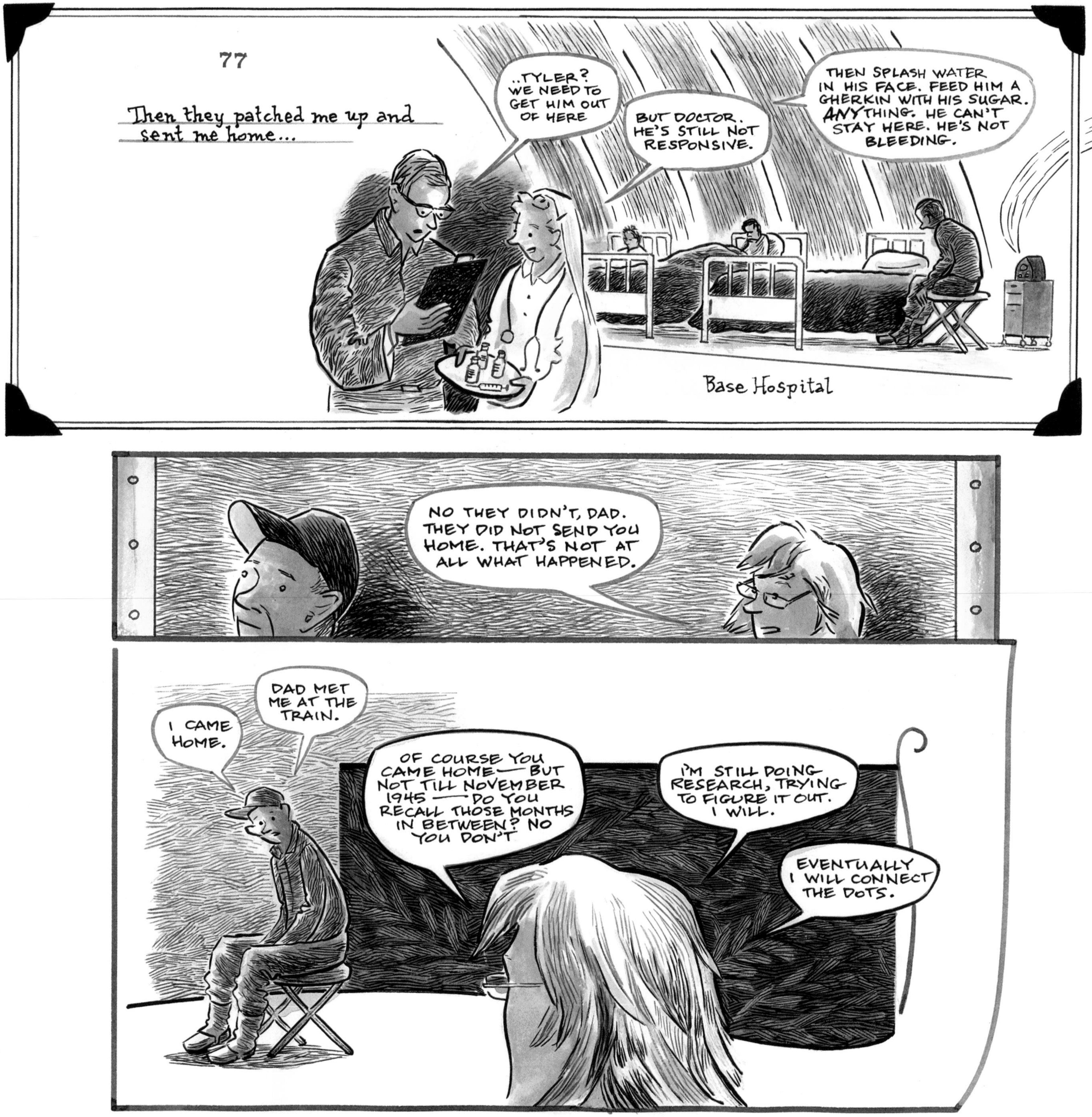
77
Then they patched me up and sent me home...
..TYLER? WE NEED TO GET HIM OUT OF HERE
BUT DOCTOR. HE'S STILL NOT RESPONSIVE.
THEN SPLASH WATER IN HIS FACE. FEED HIM A GHERKIN WITH HIS SUGAR. ANYTHING. HE CAN'T STAY HERE. HE'S NOT BLEEDING.
Base Hospital
NO THEY DIDN'T, DAD. THEY DID NOT SEND YOU HOME. THAT'S NOT AT ALL WHAT HAPPENED.
I CAME HOME.
DAD MET ME AT THE TRAIN.
OF COURSE YOU CAME HOME— BUT NOT TILL NOVEMBER 1945 — DO YOU RECALL THOSE MONTHS IN BETWEEN? NO YOU DON'T
I'M STILL DOING RESEARCH, TRYING TO FIGURE IT OUT. I WILL.
EVENTUALLY I WILL CONNECT THE DOTS.

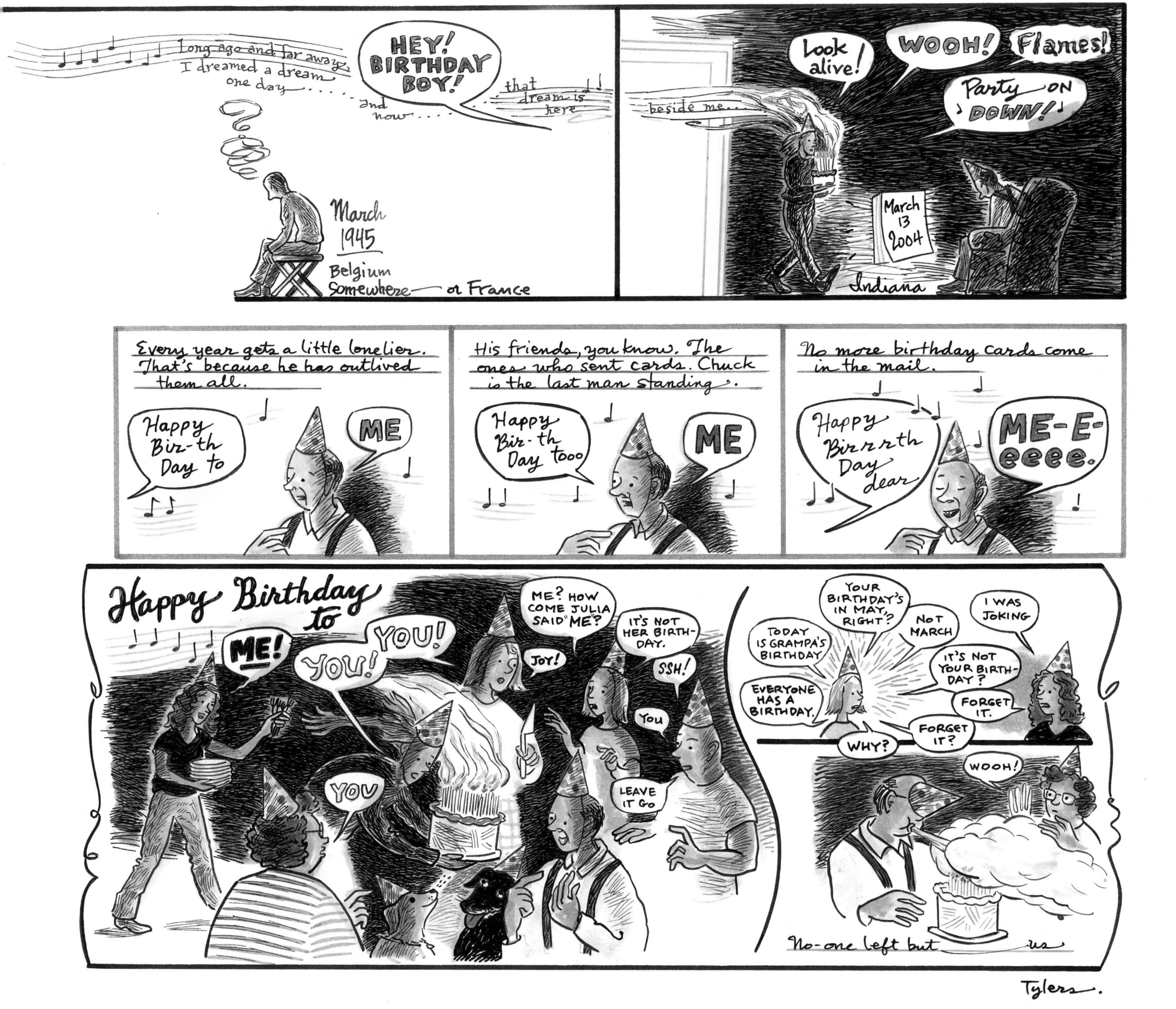

Long ago and far away, I dreamed a dream one day
HEY! BIRTHDAY BOY!
and now
that dream is here
March 1945
Belgium Somewhere — or France
beside me
Look alive!
WOOH!
Flames!
Party ON DOWN!
March 13 2004
Indiana
Every year gets a little lonelier. That's because he has outlived them all.
Happy Bir-th Day to
ME
His friends, you know. The ones who sent cards. Chuck is the last man standing.
Happy Bir-th Day tooo
ME
No more birthday cards come in the mail.
Happy Birrrth Day dear
ME-E-eeee.
Happy Birthday to
ME!
YOU!
YOU!
ME? HOW COME JULIA SAID "ME"?
JOY!
IT'S NOT HER BIRTHDAY.
SSH!
You
YOU
LEAVE IT GO
YOUR BIRTHDAY'S IN MAY, RIGHT?
TODAY IS GRAMPA'S BIRTHDAY
NOT MARCH
I WAS JOKING
IT'S NOT YOUR BIRTHDAY?
EVERYONE HAS A BIRTHDAY.
FORGET IT.
FORGET IT?
WHY?
WOOH!
No-one left but us
Tylers.

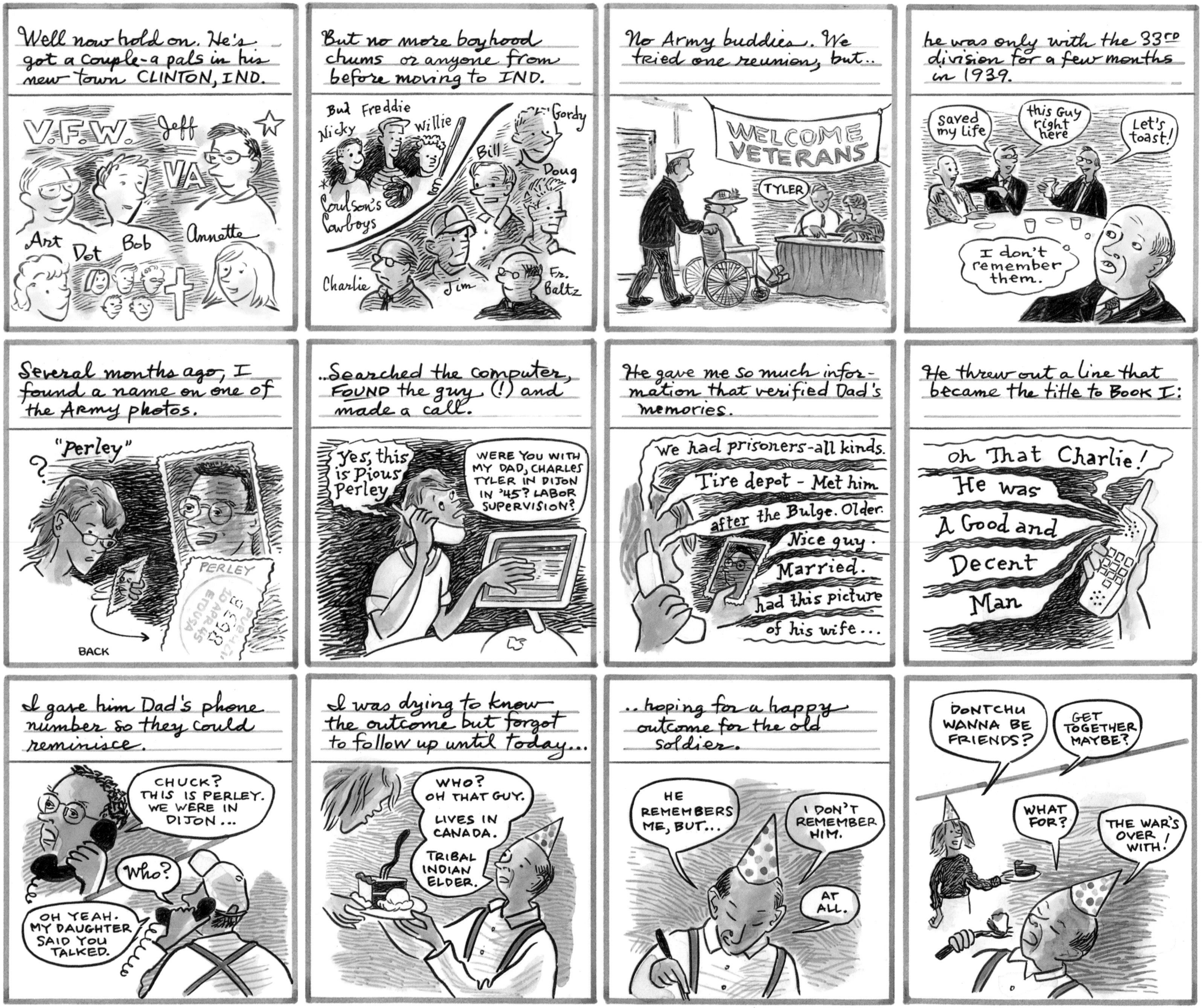
Well now hold on. He's got a couple-a pals in his new town CLINTON, IND.
V.F.W.
Jeff
VA
Art
Dot
Bob
Annette
But no more boyhood chums or anyone from before moving to IND.
Bud
Freddie
Nicky
Willie
Coulson's Cowboys
Gordy
Bill
Doug
Charlie
Jim
Fr. Baltz
No Army buddies. We tried one reunion, but..
WELCOME VETERANS
TYLER
he was only with the 33rd division for a few months in 1939.
Saved my life
this Guy right here
Let's toast!
I don't remember them.
Several months ago, I found a name on one of the Army photos.
"Perley"
?
PERLEY
BACK
..Searched the computer, FOUND the guy (!) and made a call.
Yes, this is Pious Perley
WERE YOU WITH MY DAD, CHARLES TYLER IN DIJON IN '45? LABOR SUPERVISION?
He gave me so much information that verified Dad's memories.
We had prisoners-all kinds.
Tire depot - Met him
after the Bulge. Older.
Nice guy.
Married.
had this picture
of his wife...
He threw out a line that became the title to Book I:
oh That Charlie!
He was
A Good and
Decent
Man
I gave him Dad's phone number so they could reminisce.
CHUCK? THIS IS PERLEY. WE WERE IN DIJON...
Who?
OH YEAH. MY DAUGHTER SAID YOU TALKED.
I was dying to know the outcome but forgot to follow up until today...
WHO? OH THAT GUY.
LIVES IN CANADA.
TRIBAL INDIAN ELDER.
..hoping for a happy outcome for the old soldier.
HE REMEMBERS ME, BUT...
I DON'T REMEMBER HIM.
AT ALL.
DONTCHU WANNA BE FRIENDS?
GET TOGETHER MAYBE?
WHAT FOR?
THE WAR'S OVER WITH!

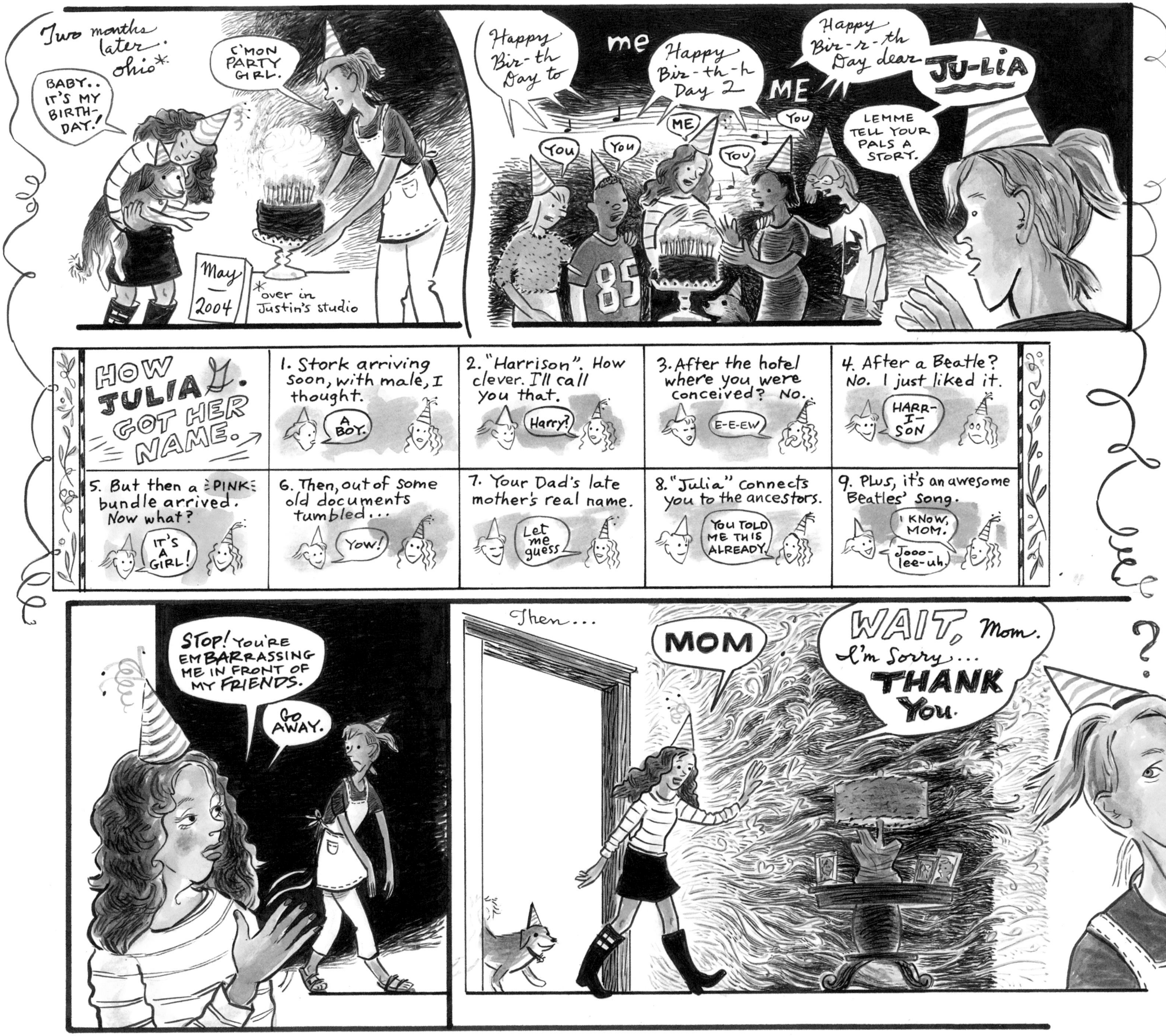
Two months later. ohio*
BABY.. IT'S MY BIRTHDAY!
C'MON PARTY GIRL.
May 2004
*over in Justin's studio
Happy Bir-th Day to
me
Happy Bir-th-h Day 2
ME
Happy Bir-r-th Day dear
JU-LIA
YOU
YOU
ME
YOU
YOU
LEMME TELL YOUR PALS A STORY.
HOW JULIA G. GOT HER NAME.
1. Stork arriving soon, with male, I thought.
A BOY.
2. "Harrison". How clever. I'll call you that.
Harry?
3. After the hotel where you were conceived? No.
E-E-EW
4. After a Beatle? No. I just liked it.
HARR-I-SON
5. But then a PINK bundle arrived. Now what?
IT'S A GIRL!
6. Then, out of some old documents tumbled...
YOW!
7. Your Dad's late mother's real name.
Let me guess
8. "Julia" connects you to the ancestors.
YOU TOLD ME THIS ALREADY.
9. Plus, it's an awesome Beatles' song.
I KNOW, MOM.
Jooo-lee-uh.
STOP! YOU'RE EMBARRASSING ME IN FRONT OF MY FRIENDS.
GO AWAY.
Then...
MOM
WAIT, Mom. I'm Sorry... THANK YOU.
?

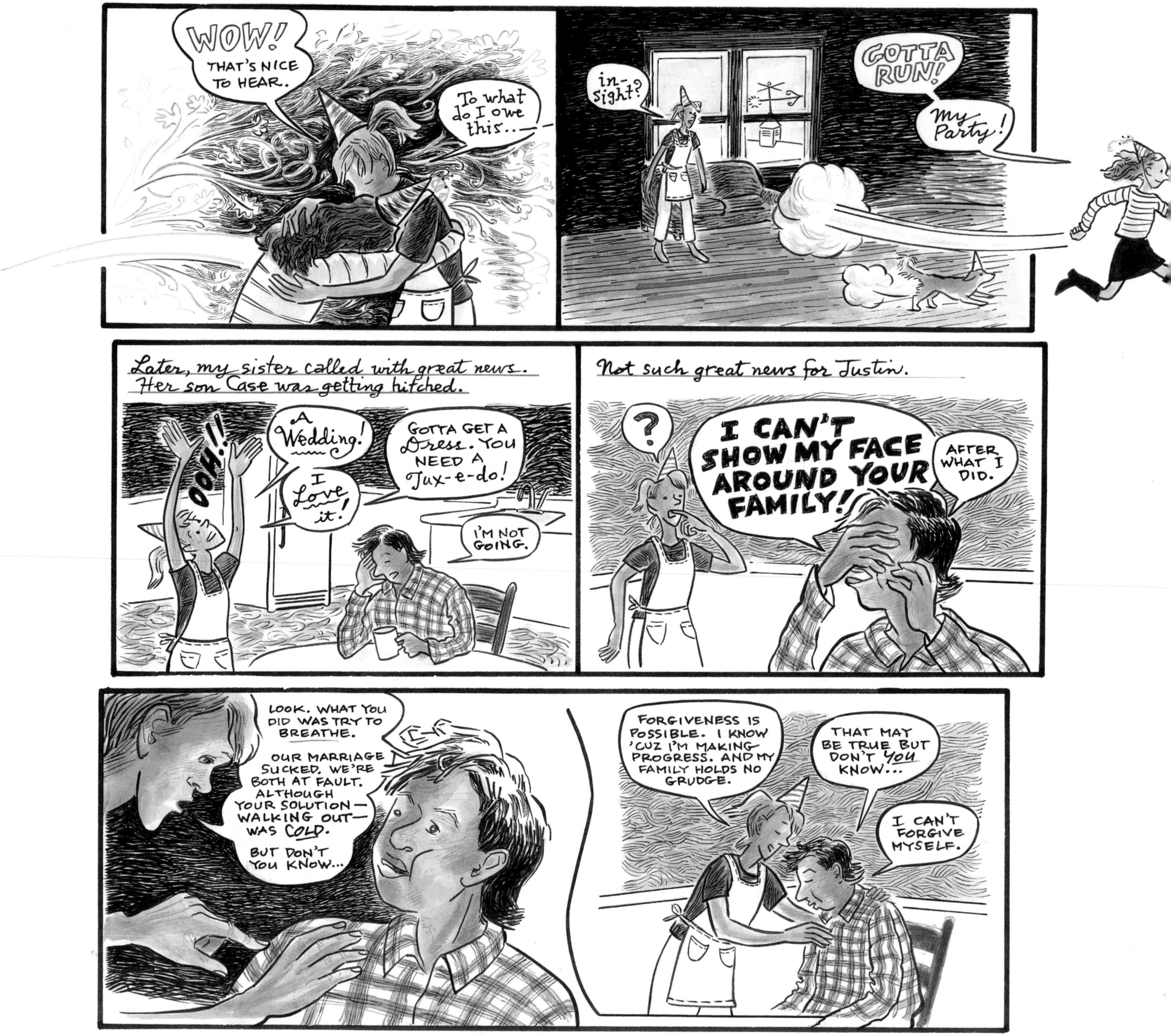
WOW! THAT'S NICE TO HEAR.
To what do I owe this...
in-sight?
GOTTA RUN!
My Party!
Later, my sister called with great news. Her son Case was getting hitched.
OOH!!
A Wedding!
I Love it!
GOTTA GET A Dress. YOU NEED A Tux-e-do!
I'M NOT GOING.
Not such great news for Justin.
?
I CAN'T SHOW MY FACE AROUND YOUR FAMILY!
AFTER WHAT I DID.
LOOK. WHAT YOU DID WAS TRY TO BREATHE.
OUR MARRIAGE SUCKED. WE'RE BOTH AT FAULT. ALTHOUGH YOUR SOLUTION— WALKING OUT— WAS COLD.
BUT DON'T YOU KNOW...
FORGIVENESS IS POSSIBLE. I KNOW 'CUZ I'M MAKING PROGRESS. AND MY FAMILY HOLDS NO GRUDGE.
THAT MAY BE TRUE BUT DON'T YOU KNOW...
I CAN'T FORGIVE MYSELF.

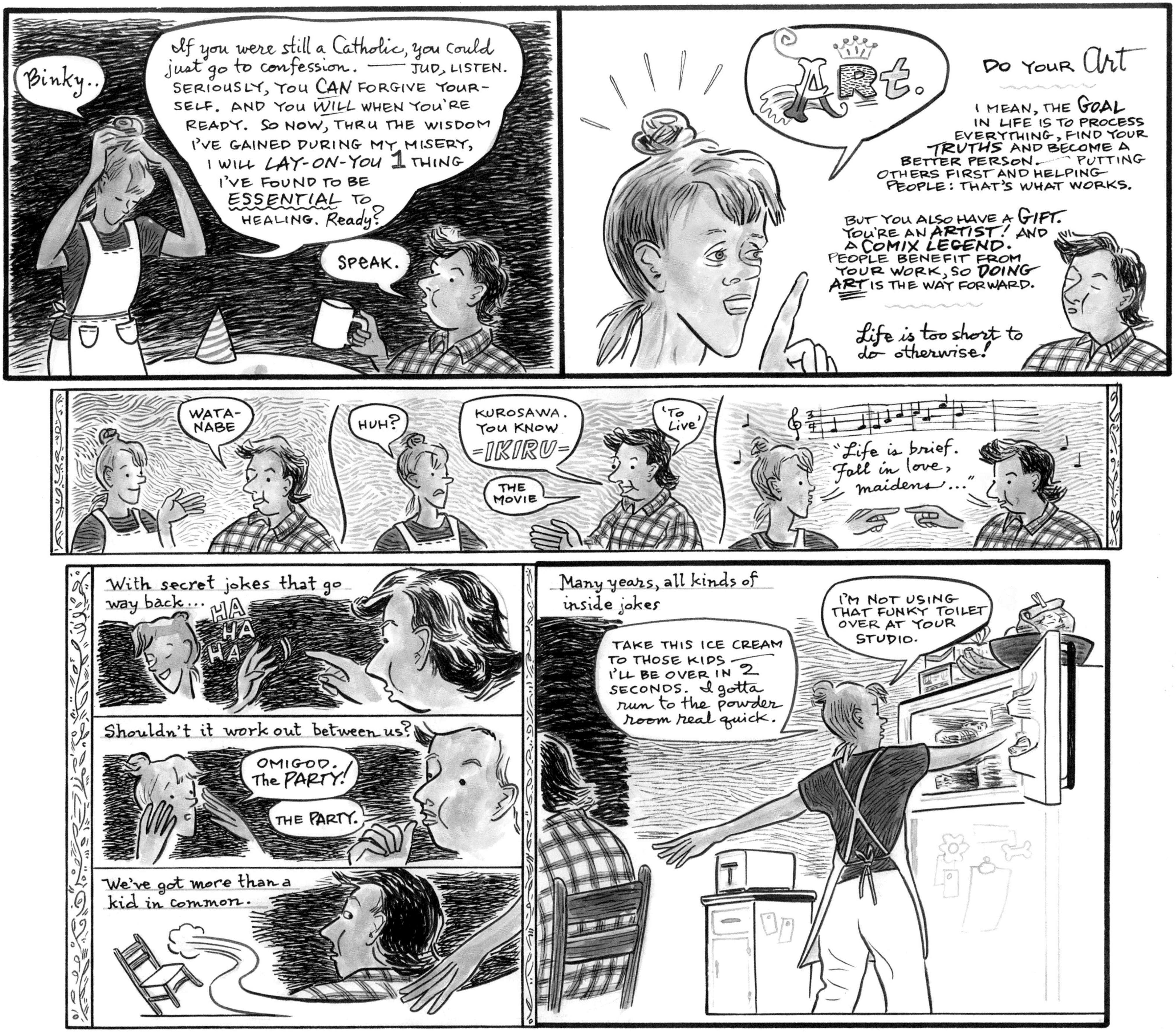

Binky..
If you were still a Catholic, you could just go to confession. — JUD, LISTEN. SERIOUSLY, YOU CAN FORGIVE YOURSELF. AND YOU WILL WHEN YOU'RE READY. SO NOW, THRU THE WISDOM I'VE GAINED DURING MY MISERY, I WILL LAY-ON-YOU 1 THING I'VE FOUND TO BE ESSENTIAL TO HEALING. Ready?
SPEAK.
ART.
DO YOUR Art
I MEAN, THE GOAL IN LIFE IS TO PROCESS EVERYTHING, FIND YOUR TRUTHS AND BECOME A BETTER PERSON. — PUTTING OTHERS FIRST AND HELPING PEOPLE: THAT'S WHAT WORKS.
BUT YOU ALSO HAVE A GIFT. YOU'RE AN ARTIST! AND A COMIX LEGEND. PEOPLE BENEFIT FROM YOUR WORK, SO DOING ART IS THE WAY FORWARD.
Life is too short to do otherwise!
WATA-NABE
HUH?
KUROSAWA. YOU KNOW =IKIRU=
THE MOVIE
'To Live'
"Life is brief. Fall in love, maidens..."
With secret jokes that go way back...
HA HA HA
Shouldn't it work out between us?
OMIGOD. The PARTY!
THE PARTY.
We've got more than a kid in common.
Many years, all kinds of inside jokes
TAKE THIS ICE CREAM TO THOSE KIDS — I'LL BE OVER IN 2 SECONDS. I gotta run to the powder room real quick.
I'M NOT USING THAT FUNKY TOILET OVER AT YOUR STUDIO.

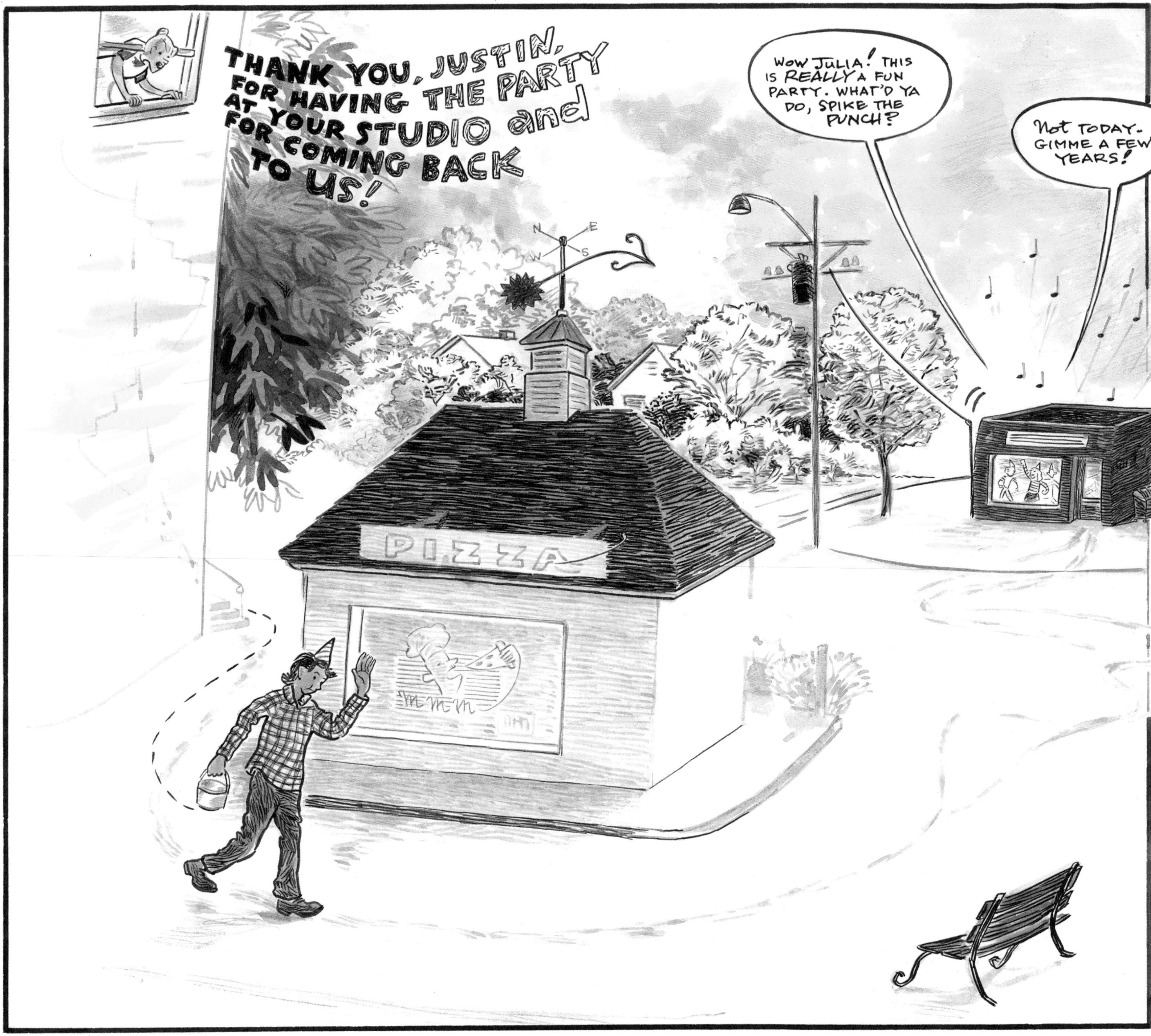
THANK YOU, JUSTIN, FOR HAVING THE PARTY AT YOUR STUDIO and FOR COMING BACK TO US!
WOW JULIA! THIS IS REALLY A FUN PARTY. WHAT'D YA DO, SPIKE THE PUNCH?
Not TODAY. GIMME A FEW YEARS!
PIZZA
N E W S

☆Attention Reader: ☆

This next chapter is about
going to St. Louis, Missouri
with my parents.

Due to space limitations,
a lot of writing is krammed
on onto each journal
page. My request: that
you SLOW DOWN, especially
after each sentence. Put
some miles between them.
Have a sip of Coke. It's
the pause that refreshes!

And also: take the time
to listen to the songs

each one.

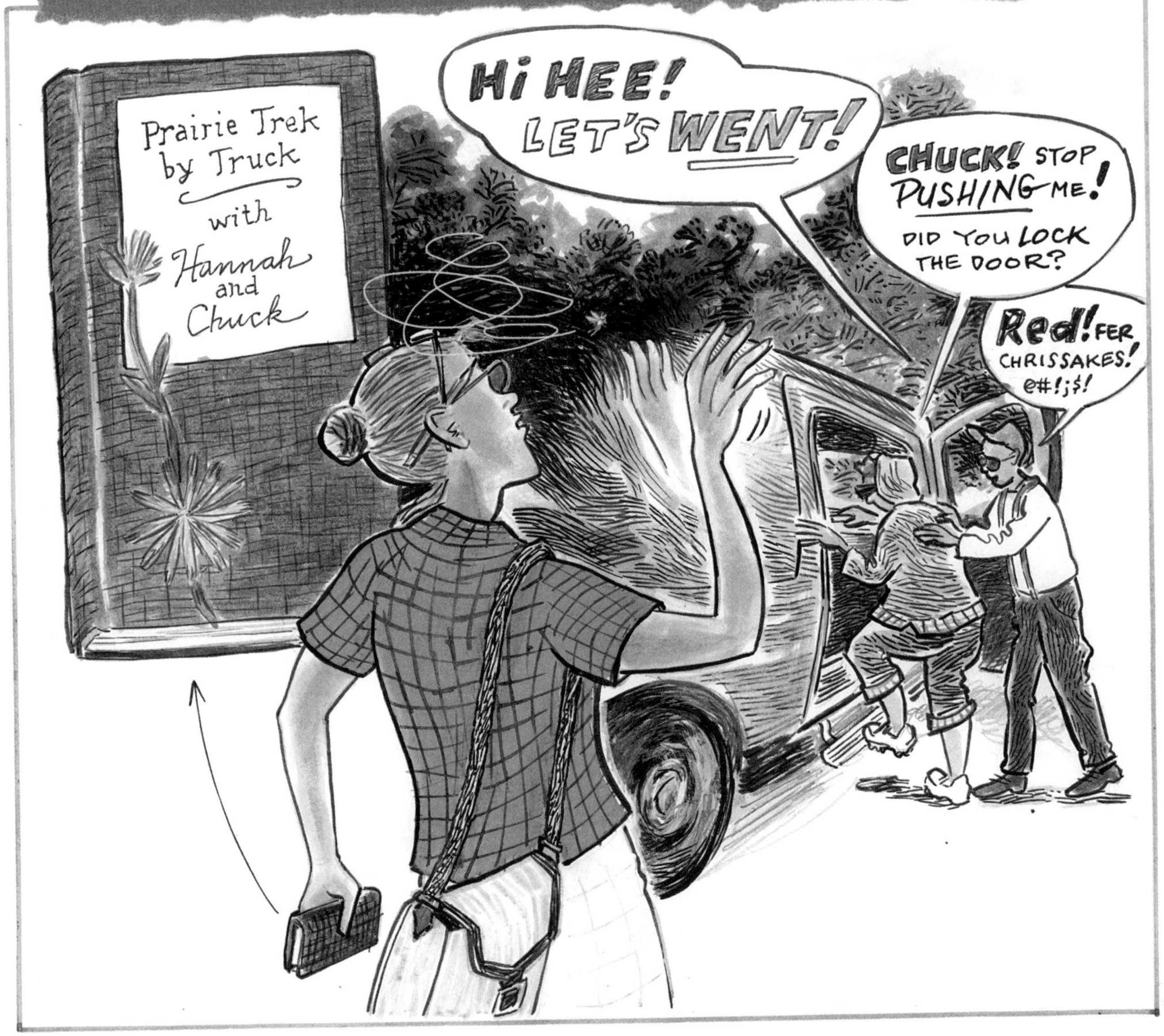

Prairie Trek by Truck with Hannah and Chuck
Hi HEE! LET'S WENT!
CHUCK! STOP PUSHING ME! DID YOU LOCK THE DOOR?
Red! FER CHRISSAKES! @#!;$!

Started the day with a spare tire-sized flapjack, topped with a hunk-a hunk-a big ol' butter, some maple syrup (the real stuff) and 2 skillfully browned piggie links. This is how Dad fixes breakfast. It's the meal he does best—.

Julia was gonna come stay with her Grandma, but at the last minute she got called in by the art camp to paint a pig, so Mom'll be coming with us. Awww no Dr. Phil today.

Dad's wearing his usual, Mom's in seersucker from the Penney's catalogue, and my pedal-pushers are stitched together out of an old tablecloth. Sew 4-H of me!

Everything on this trek—to the Army Records Office in St. Louis will be noted in this handsome, vintage Boorum & Pease Memo book, No. 6553. Got it at a yard sale back in Calif. in the 1980s. Totally rad! They don't make 'em anymore. Can't find 'em thriftin' or on the internet. So what I've got here is FINITE and rare, which makes me appreciate it even more. So—

with a full tank of gas, it's Hi-Hi-Hee as our caisson goes rolling along. I get to be the kid in the back seat again. And with Chuck Tyler at the wheel, there's nothing to fear. He's an EXCELLENT driver. One of Patton's boys, so call this a 'LUCKY FORWARD' roll. This means NO STOPPING, NO side trips. "Ladies, do what you gotta do while I gas-up."

Control over the wheel includes dominion over the radio... Turned VERY LOW. Barely audible songs from the American Songbook HINT at us. Because, the radio is on "in case of a bulletin from the authorities." Out here. In the middle of nowhere. On a spectacular day. ♫ Whispering towards us now: TRAVELING MAN by Rick Nelson. ♫ ♩ . . .

So much preparation went into this 2 day Road jolly to Missouri. You can't just show up. Micro-film viewing requires clearance. Something about the FREEDOM of INFORMATION Act. Bunch of forms faxed back and forth, signatures, SSNs. Blood promises. ☐ SIGN HERE

We are running with the big rigs and their 'naughty' mud flaps, to ♫ Terry Stafford's Amarillo by Morning. Unfolding before us is the great American landscape: waving prairies edging corn, corn, corn and soybeans. The breadbasket! One grand country, ours. The one Soldiers defend and die for. — Just saw a sign that reads GUNS SAVE LIVES. (!)

Mom and I are already SICK of Dad's STINKING pipe. Click the Zippo open. Light the bowl. Clank it SHUT. Fill the bowl again from the tobacco-pouch on lap. Click-PUFF-PUFF-Clank. Click-PUFF-PUFF-Clank. At least the window is cracked open just enough to suck out our complaints, along with ♫ Handy Man by ♩ James Taylor. The KHHKHHHKKH noise from the window, clicking, clanking RRR engines WWR wheels. So noisy! I can't ponder my angst over Justin and Rod, I conclude, as George's guitar gently weeps... ♫

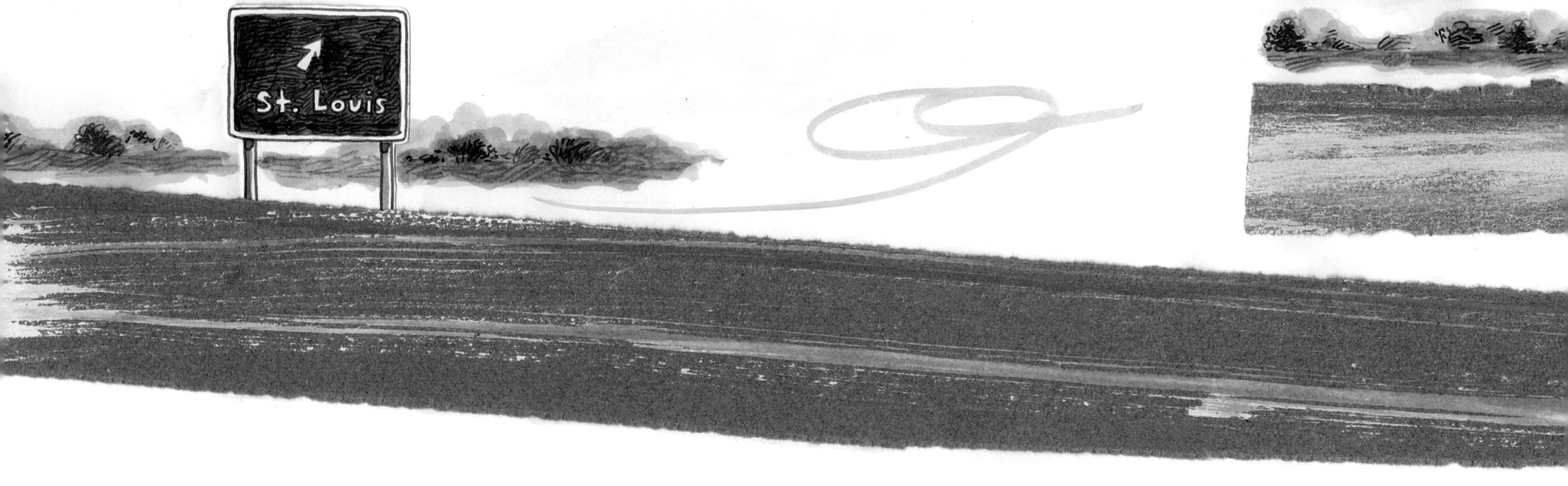

St. Louis

Hour 3. Still on the heartland conveyor belt. Remembering... 1961 It was cee-gars while driving. Outta the side of his mouth. DAD. He smoked and cussed at Janes for 'sitting on the pot' when they shoulda been speeding like he was. HONK HONK 'Gonna cause a Pile-up for Chrissakes.' Mom's reaction never varied: (sucking sound through her teeth) 'You're taking a chance, Chuck!' and her motion was to hit the fictitious passenger-side brake while tapping a non-existent steering wheel. Still does it.

♫ Lilting on the airwaves now: Gogi Grant ♪ Oh the way-ward wind.. is a restless wind...

Mom is a tree watcher. Not signs, not architecture.

She notices them out loud. "Look how big THAT one is!" Or, of one hacked by a storm, "Oh that poor sad fellow." But out in the wide open she becomes a CLOUD WATCHER. Not so much to shape out a lady's profile, but to marvel at the Magnificence of something so much bigger than she is, with the same awe she has for trees — I didn't know until just recently that she requests to have her ashes buried in a tree trunk. It's in her will.

Dad wishes to be up by his parents in Chicago. Ann is there, too. The plot was paid for years ago, "why waste money", he says. He's ok with Mom's tree wishes. "When you're gone, you're

gone. That's it." ♫♪

♪ ...and she was born the next of kin... to the wayward wind. ♪♪

M: "That blue stuff on the side of the road: CHICORY. Dad complained when they'd use too much of it. To stretch coffee during the Depression." Later, Dad (D) says "I'm gonna shoot BUSH if he takes away my Social Security." M: "You can't talk that way any more, Chuck. Zero tolerance. They'll lock you up." D: "Why not! The stock market's gonna go broke and there's no more poor farm. I'll be better off in prison." M: "Maybe. If you like chicory."

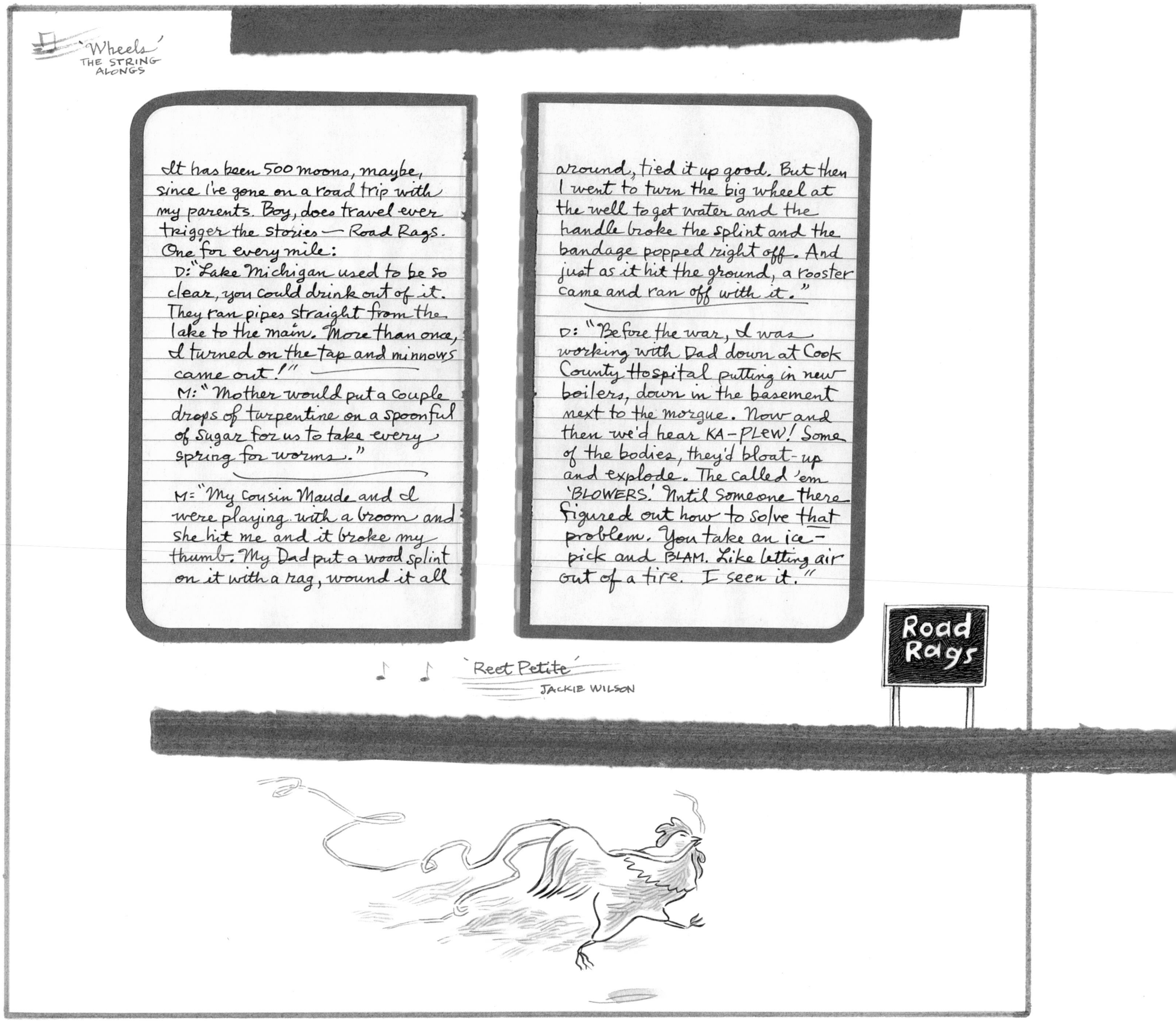
'Wheels'
THE STRING ALONGS
It has been 500 moons, maybe, since I've gone on a road trip with my parents. Boy, does travel ever trigger the stories — Road Rags. One for every mile:
D: "Lake Michigan used to be so clear, you could drink out of it. They ran pipes straight from the lake to the main. More than once, I turned on the tap and minnows came out!"
M: "Mother would put a couple drops of turpentine on a spoonful of sugar for us to take every spring for worms."
M: "My cousin Maude and I were playing with a broom and she hit me and it broke my thumb. My Dad put a wood splint on it with a rag, wound it all around, tied it up good. But then I went to turn the big wheel at the well to get water and the handle broke the splint and the bandage popped right off. And just as it hit the ground, a rooster came and ran off with it."
D: "Before the war, I was working with Dad down at Cook County Hospital putting in new boilers, down in the basement next to the morgue. Now and then we'd hear KA-PLEW! Some of the bodies, they'd bloat-up and explode. The called 'em 'BLOWERS.' Until someone there figured out how to solve that problem. You take an ice-pick and BLAM. Like letting air out of a tire. I seen it."
'Reet Petite'
JACKIE WILSON
Road Rags

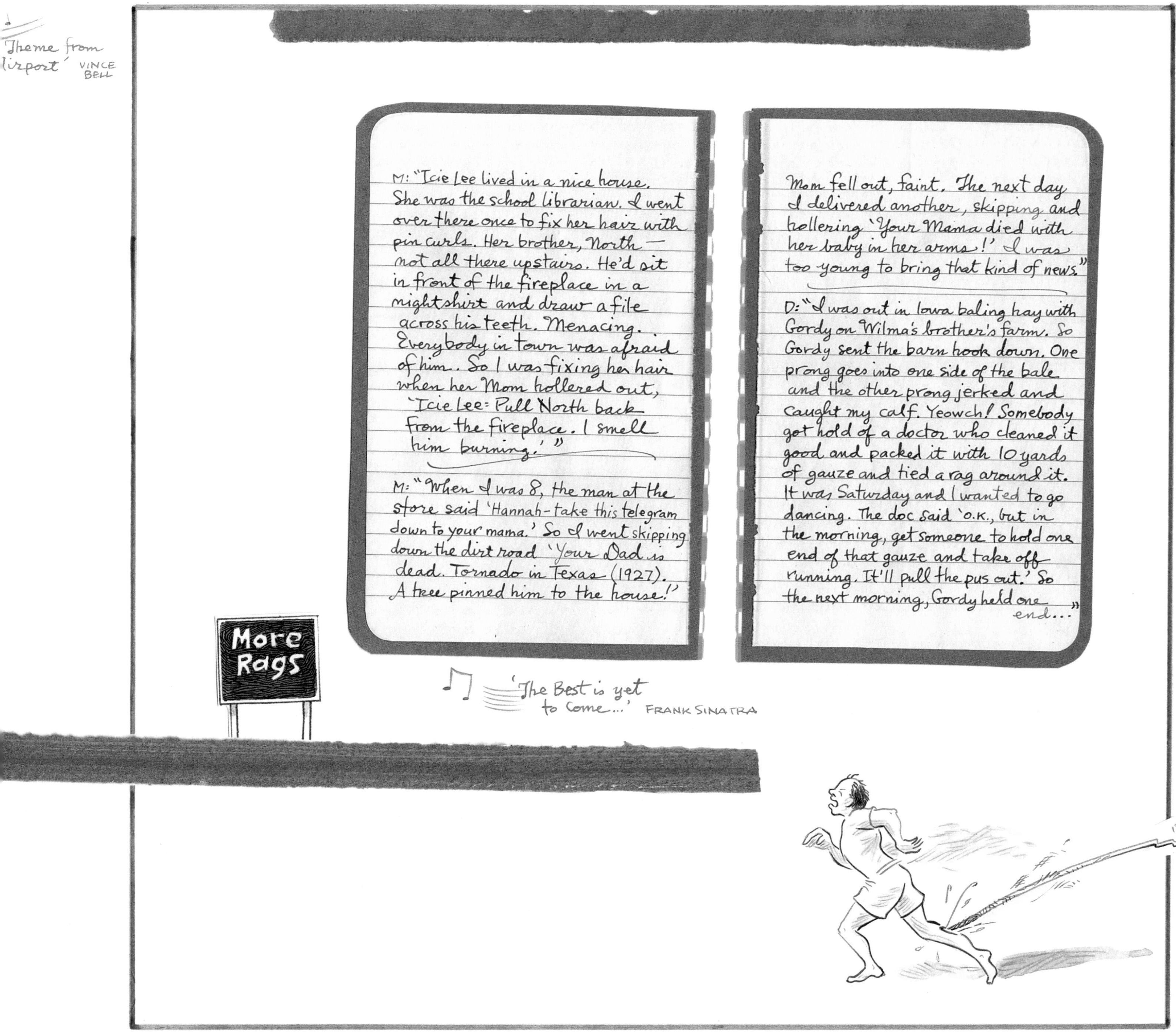
'Theme from Airport' VINCE BELL
M: "Icie Lee lived in a nice house. She was the school librarian. I went over there once to fix her hair with pin curls. Her brother, North — not all there upstairs. He'd sit in front of the fireplace in a nightshirt and draw a file across his teeth. Menacing. Everybody in town was afraid of him. So I was fixing her hair when her Mom hollered out, 'Icie Lee: Pull North back from the fireplace. I smell him burning.'"
M: "When I was 8, the man at the store said 'Hannah-take this telegram down to your mama.' So I went skipping down the dirt road 'Your Dad is dead. Tornado in Texas (1927). A tree pinned him to the house!'
Mom fell out, faint. The next day I delivered another, skipping and hollering 'Your Mama died with her baby in her arms!' I was too young to bring that kind of news."
D: "I was out in Iowa baling hay with Gordy on Wilma's brother's farm. So Gordy sent the barn hook down. One prong goes into one side of the bale and the other prong jerked and caught my calf. Yeowch! Somebody got hold of a doctor who cleaned it good and packed it with 10 yards of gauze and tied a rag around it. It was Saturday and I wanted to go dancing. The doc said 'O.K., but in the morning, get someone to hold one end of that gauze and take off running. It'll pull the pus out.' So the next morning, Gordy held one end..."
More Rags
'The Best is yet to Come...' FRANK SINATRA

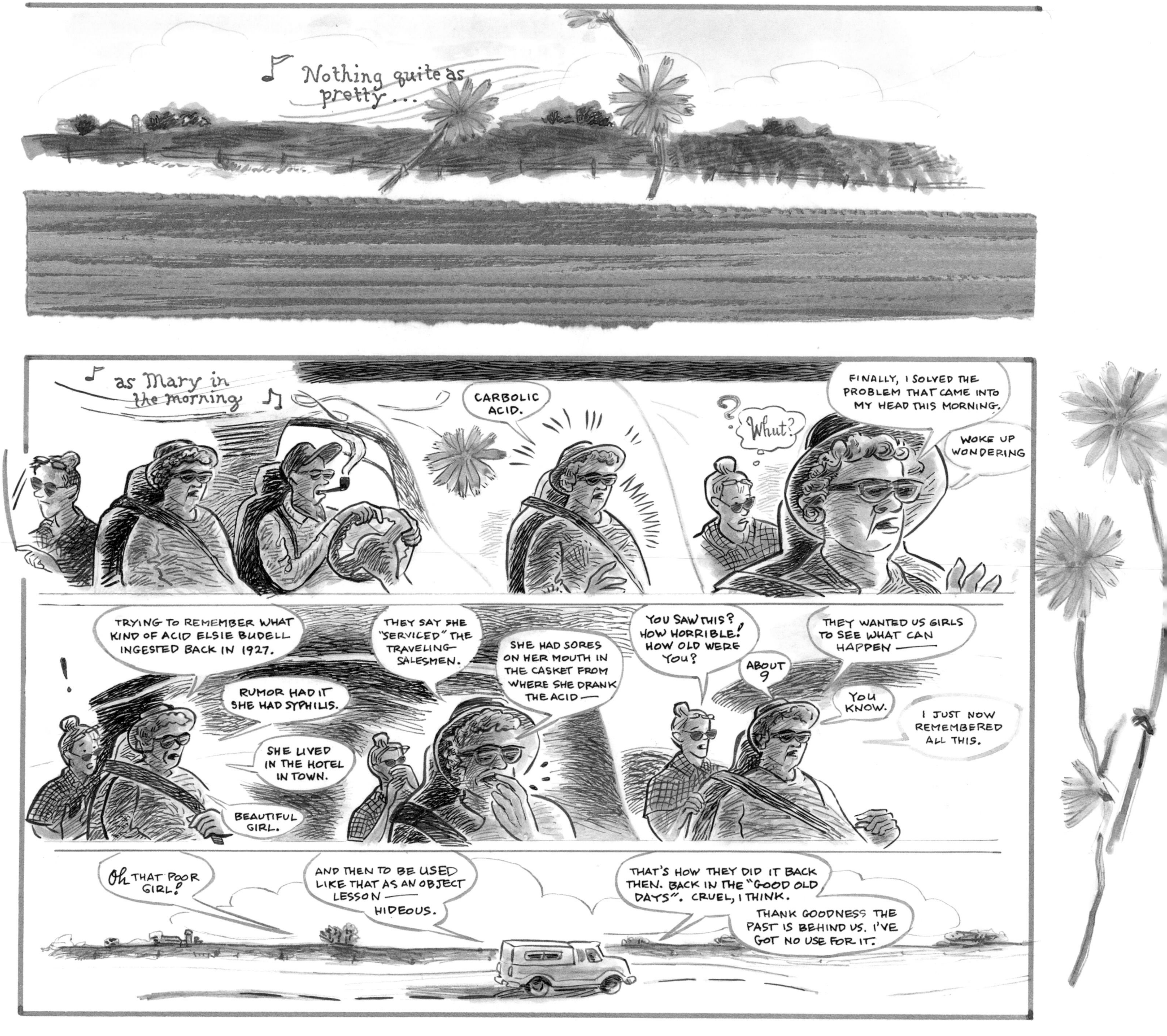
Nothing quite as pretty...
as Mary in the morning
CARBOLIC ACID.
Whut?
FINALLY, I SOLVED THE PROBLEM THAT CAME INTO MY HEAD THIS MORNING.
WOKE UP WONDERING
TRYING TO REMEMBER WHAT KIND OF ACID ELSIE BUDELL INGESTED BACK IN 1927.
!
RUMOR HAD IT SHE HAD SYPHILIS.
SHE LIVED IN THE HOTEL IN TOWN.
BEAUTIFUL GIRL.
THEY SAY SHE "SERVICED" THE TRAVELING SALESMEN.
SHE HAD SORES ON HER MOUTH IN THE CASKET FROM WHERE SHE DRANK THE ACID—
YOU SAW THIS? HOW HORRIBLE! HOW OLD WERE YOU?
ABOUT 9
THEY WANTED US GIRLS TO SEE WHAT CAN HAPPEN—
YOU KNOW.
I JUST NOW REMEMBERED ALL THIS.
Oh THAT POOR GIRL!
AND THEN TO BE USED LIKE THAT AS AN OBJECT LESSON— HIDEOUS.
THAT'S HOW THEY DID IT BACK THEN. BACK IN THE "GOOD OLD DAYS". CRUEL, I THINK.
THANK GOODNESS THE PAST IS BEHIND US. I'VE GOT NO USE FOR IT.

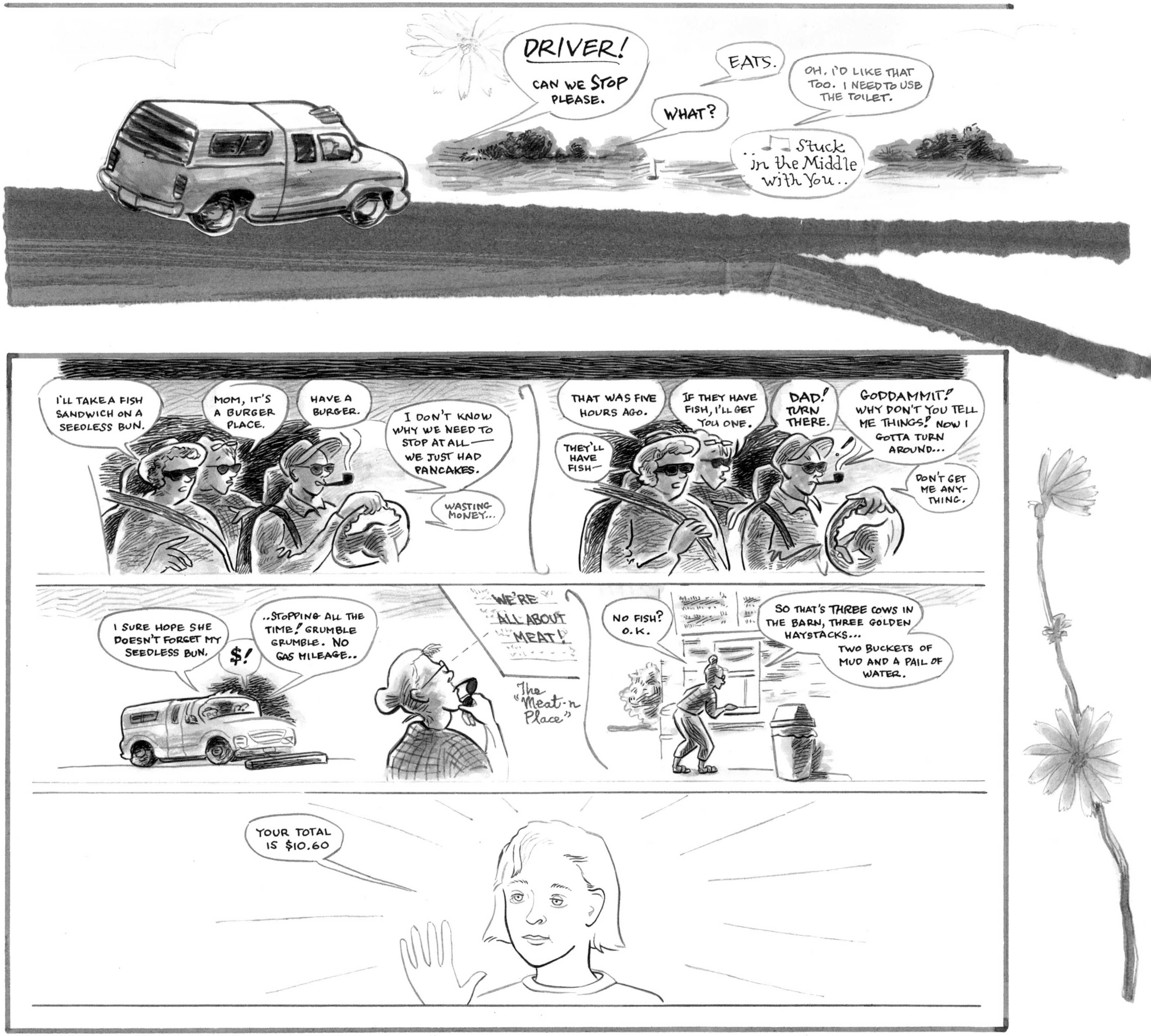
DRIVER!
CAN WE STOP PLEASE.
WHAT?
EATS.
OH. I'D LIKE THAT TOO. I NEED TO USE THE TOILET.
Stuck in the Middle with You..
I'LL TAKE A FISH SANDWICH ON A SEEDLESS BUN.
MOM, IT'S A BURGER PLACE.
HAVE A BURGER.
I DON'T KNOW WHY WE NEED TO STOP AT ALL— WE JUST HAD PANCAKES.
WASTING MONEY...
THAT WAS FIVE HOURS AGO.
THEY'LL HAVE FISH—
IF THEY HAVE FISH, I'LL GET YOU ONE.
DAD! TURN THERE.
GODDAMMIT! WHY DON'T YOU TELL ME THINGS! NOW I GOTTA TURN AROUND...
DON'T GET ME ANYTHING.
I SURE HOPE SHE DOESN'T FORGET MY SEEDLESS BUN.
$!
..STOPPING ALL THE TIME! GRUMBLE GRUMBLE. NO GAS MILEAGE..
WE'RE ALL ABOUT MEAT!
The "Meat-n Place"
NO FISH? O.K.
SO THAT'S THREE COWS IN THE BARN, THREE GOLDEN HAYSTACKS...
TWO BUCKETS OF MUD AND A PAIL OF WATER.
YOUR TOTAL IS $10.60

♪ Shoo bop shoo bop
my baby shoo
bop shoo bop ♪♪
♪♪ Hello Stranger ♪♪ (Hello
Barbara Lewis!)

That girl back there who
served us: Wearing an expression
I've seen in a painting. The
Mona Lisa, I think. In fact,
I'll call her that. Mona Lisa
of the Midwest, I love you.
Or, she could be someone Dorothea
Lange would have photographed.
♪♪ oooo seems like a
mighty long time ... shoo bop
shoo bop

Mom says she's got no use
for the past. It's true that
things have to change, but I
love their stories. I love them
juxtaposed on this prairie
trek. ── Mom and Dad
are so-o-o WPA mural.

They are ART to me, as much as
Grant Wood or Edward Hopper.
American Art, as in Jackson
Pollock. Heartland + Ashcan +
Action + 20TH Century = these
true people. But unlike art,
experience is VAPOR ──. I'm
doing my best to catch it and
hold it on these pages before it's
out the window with Dad's smoke.
♪ ♪

♪ On a day ── like today ──
we'll pass the time away ── writing
Love Letters in .. the sand ♪
Pat Boone croons.

M: "I wrote your Dad a letter
every day during the war."
me: "Really? A year and a half?
Wow, that's a lot of letters. What
happened to them?" = INTERRUPTION
D "HEY. Which exit now. We're
here"

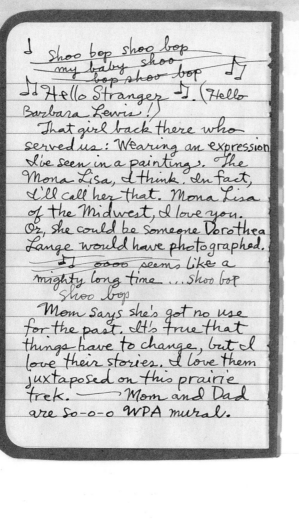

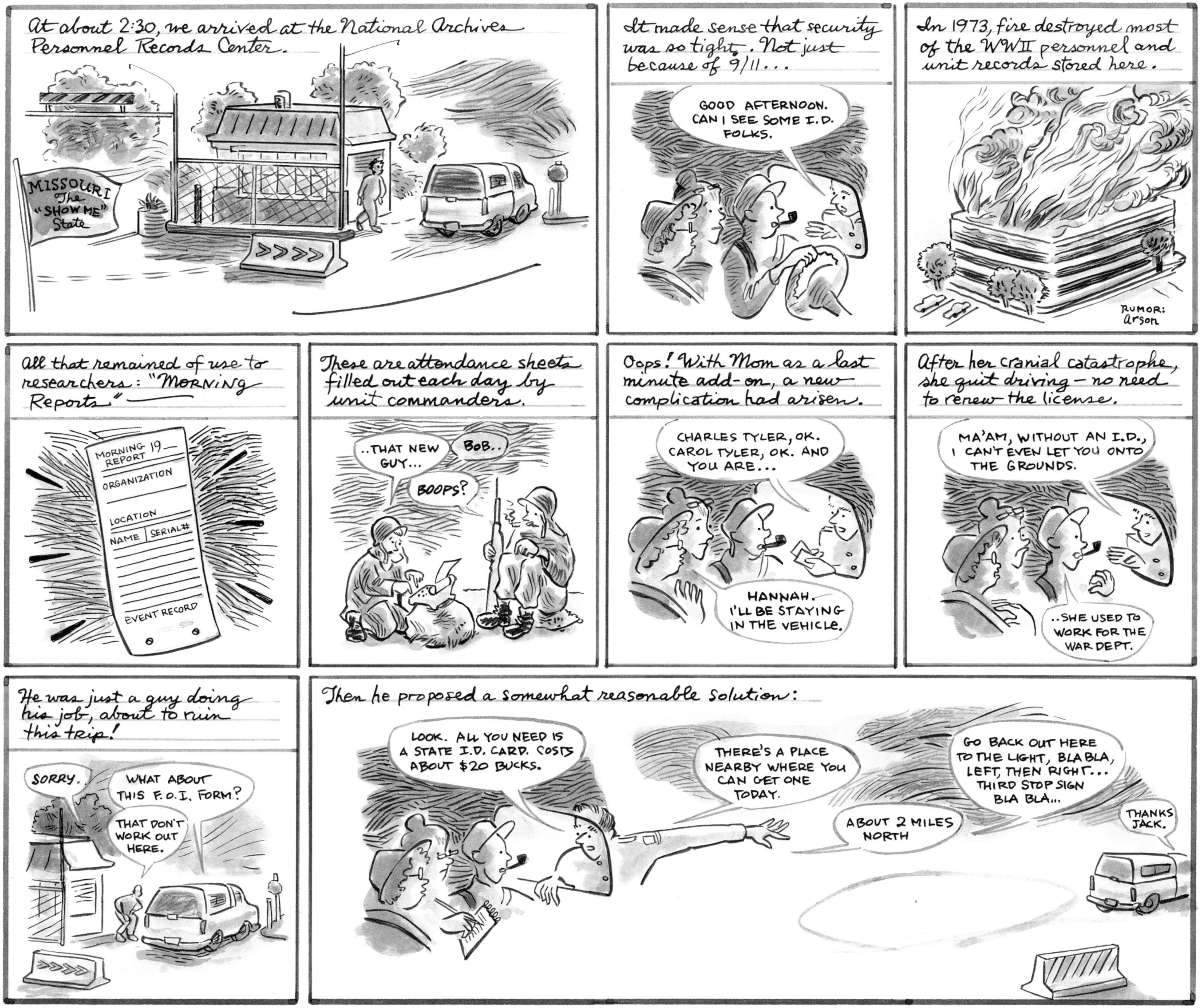
At about 2:30, we arrived at the National Archives Personnel Records Center.
MISSOURI The "SHOW ME" State
>>>>
It made sense that security was so tight. Not just because of 9/11...
GOOD AFTERNOON. CAN I SEE SOME I.D. FOLKS.
In 1973, fire destroyed most of the WWII personnel and unit records stored here.
RUMOR: arson
All that remained of use to researchers: "MORNING Reports"
MORNING REPORT 19__
ORGANIZATION
LOCATION
NAME
SERIAL#
EVENT RECORD
These are attendance sheets filled out each day by unit commanders.
..THAT NEW GUY...
BOB..
BOOPS?
Oops! With Mom as a last minute add-on, a new complication had arisen.
CHARLES TYLER, OK. CAROL TYLER, OK. AND YOU ARE...
HANNAH. I'LL BE STAYING IN THE VEHICLE.
After her cranial catastrophe, she quit driving—no need to renew the license.
MA'AM, WITHOUT AN I.D., I CAN'T EVEN LET YOU ONTO THE GROUNDS.
..SHE USED TO WORK FOR THE WAR DEPT.
He was just a guy doing his job, about to ruin this trip!
SORRY..
WHAT ABOUT THIS F.O.I. FORM?
THAT DON'T WORK OUT HERE.
Then he proposed a somewhat reasonable solution:
LOOK. ALL YOU NEED IS A STATE I.D. CARD. COSTS ABOUT $20 BUCKS.
THERE'S A PLACE NEARBY WHERE YOU CAN GET ONE TODAY.
ABOUT 2 MILES NORTH
GO BACK OUT HERE TO THE LIGHT, BLA BLA, LEFT, THEN RIGHT... THIRD STOP SIGN BLA BLA...
THANKS JACK.

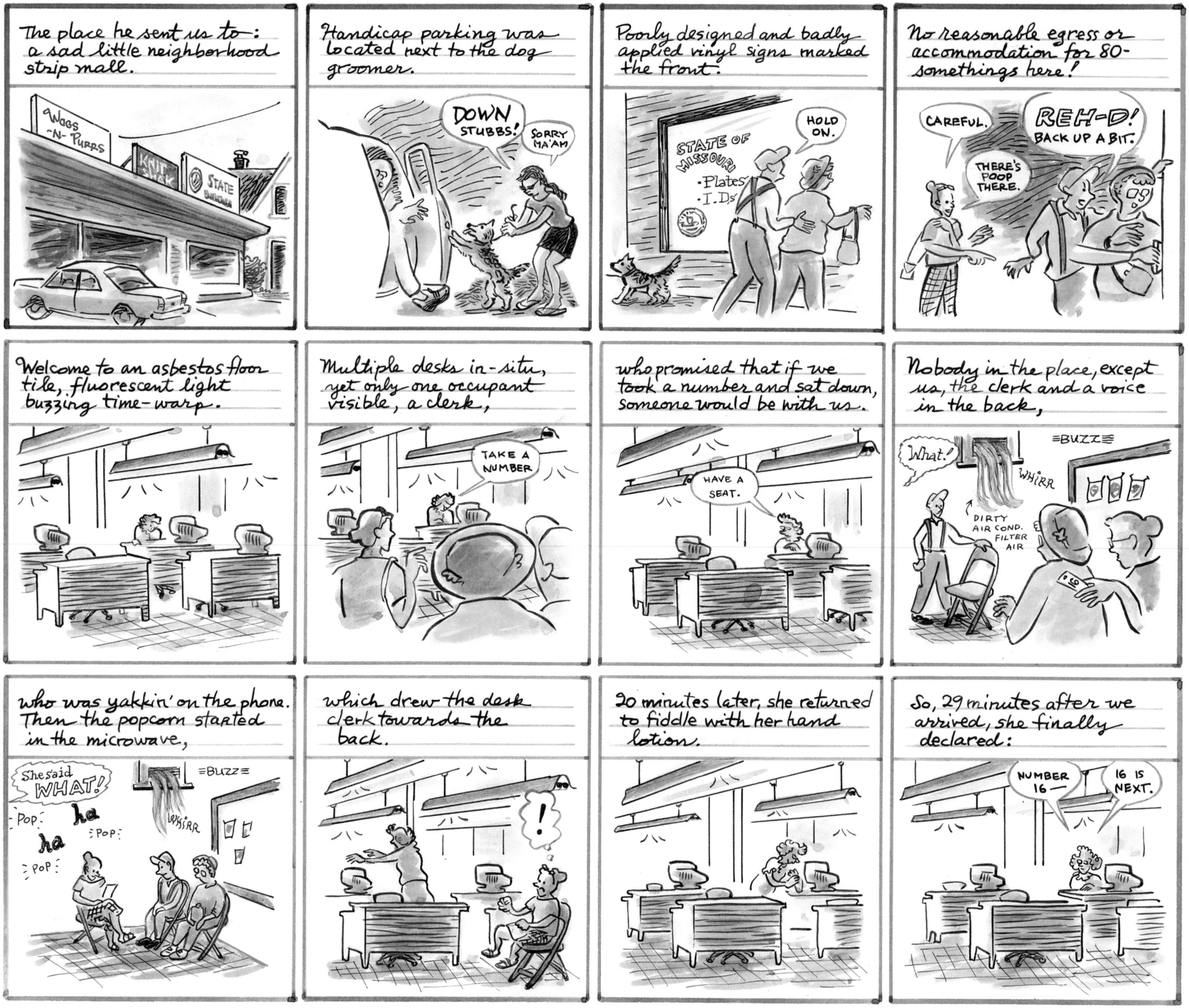
The place he sent us to: a sad little neighborhood strip mall.
Wags -N- Purrs
Knit Shak
State
Handicap parking was located next to the dog groomer.
DOWN STUBBS!
SORRY MA'AM
Poorly designed and badly applied vinyl signs marked the front.
STATE OF MISSOURI
•Plates
•I.Ds
HOLD ON.
No reasonable egress or accommodation for 80-somethings here!
CAREFUL.
THERE'S POOP THERE.
REH-D!
BACK UP A BIT.
Welcome to an asbestos floor tile, fluorescent light buzzing time-warp.
Multiple desks in-situ, yet only one occupant visible, a clerk,
TAKE A NUMBER
who promised that if we took a number and sat down, someone would be with us.
HAVE A SEAT.
Nobody in the place, except us, the clerk and a voice in the back,
What!
BUZZ
WHIRR
DIRTY AIR COND. FILTER AIR
who was yakkin' on the phone. Then the popcorn started in the microwave,
She said WHAT!
BUZZ
POP
ha
POP
ha
POP
WHIRR
which drew the desk clerk towards the back.
!
20 minutes later, she returned to fiddle with her hand lotion.
So, 29 minutes after we arrived, she finally declared:
NUMBER 16 —
16 IS NEXT.

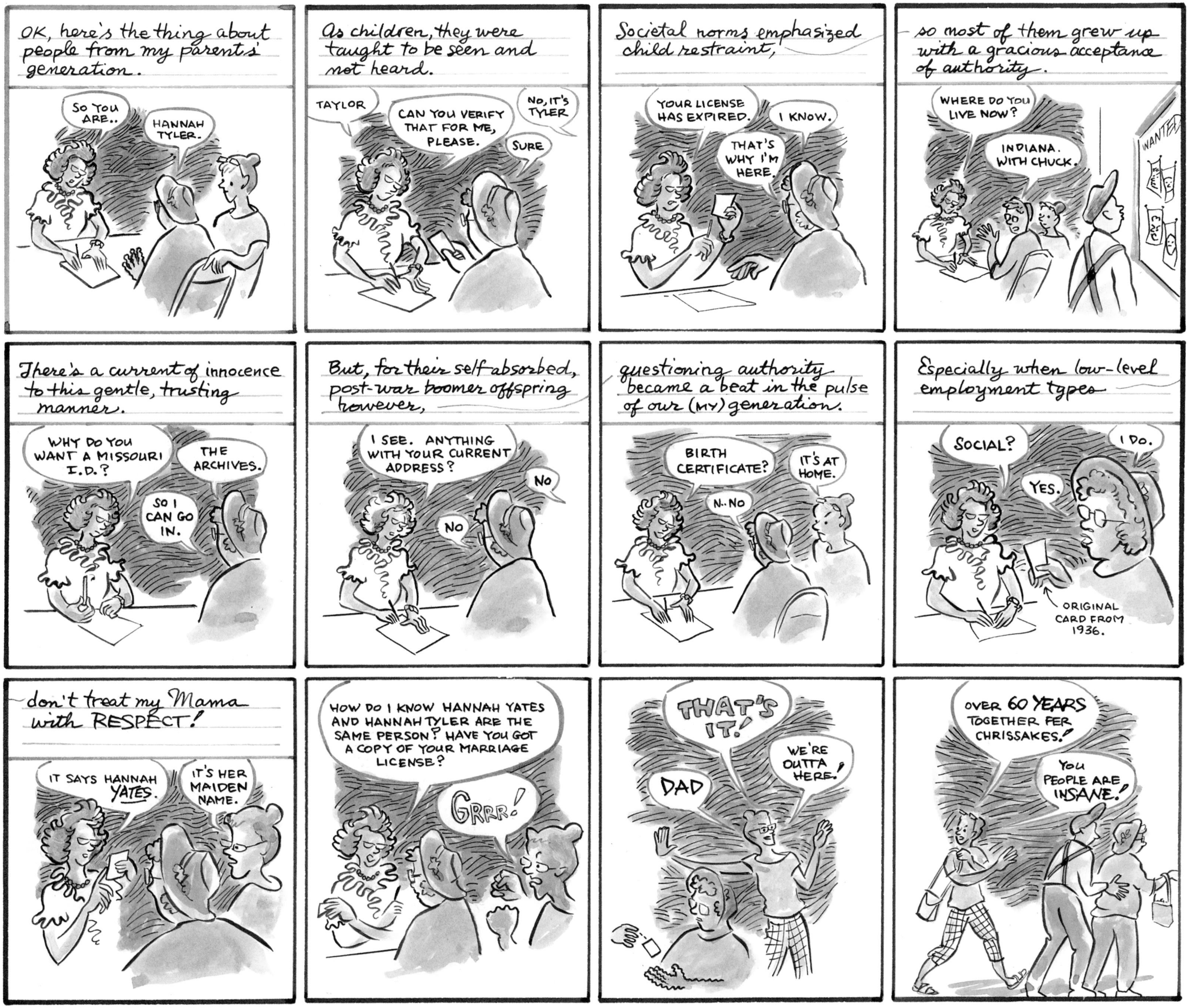
OK, here's the thing about people from my parents' generation.
SO YOU ARE..
HANNAH TYLER.
As children, they were taught to be seen and not heard.
TAYLOR
CAN YOU VERIFY THAT FOR ME, PLEASE.
NO, IT'S TYLER
SURE
Societal norms emphasized child restraint,
YOUR LICENSE HAS EXPIRED.
I KNOW.
THAT'S WHY I'M HERE.
so most of them grew up with a gracious acceptance of authority.
WHERE DO YOU LIVE NOW?
INDIANA. WITH CHUCK.
WANTED
There's a current of innocence to this gentle, trusting manner.
WHY DO YOU WANT A MISSOURI I.D.?
THE ARCHIVES.
SO I CAN GO IN.
But, for their self absorbed, post-war boomer offspring however,
I SEE. ANYTHING WITH YOUR CURRENT ADDRESS?
NO
NO
questioning authority became a beat in the pulse of our (MY) generation.
BIRTH CERTIFICATE?
IT'S AT HOME.
N..NO
Especially when low-level employment types
SOCIAL?
I DO.
YES.
ORIGINAL CARD FROM 1936.
don't treat my Mama with RESPECT!
IT SAYS HANNAH YATES.
IT'S HER MAIDEN NAME.
HOW DO I KNOW HANNAH YATES AND HANNAH TYLER ARE THE SAME PERSON? HAVE YOU GOT A COPY OF YOUR MARRIAGE LICENSE?
GRRR!
THAT'S IT!
DAD
WE'RE OUTTA HERE!
OVER 60 YEARS TOGETHER FER CHRISSAKES!
YOU PEOPLE ARE INSANE!

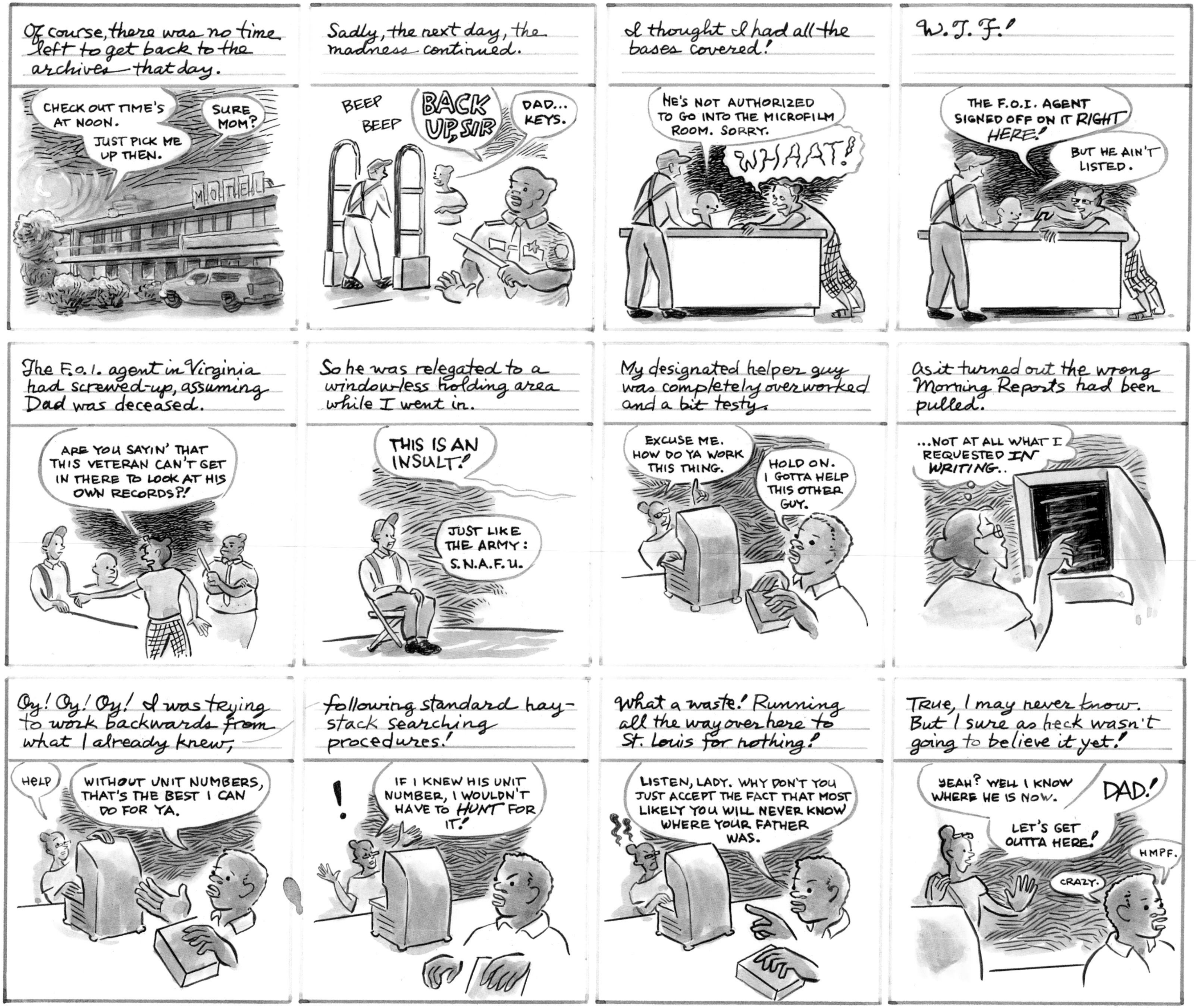
Of course, there was no time left to get back to the archives that day.
CHECK OUT TIME'S AT NOON.
SURE MOM?
JUST PICK ME UP THEN.
Sadly, the next day, the madness continued.
BEEP
BEEP
BACK UP, SIR
DAD... KEYS.
I thought I had all the bases covered!
HE'S NOT AUTHORIZED TO GO INTO THE MICROFILM ROOM. SORRY.
WHAAT!
W.T.F.!
THE F.O.I. AGENT SIGNED OFF ON IT RIGHT HERE!
BUT HE AIN'T LISTED.
The F.O.I. agent in Virginia had screwed-up, assuming Dad was deceased.
ARE YOU SAYIN' THAT THIS VETERAN CAN'T GET IN THERE TO LOOK AT HIS OWN RECORDS?!
So he was relegated to a windowless holding area while I went in.
THIS IS AN INSULT!
JUST LIKE THE ARMY: S.N.A.F.U.
My designated helper guy was completely overworked and a bit testy.
EXCUSE ME. HOW DO YA WORK THIS THING.
HOLD ON. I GOTTA HELP THIS OTHER GUY.
As it turned out the wrong Morning Reports had been pulled.
...NOT AT ALL WHAT I REQUESTED IN WRITING..
Oy! Oy! Oy! I was trying to work backwards from what I already knew,
HELP
WITHOUT UNIT NUMBERS, THAT'S THE BEST I CAN DO FOR YA.
following standard hay-stack searching procedures!
!
IF I KNEW HIS UNIT NUMBER, I WOULDN'T HAVE TO HUNT FOR IT!
What a waste! Running all the way over here to St. Louis for nothing!
LISTEN, LADY. WHY DON'T YOU JUST ACCEPT THE FACT THAT MOST LIKELY YOU WILL NEVER KNOW WHERE YOUR FATHER WAS.
True, I may never know. But I sure as heck wasn't going to believe it yet!
YEAH? WELL I KNOW WHERE HE IS NOW.
DAD!
LET'S GET OUTTA HERE!
HMPF.
CRAZY.

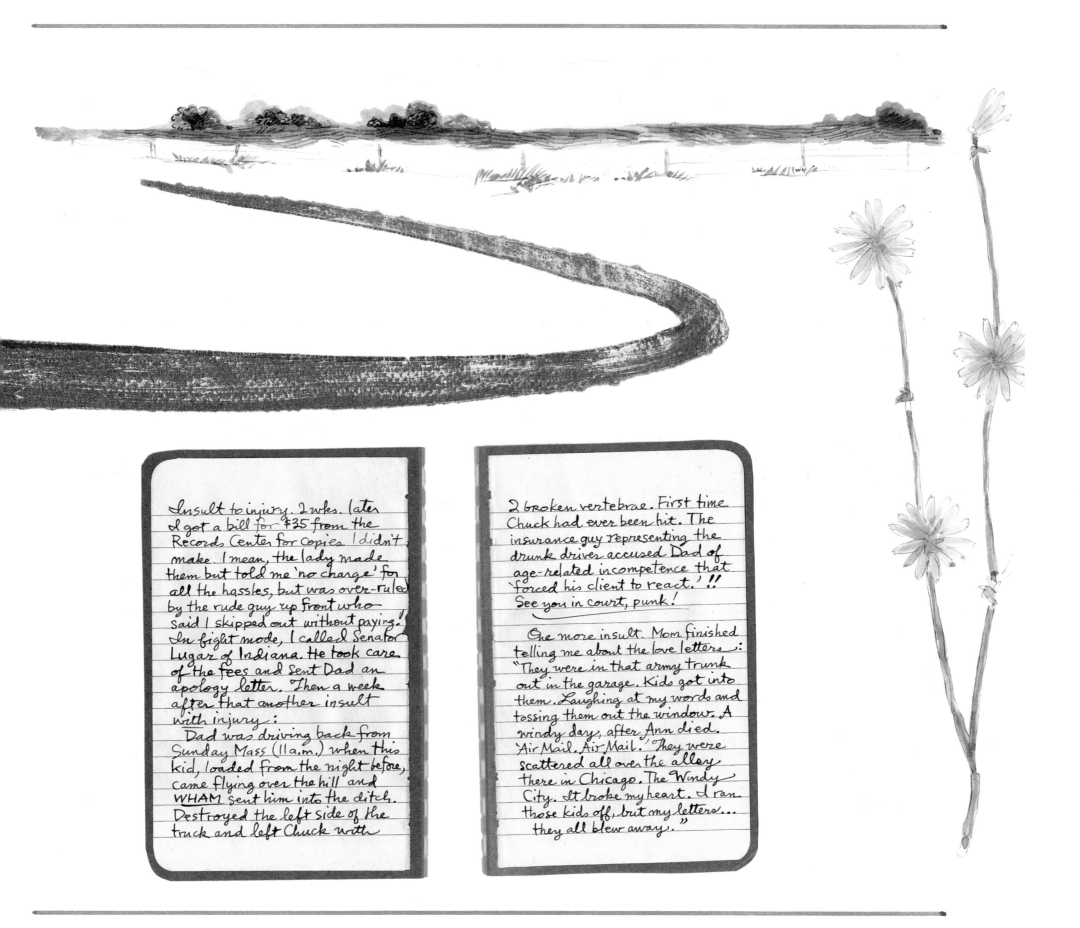

Insult to injury. 2 wks. later
I got a bill for $35 from the
Records Center for copies I didn't
make. I mean, the lady made
them but told me 'no charge' for
all the hassles, but was over-ruled
by the rude guy up front who
said I skipped out without paying!
In fight mode, I called Senator
Lugar of Indiana. He took care
of the fees and sent Dad an
apology letter. Then a week
after that another insult
with injury:
Dad was driving back from
Sunday Mass (11 a.m.) when this
kid, loaded from the night before,
came flying over the hill and
WHAM sent him into the ditch.
Destroyed the left side of the
truck and left Chuck with

2 broken vertebrae. First time
Chuck had ever been hit. The
insurance guy representing the
drunk driver accused Dad of
age-related incompetence that
'forced his client to react.' !!
See you in court, punk!

One more insult. Mom finished
telling me about the love letters:
"They were in that army trunk
out in the garage. Kids got into
them. Laughing at my words and
tossing them out the window. A
windy day, after Ann died.
'Air Mail. Air Mail.' They were
scattered all over the alley
there in Chicago. The Windy
City. It broke my heart. I ran
those kids off, but my letters...
they all blew away."

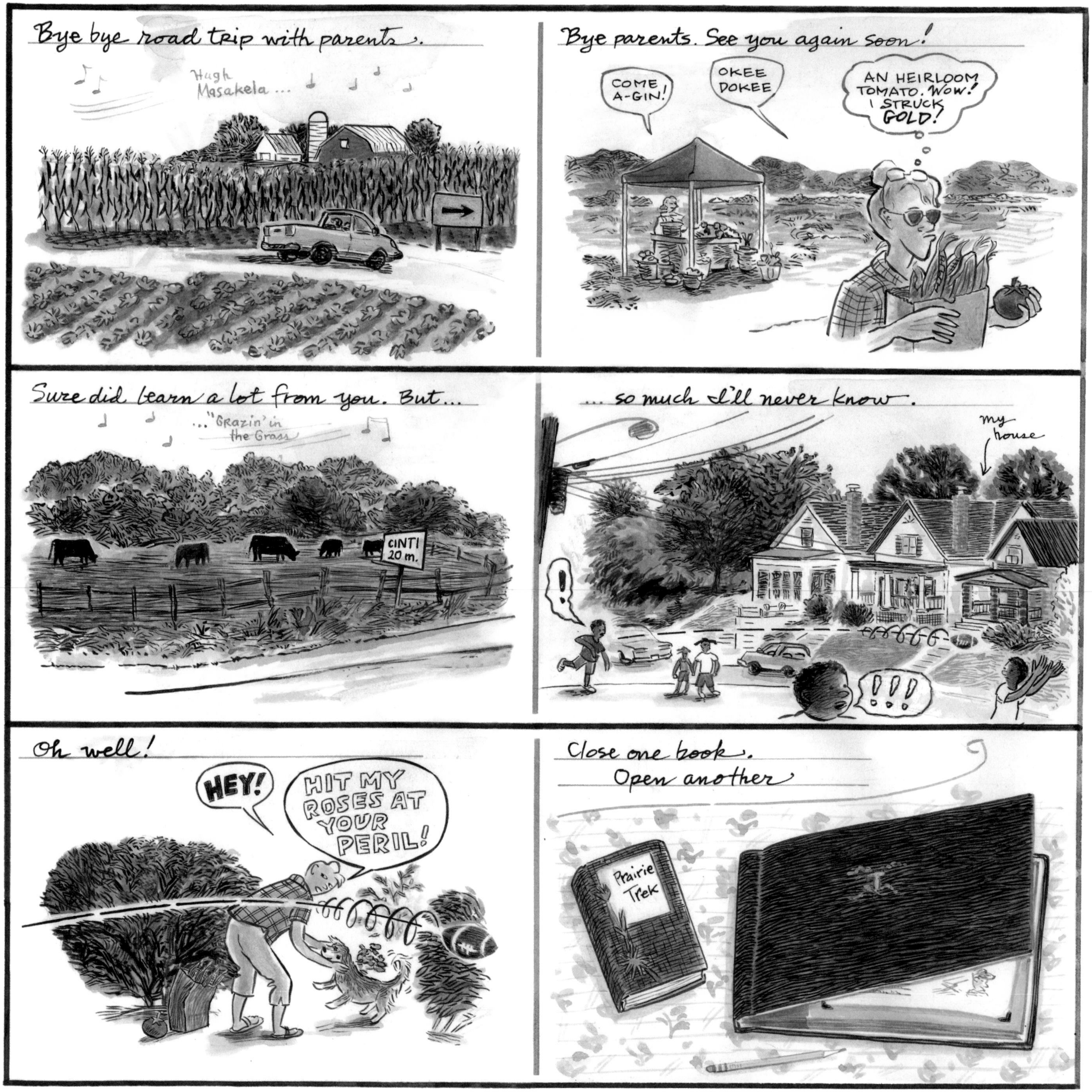
Bye bye road trip with parents.
Hugh Masakela ...
Bye parents. See you again soon!
COME A-GIN!
OKEE DOKEE
AN HEIRLOOM TOMATO. WOW! I STRUCK GOLD!
Sure did learn a lot from you. But...
..."Grazin' in the Grass
CINTI 20 m.
... so much I'll never know.
my house
!
!!!
Oh well!
HEY!
HIT MY ROSES AT YOUR PERIL!
Close one book.
Open another
Prairie Trek

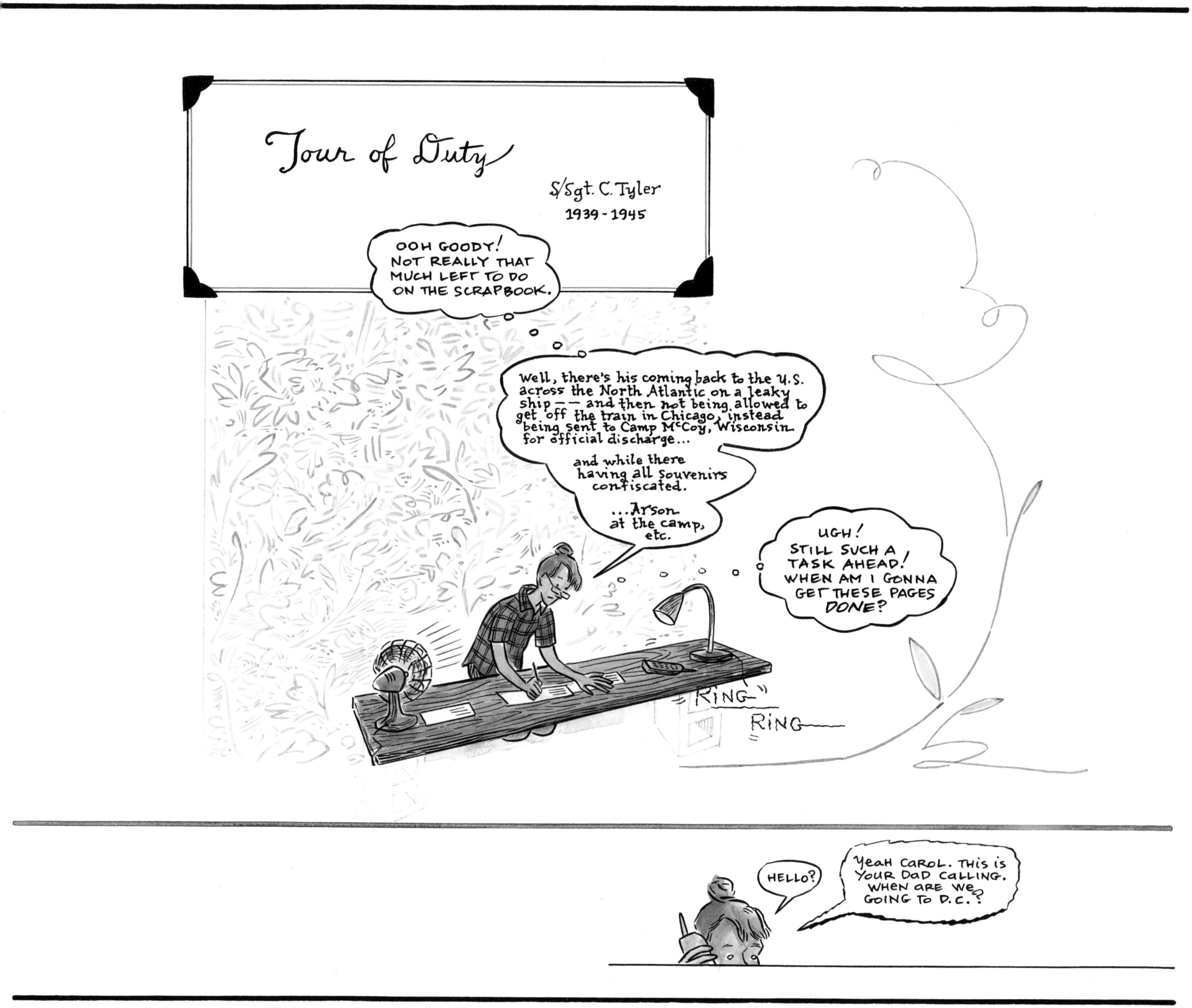

Tour of Duty
S/Sgt. C. Tyler
1939 - 1945
OOH GOODY! NOT REALLY THAT MUCH LEFT TO DO ON THE SCRAPBOOK.
Well, there's his coming back to the U.S. across the North Atlantic on a leaky ship -- and then not being allowed to get off the train in Chicago, instead being sent to Camp McCoy, Wisconsin for official discharge...
and while there having all souvenirs confiscated.
...Arson at the camp, etc.
UGH! STILL SUCH A TASK AHEAD! WHEN AM I GONNA GET THESE PAGES DONE?
RING
RING
HELLO?
YEAH CAROL. THIS IS YOUR DAD CALLING. WHEN ARE WE GOING TO D.C.?

TRIP TO THE NATIONAL ARCHIVES AND THE WWII MEMORIAL

WASHINGTON, D.C.
JULY, 2004

"*What is Past is Prologue*"   Shakespeare quote on Archives.

"THE PAST IS NEVER DEAD. IT'S NOT EVEN PAST."

Faulkner quote – at local library history section

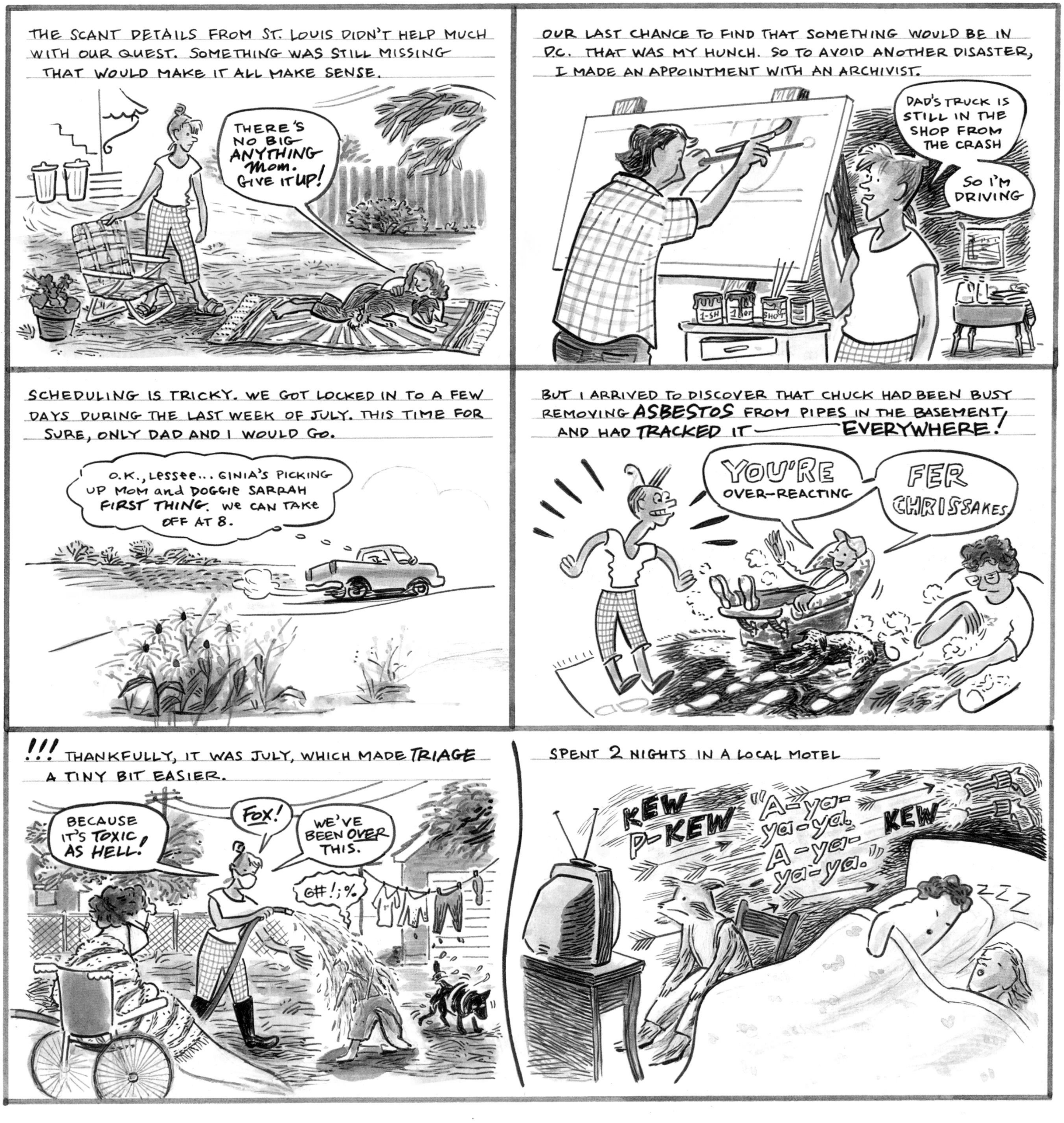
THE SCANT DETAILS FROM ST. LOUIS DIDN'T HELP MUCH WITH OUR QUEST. SOMETHING WAS STILL MISSING THAT WOULD MAKE IT ALL MAKE SENSE.
THERE'S NO BIG ANYTHING MOM. GIVE IT UP!
OUR LAST CHANCE TO FIND THAT SOMETHING WOULD BE IN D.C. THAT WAS MY HUNCH. SO TO AVOID ANOTHER DISASTER, I MADE AN APPOINTMENT WITH AN ARCHIVIST.
DAD'S TRUCK IS STILL IN THE SHOP FROM THE CRASH
SO I'M DRIVING
SCHEDULING IS TRICKY. WE GOT LOCKED IN TO A FEW DAYS DURING THE LAST WEEK OF JULY. THIS TIME FOR SURE, ONLY DAD AND I WOULD GO.
O.K., LESSEE... GINIA'S PICKING UP MOM AND DOGGIE SARRAH FIRST THING. WE CAN TAKE OFF AT 8.
BUT I ARRIVED TO DISCOVER THAT CHUCK HAD BEEN BUSY REMOVING ASBESTOS FROM PIPES IN THE BASEMENT, AND HAD TRACKED IT — EVERYWHERE!
YOU'RE OVER-REACTING
FER CHRISSAKES
!!! THANKFULLY, IT WAS JULY, WHICH MADE TRIAGE A TINY BIT EASIER.
BECAUSE IT'S TOXIC AS HELL!
FOX!
WE'VE BEEN OVER THIS.
G#!;%
SPENT 2 NIGHTS IN A LOCAL MOTEL
KEW
P-KEW
"A-YA-YA-YA. A-YA-YA-YA."
KEW
Z Z Z

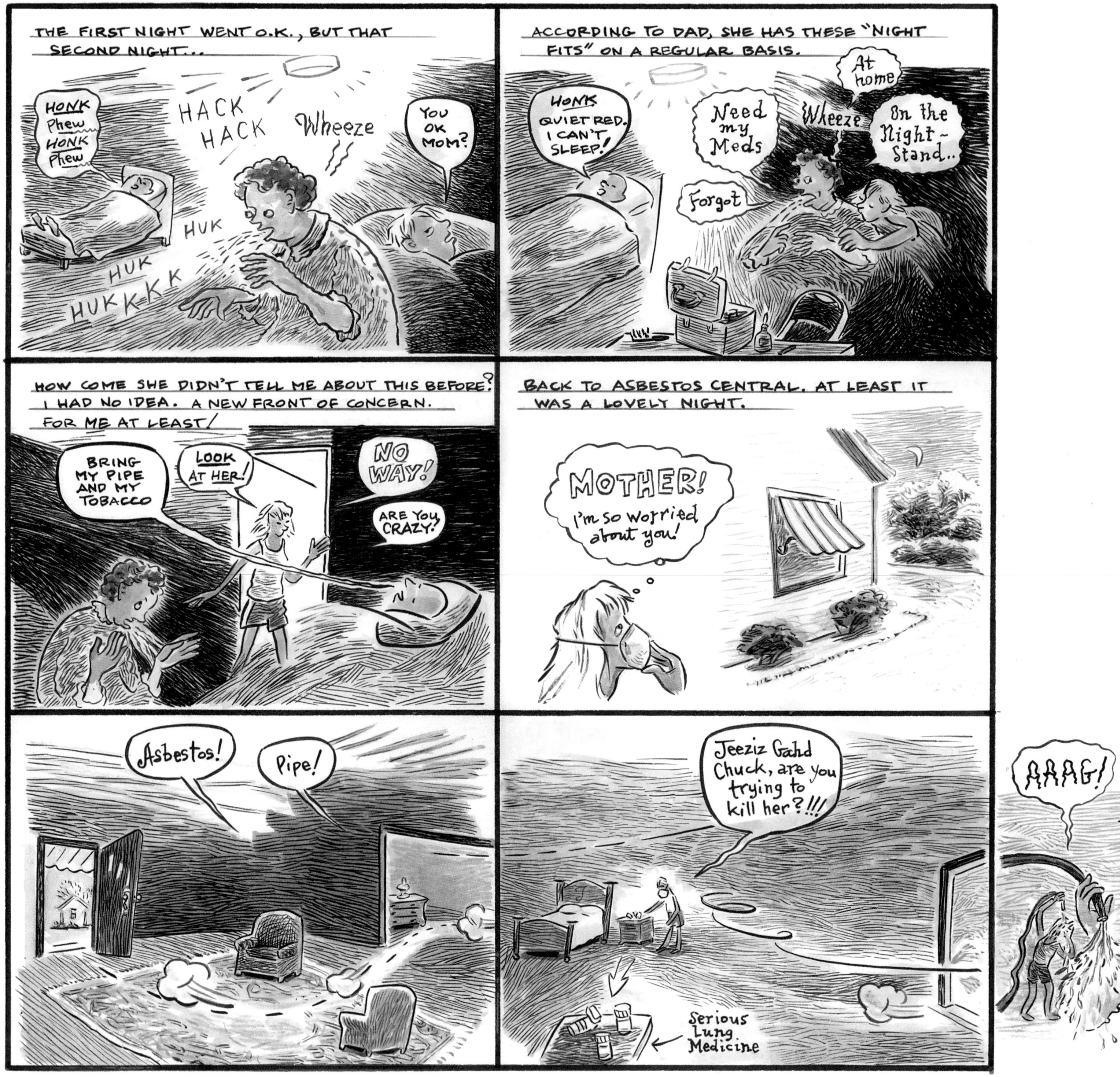
THE FIRST NIGHT WENT O.K., BUT THAT SECOND NIGHT...
HONK Phew HONK Phew
HACK HACK
Wheeze
You OK MOM?
HUK
HUK
HUKKKK
ACCORDING TO DAD, SHE HAS THESE "NIGHT FITS" ON A REGULAR BASIS.
HONK QUIET RED. I CAN'T SLEEP!
Need my Meds
Wheeze
At home
On the Night-Stand..
Forgot
HOW COME SHE DIDN'T TELL ME ABOUT THIS BEFORE? I HAD NO IDEA. A NEW FRONT OF CONCERN. FOR ME AT LEAST!
BRING MY PIPE AND MY TOBACCO
LOOK AT HER!
NO WAY!
ARE YOU CRAZY!
BACK TO ASBESTOS CENTRAL. AT LEAST IT WAS A LOVELY NIGHT.
MOTHER! I'm so worried about you!
Asbestos!
Pipe!
Jeeziz Gahd Chuck, are you trying to kill her?!!!
Serious Lung Medicine
AAAG!

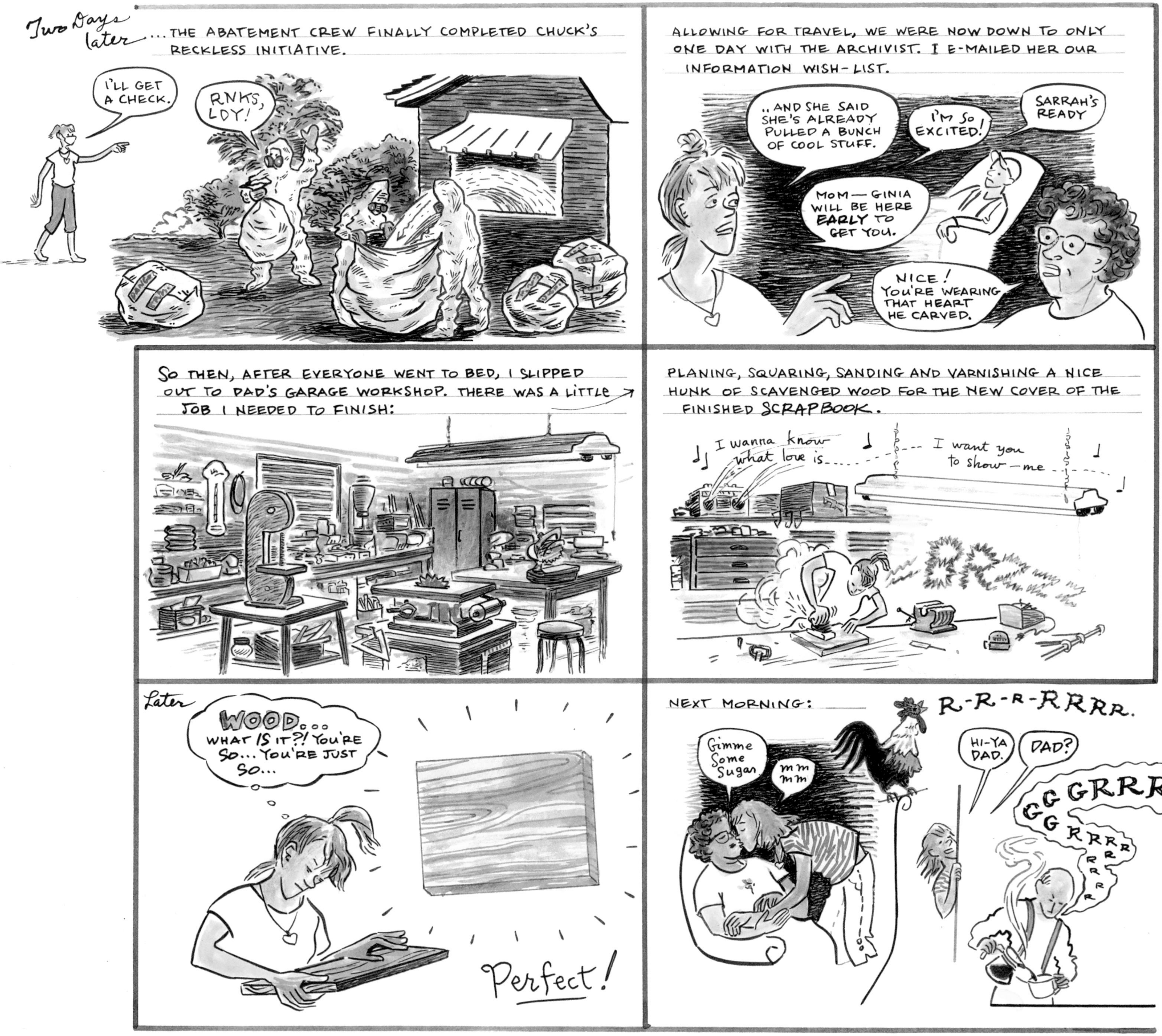
Two Days later ...THE ABATEMENT CREW FINALLY COMPLETED CHUCK'S RECKLESS INITIATIVE.
I'LL GET A CHECK.
RNKS, LDY!
ALLOWING FOR TRAVEL, WE WERE NOW DOWN TO ONLY ONE DAY WITH THE ARCHIVIST. I E-MAILED HER OUR INFORMATION WISH-LIST.
..AND SHE SAID SHE'S ALREADY PULLED A BUNCH OF COOL STUFF.
I'M SO EXCITED!
SARRAH'S READY
MOM— GINIA WILL BE HERE EARLY TO GET YOU.
NICE! YOU'RE WEARING THAT HEART HE CARVED.
SO THEN, AFTER EVERYONE WENT TO BED, I SLIPPED OUT TO DAD'S GARAGE WORKSHOP. THERE WAS A LITTLE JOB I NEEDED TO FINISH:
PLANING, SQUARING, SANDING AND VARNISHING A NICE HUNK OF SCAVENGED WOOD FOR THE NEW COVER OF THE FINISHED SCRAPBOOK.
I wanna know what love is... I want you to show—me
Later
WOOD... WHAT IS IT?! YOU'RE SO... YOU'RE JUST SO...
Perfect!
NEXT MORNING:
R-R-R-RRRR.
Gimme Some Sugar
mm mm
HI-YA DAD.
DAD?
GGGRRR!
GGRRRRRRR

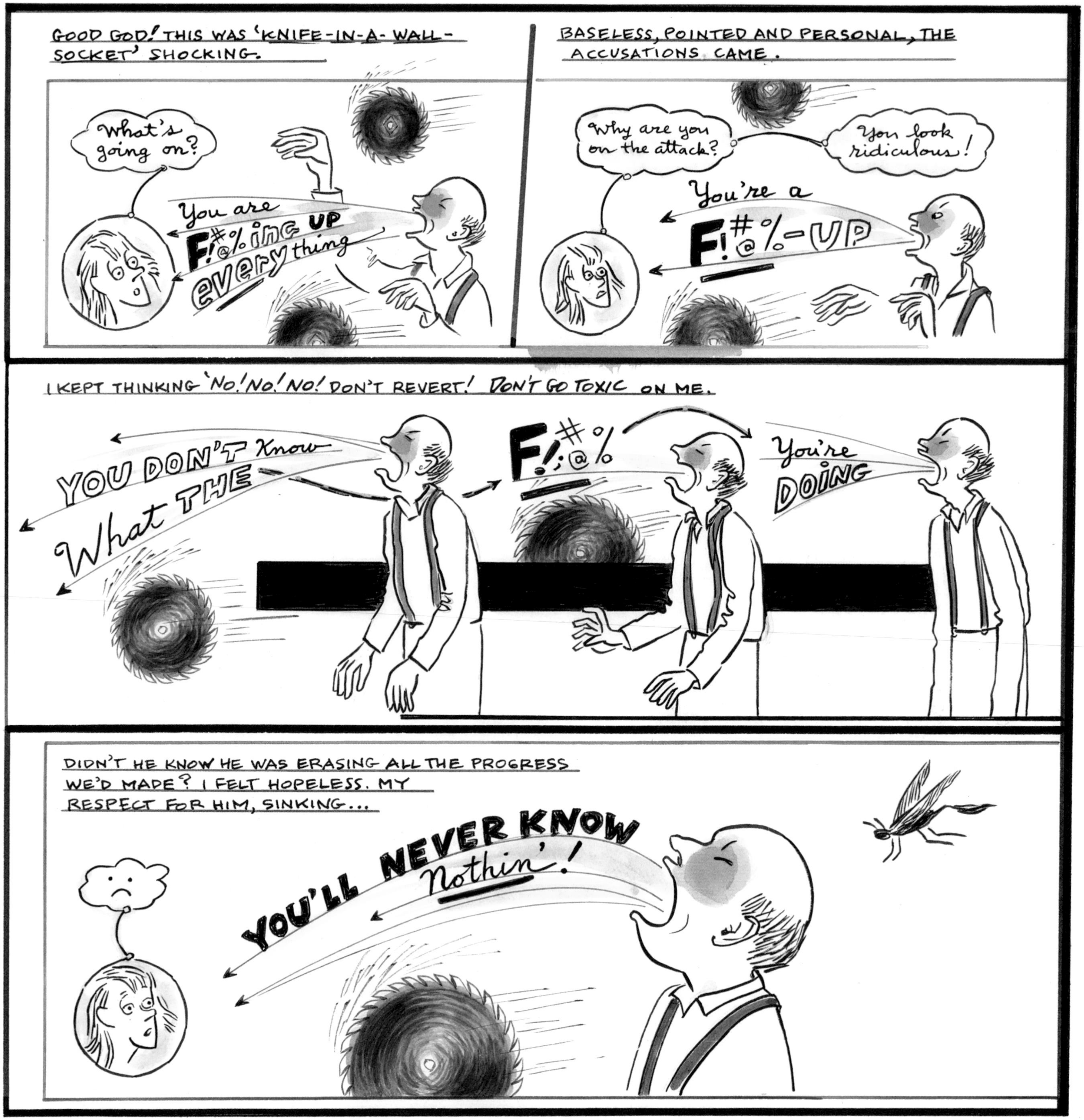
GOOD GOD! THIS WAS 'KNIFE-IN-A-WALL-SOCKET' SHOCKING.
What's going on?
You are F!#@%ing UP everything
BASELESS, POINTED AND PERSONAL, THE ACCUSATIONS CAME.
Why are you on the attack?
You look ridiculous!
You're a F!#@%-UP
I KEPT THINKING 'NO! NO! NO! DON'T REVERT! DON'T GO TOXIC ON ME.
YOU DON'T Know What THE
F!#@%
You're DOING
DIDN'T HE KNOW HE WAS ERASING ALL THE PROGRESS WE'D MADE? I FELT HOPELESS. MY RESPECT FOR HIM, SINKING...
YOU'LL NEVER KNOW Nothin'!

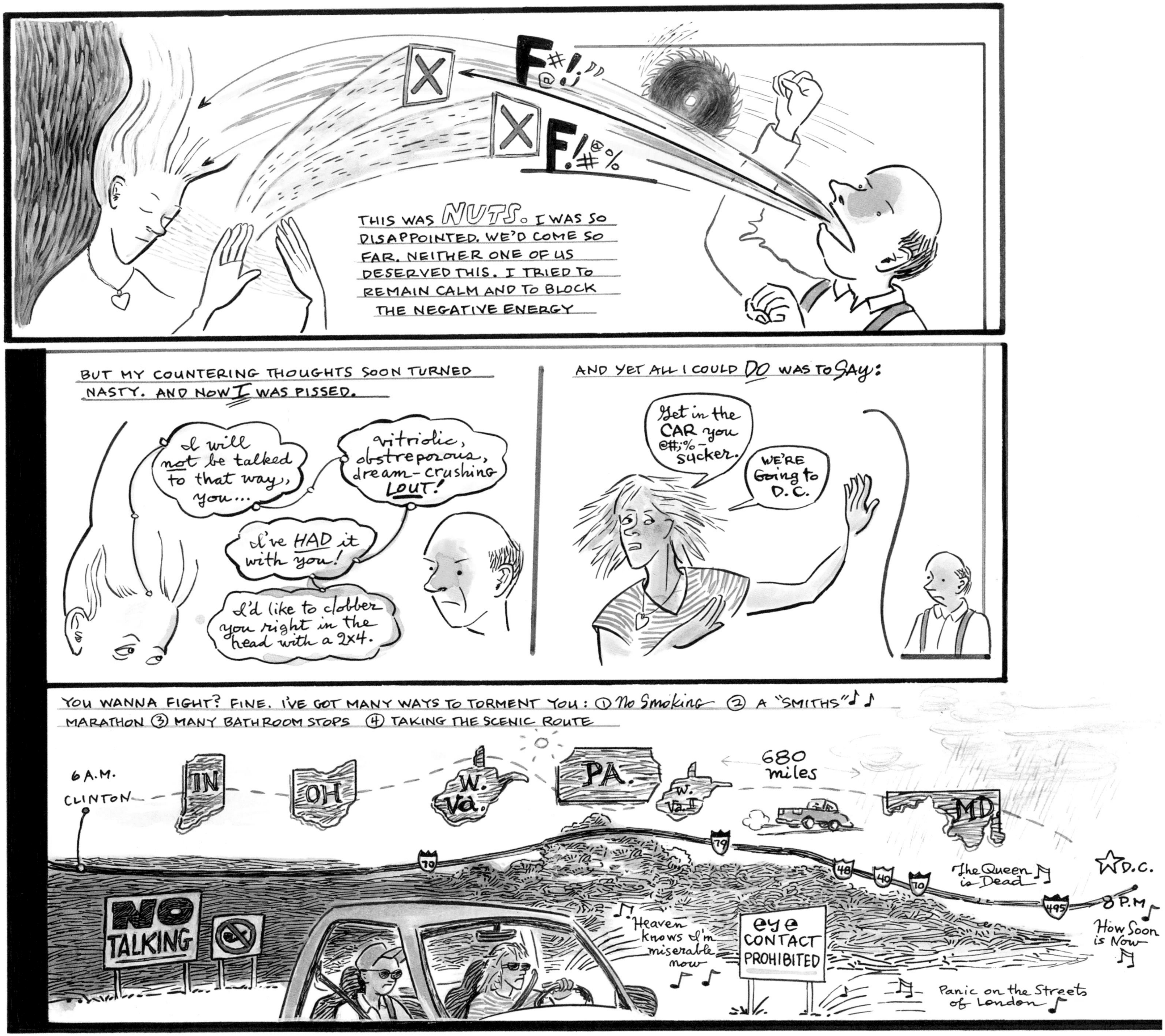
F#@!;"
F!#@%
THIS WAS NUTS. I WAS SO DISAPPOINTED. WE'D COME SO FAR. NEITHER ONE OF US DESERVED THIS. I TRIED TO REMAIN CALM AND TO BLOCK THE NEGATIVE ENERGY
BUT MY COUNTERING THOUGHTS SOON TURNED NASTY. AND NOW I WAS PISSED.
I will not be talked to that way, you...
vitriolic, obstreperous, dream-crushing LOUT!
I've HAD it with you!
I'd like to clobber you right in the head with a 2x4.
AND YET ALL I COULD DO WAS TO SAY:
Get in the CAR you @#;%-sucker.
WE'RE Going to D.C.
YOU WANNA FIGHT? FINE. I'VE GOT MANY WAYS TO TORMENT YOU: ① No Smoking ② A "SMITHS" MARATHON ③ MANY BATHROOM STOPS ④ TAKING THE SCENIC ROUTE
6 A.M.
CLINTON
IN
OH
W. Va.
PA.
W. Va.
680 miles
MD
79
70
48
40
70
495
D.C.
8 P.M
The Queen is Dead
How Soon is Now
NO TALKING
Heaven knows I'm miserable now
eye CONTACT PROHIBITED
Panic on the Streets of London

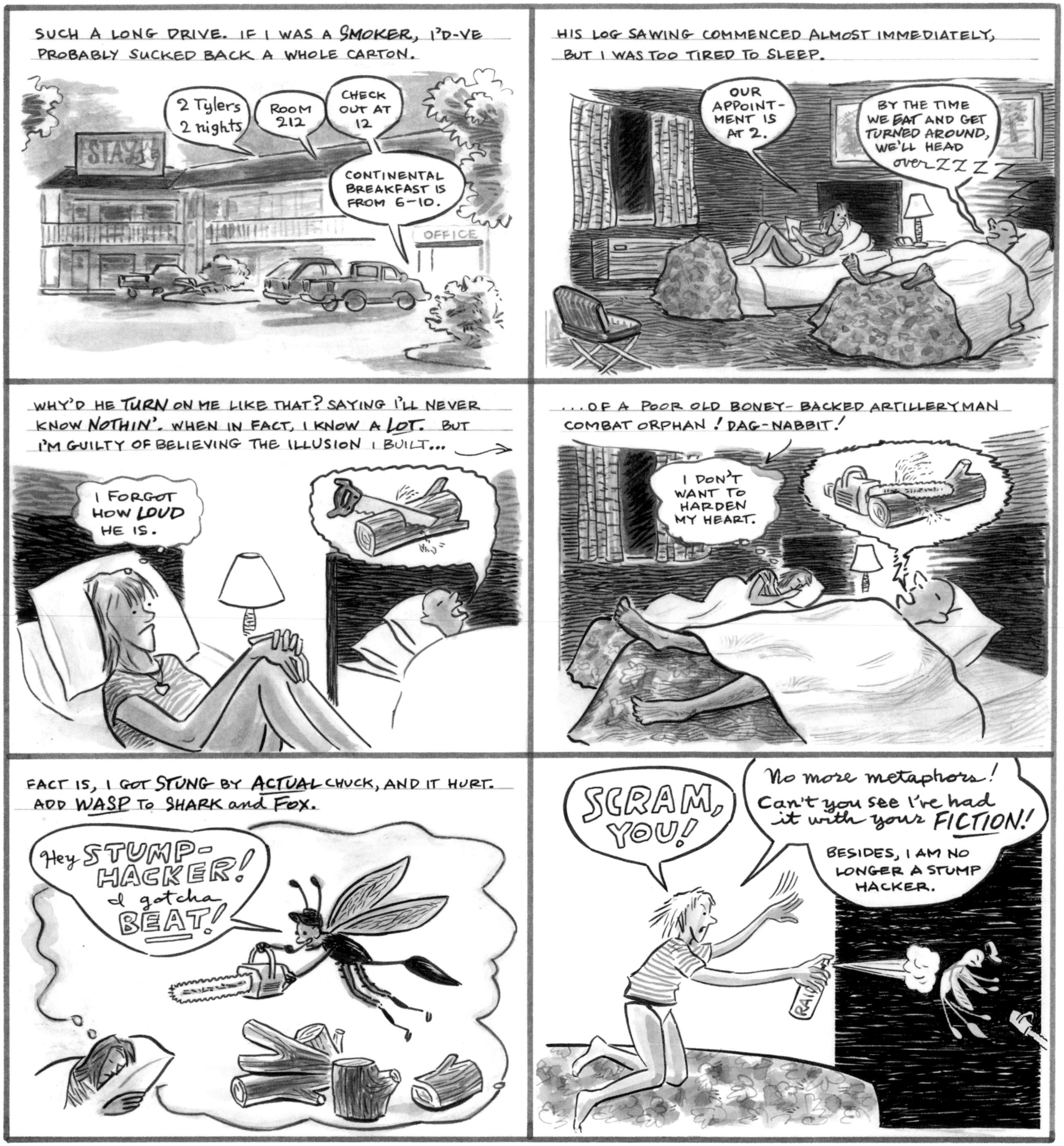
SUCH A LONG DRIVE. IF I WAS A SMOKER, I'D-VE PROBABLY SUCKED BACK A WHOLE CARTON.
2 Tylers 2 nights
ROOM 212
CHECK OUT AT 12
CONTINENTAL BREAKFAST IS FROM 6-10.
OFFICE
HIS LOG SAWING COMMENCED ALMOST IMMEDIATELY, BUT I WAS TOO TIRED TO SLEEP.
OUR APPOINTMENT IS AT 2.
BY THE TIME WE EAT AND GET TURNED AROUND, WE'LL HEAD overZZZ
WHY'D HE TURN ON ME LIKE THAT? SAYING I'LL NEVER KNOW NOTHIN'. WHEN IN FACT, I KNOW A LOT. BUT I'M GUILTY OF BELIEVING THE ILLUSION I BUILT...
I FORGOT HOW LOUD HE IS.
...OF A POOR OLD BONEY-BACKED ARTILLERYMAN COMBAT ORPHAN! DAG-NABBIT!
I DON'T WANT TO HARDEN MY HEART.
FACT IS, I GOT STUNG BY ACTUAL CHUCK, AND IT HURT. ADD WASP TO SHARK and FOX.
Hey STUMP-HACKER! I gotcha BEAT!
SCRAM, YOU!
No more metaphors! Can't you see I've had it with your FICTION!
BESIDES, I AM NO LONGER A STUMP HACKER.

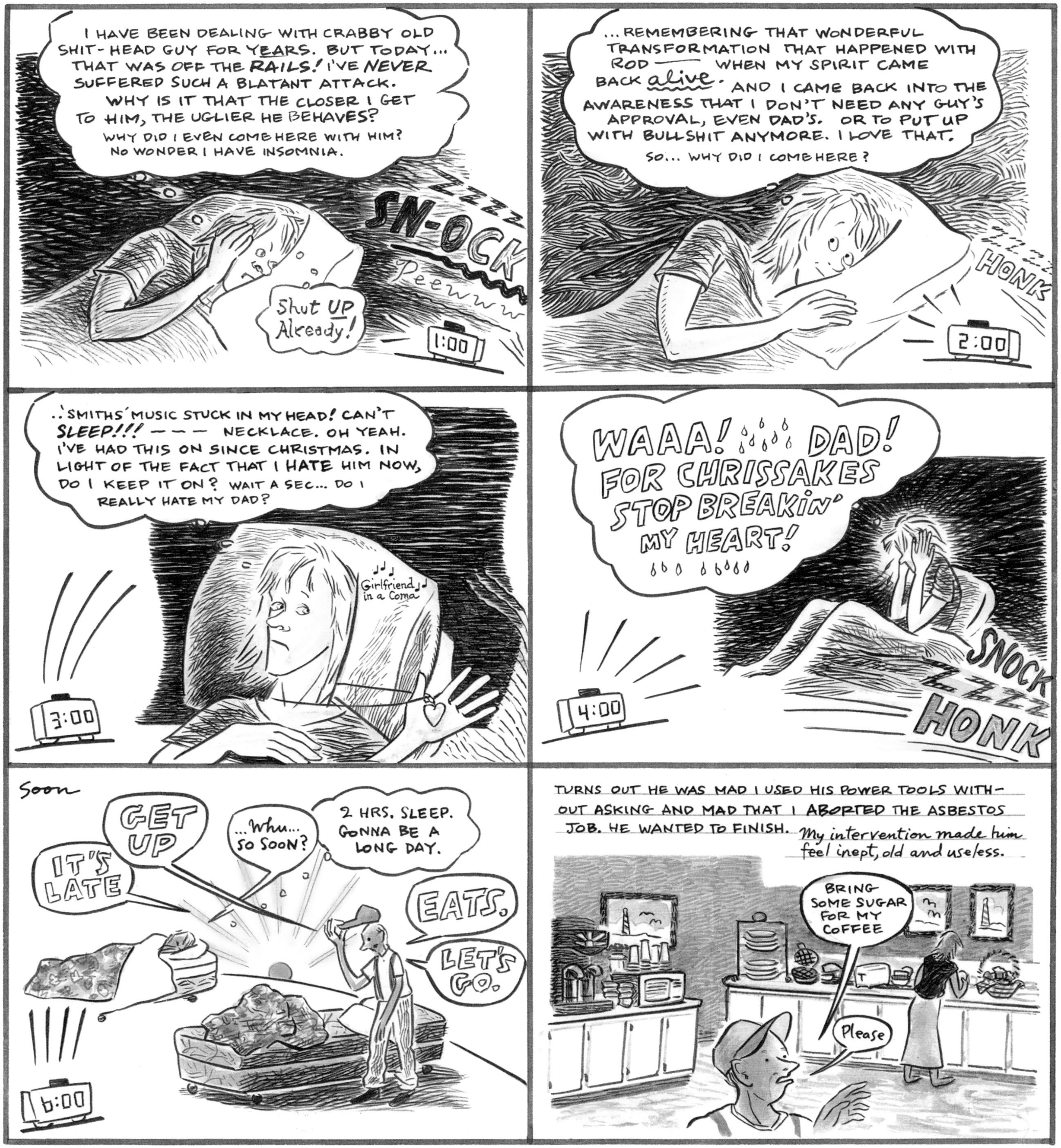

I HAVE BEEN DEALING WITH CRABBY OLD SHIT-HEAD GUY FOR YEARS. BUT TODAY... THAT WAS OFF THE RAILS! I'VE NEVER SUFFERED SUCH A BLATANT ATTACK. WHY IS IT THAT THE CLOSER I GET TO HIM, THE UGLIER HE BEHAVES? WHY DID I EVEN COME HERE WITH HIM? NO WONDER I HAVE INSOMNIA.
ZZZZ
SN-OCK
Peewww
Shut UP Already!
1:00
...REMEMBERING THAT WONDERFUL TRANSFORMATION THAT HAPPENED WITH ROD — WHEN MY SPIRIT CAME BACK alive. AND I CAME BACK INTO THE AWARENESS THAT I DON'T NEED ANY GUY'S APPROVAL, EVEN DAD'S. OR TO PUT UP WITH BULLSHIT ANYMORE. I LOVE THAT. SO... WHY DID I COME HERE?
ZZZZ
HONK
2:00
..'SMITHS' MUSIC STUCK IN MY HEAD! CAN'T SLEEP!!! ——— NECKLACE. OH YEAH. I'VE HAD THIS ON SINCE CHRISTMAS. IN LIGHT OF THE FACT THAT I HATE HIM NOW, DO I KEEP IT ON? WAIT A SEC... DO I REALLY HATE MY DAD?
Girlfriend in a Coma
3:00
WAAA! DAD! FOR CHRISSAKES STOP BREAKIN' MY HEART!
SNOCK
ZZZZ
HONK
4:00
Soon
GET UP
IT'S LATE
...Whu... SO SOON?
2 HRS. SLEEP. GONNA BE A LONG DAY.
EATS,
LET'S GO.
6:00
TURNS OUT HE WAS MAD I USED HIS POWER TOOLS WITHOUT ASKING AND MAD THAT I ABORTED THE ASBESTOS JOB. HE WANTED TO FINISH. My intervention made him feel inept, old and useless.
BRING SOME SUGAR FOR MY COFFEE
Please

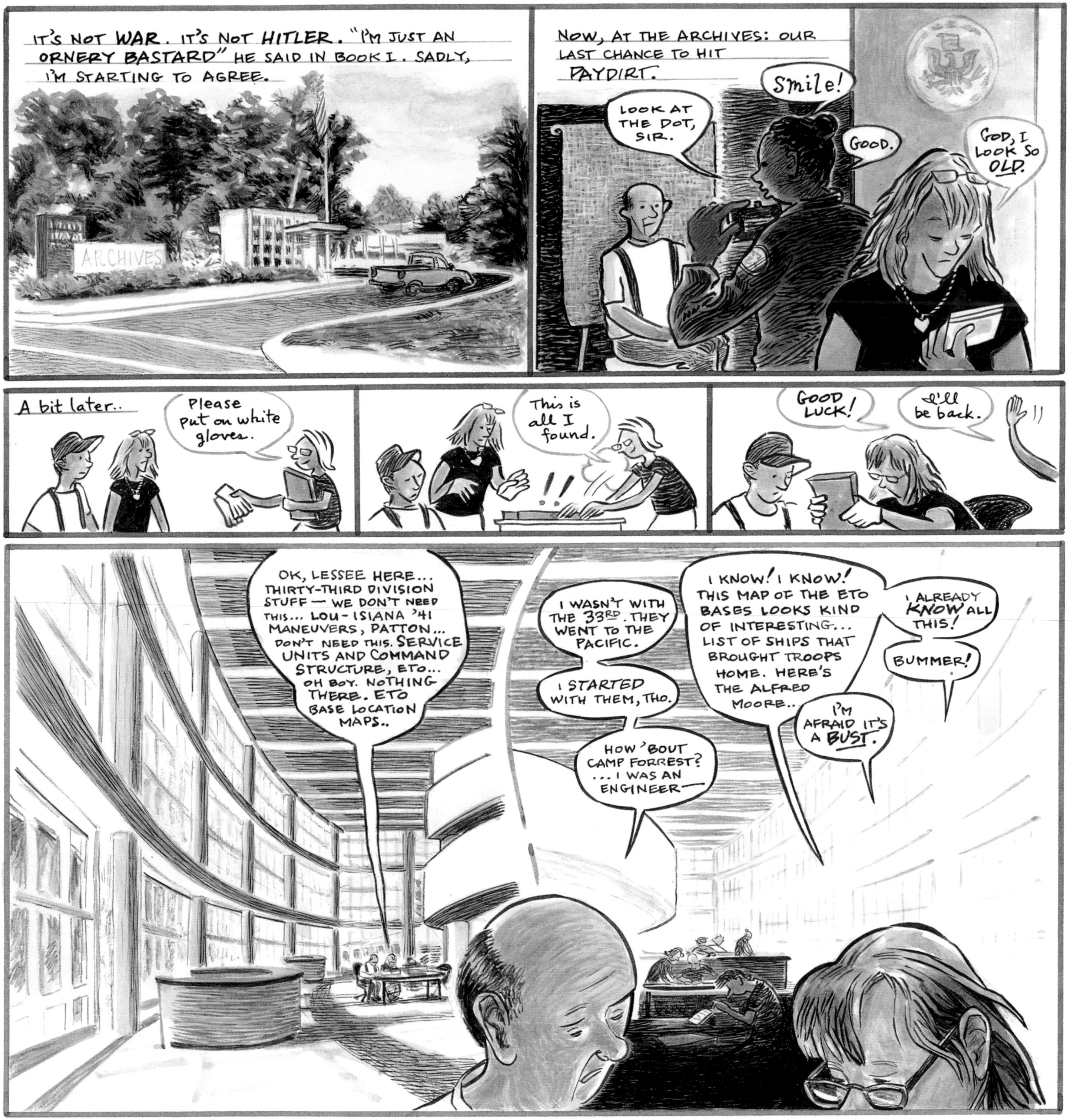
IT'S NOT WAR. IT'S NOT HITLER. "I'M JUST AN ORNERY BASTARD" HE SAID IN BOOK I. SADLY, I'M STARTING TO AGREE.
ARCHIVES
NOW, AT THE ARCHIVES: OUR LAST CHANCE TO HIT PAYDIRT.
LOOK AT THE DOT, SIR.
Smile!
GOOD.
GOD, I LOOK SO OLD.
A bit later..
Please put on white gloves.
This is all I found.
!!
GOOD LUCK!
I'll be back.
OK, LESSEE HERE... THIRTY-THIRD DIVISION STUFF — WE DON'T NEED THIS... LOU-ISIANA '41 MANEUVERS, PATTON... DON'T NEED THIS. SERVICE UNITS AND COMMAND STRUCTURE, ETO... OH BOY. NOTHING THERE. ETO BASE LOCATION MAPS..
I WASN'T WITH THE 33RD. THEY WENT TO THE PACIFIC.
I STARTED WITH THEM, THO.
HOW 'BOUT CAMP FORREST? ...I WAS AN ENGINEER—
I KNOW! I KNOW! THIS MAP OF THE ETO BASES LOOKS KIND OF INTERESTING... LIST OF SHIPS THAT BROUGHT TROOPS HOME. HERE'S THE ALFRED MOORE...
I ALREADY KNOW ALL THIS!
BUMMER!
I'M AFRAID IT'S A BUST.

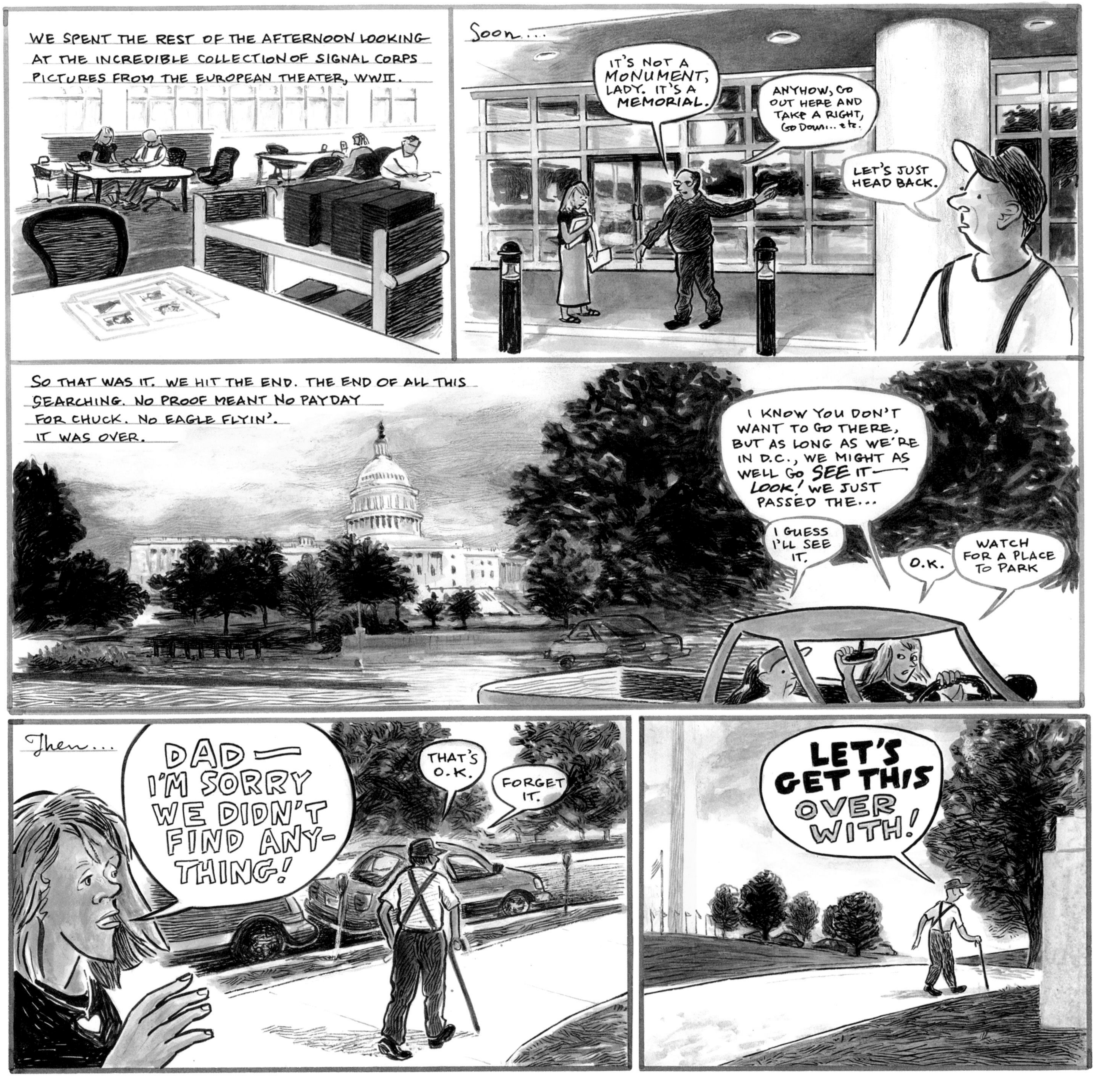
WE SPENT THE REST OF THE AFTERNOON LOOKING AT THE INCREDIBLE COLLECTION OF SIGNAL CORPS PICTURES FROM THE EUROPEAN THEATER, WWII.
Soon...
IT'S NOT A MONUMENT, LADY. IT'S A MEMORIAL.
ANYHOW, GO OUT HERE AND TAKE A RIGHT, GO DOWN... etc.
LET'S JUST HEAD BACK.
SO THAT WAS IT. WE HIT THE END. THE END OF ALL THIS SEARCHING. NO PROOF MEANT NO PAYDAY FOR CHUCK. NO EAGLE FLYIN'. IT WAS OVER.
I KNOW YOU DON'T WANT TO GO THERE, BUT AS LONG AS WE'RE IN D.C., WE MIGHT AS WELL GO SEE IT— LOOK! WE JUST PASSED THE...
I GUESS I'LL SEE IT.
O.K.
WATCH FOR A PLACE TO PARK
Then...
DAD— I'M SORRY WE DIDN'T FIND ANY-THING!
THAT'S O.K.
FORGET IT.
LET'S GET THIS OVER WITH!

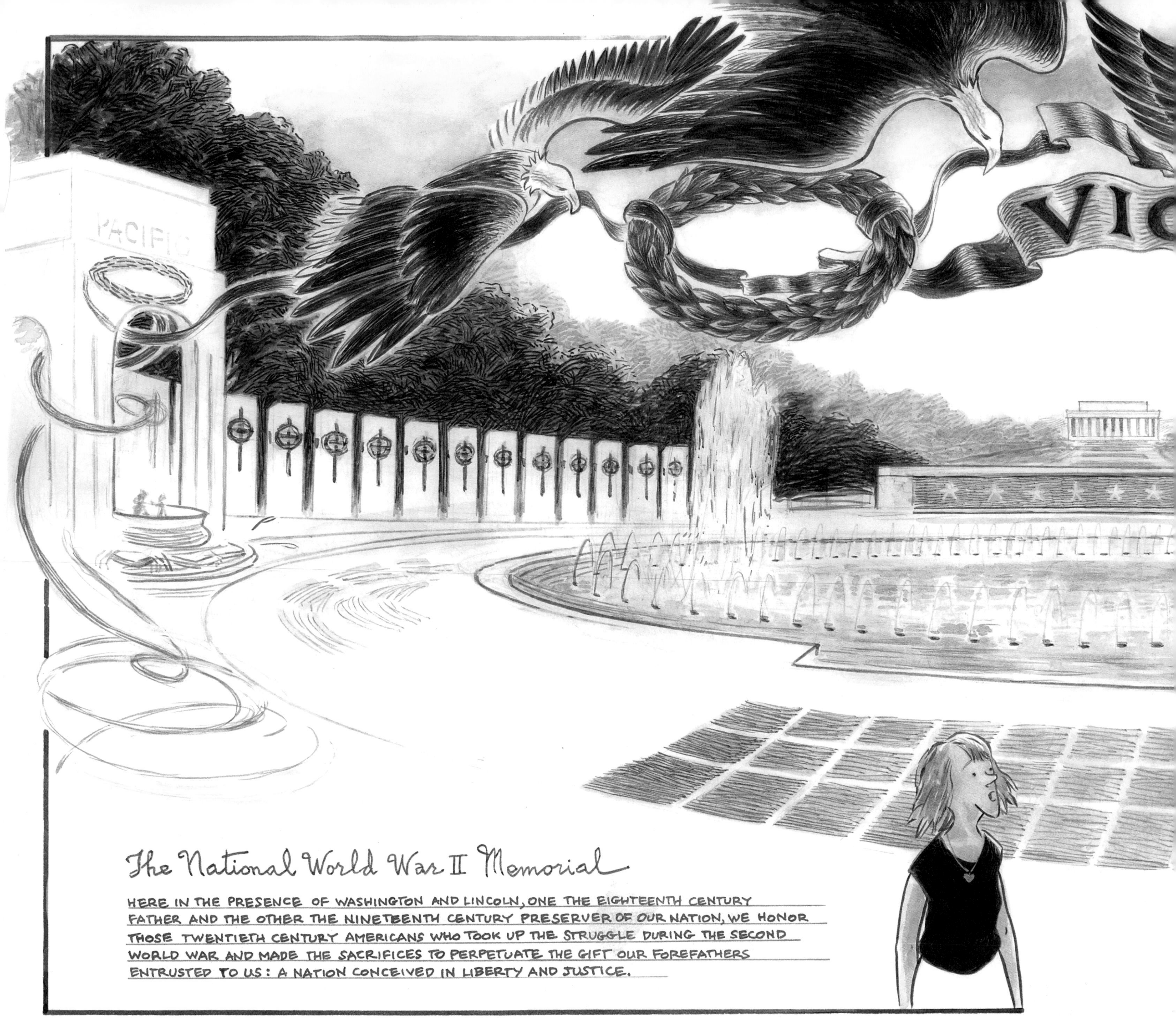
PACIFIC
VIC
The National World War II Memorial
HERE IN THE PRESENCE OF WASHINGTON AND LINCOLN, ONE THE EIGHTEENTH CENTURY FATHER AND THE OTHER THE NINETEENTH CENTURY PRESERVER OF OUR NATION, WE HONOR THOSE TWENTIETH CENTURY AMERICANS WHO TOOK UP THE STRUGGLE DURING THE SECOND WORLD WAR AND MADE THE SACRIFICES TO PERPETUATE THE GIFT OUR FOREFATHERS ENTRUSTED TO US: A NATION CONCEIVED IN LIBERTY AND JUSTICE.

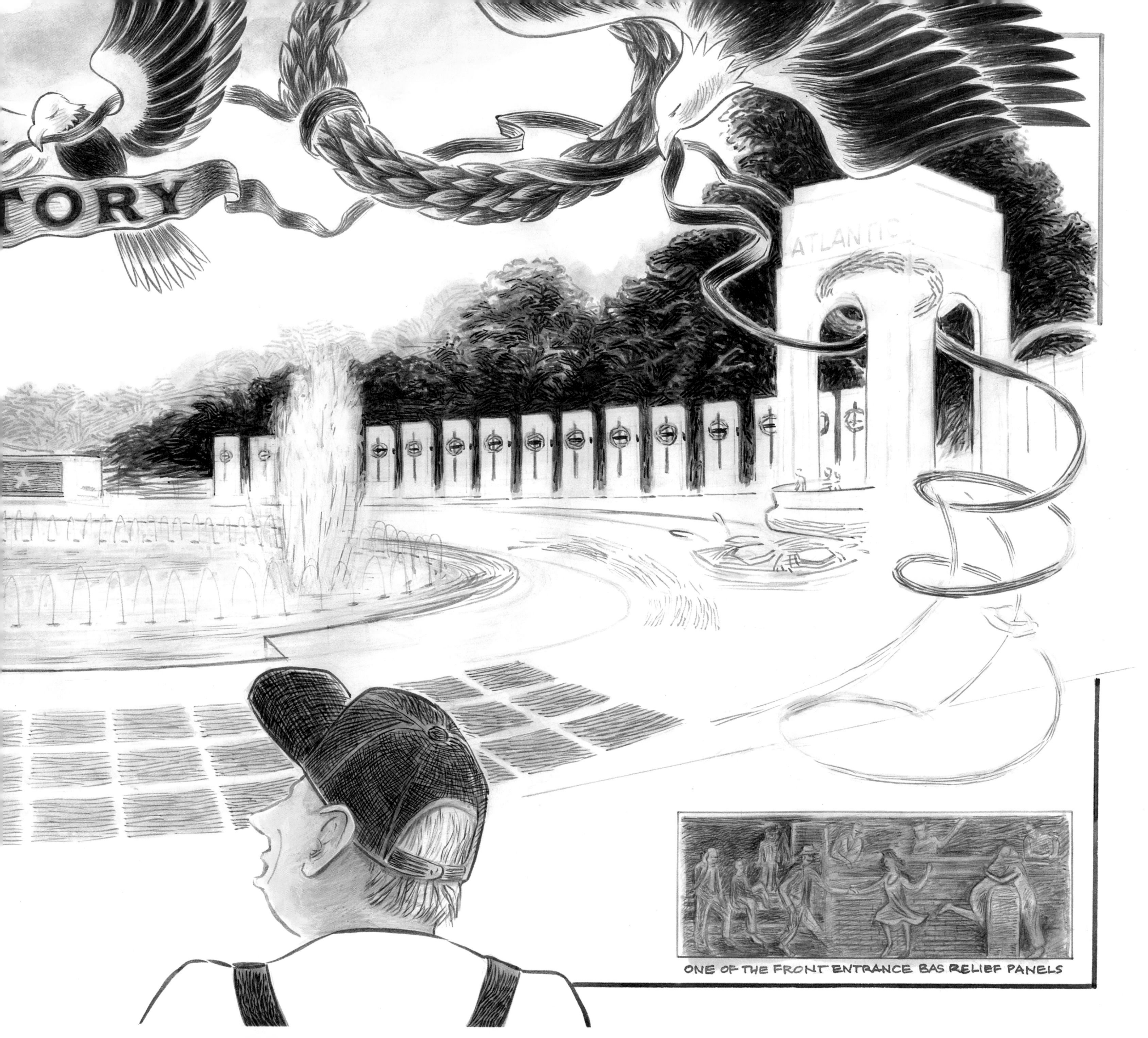

TORY
ATLANTIC
ONE OF THE FRONT ENTRANCE BAS RELIEF PANELS

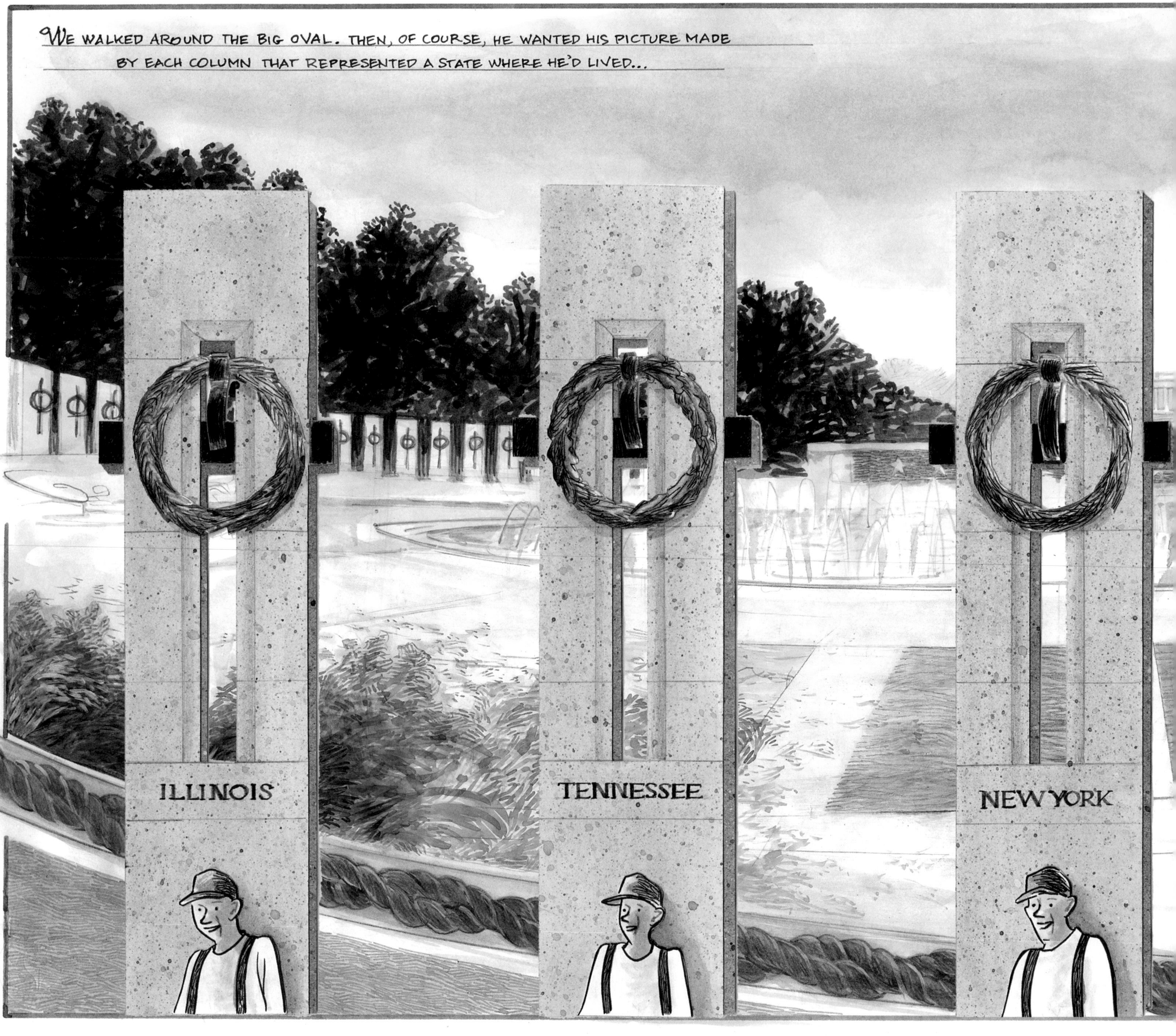
WE WALKED AROUND THE BIG OVAL. THEN, OF COURSE, HE WANTED HIS PICTURE MADE BY EACH COLUMN THAT REPRESENTED A STATE WHERE HE'D LIVED...
ILLINOIS
TENNESSEE
NEW YORK

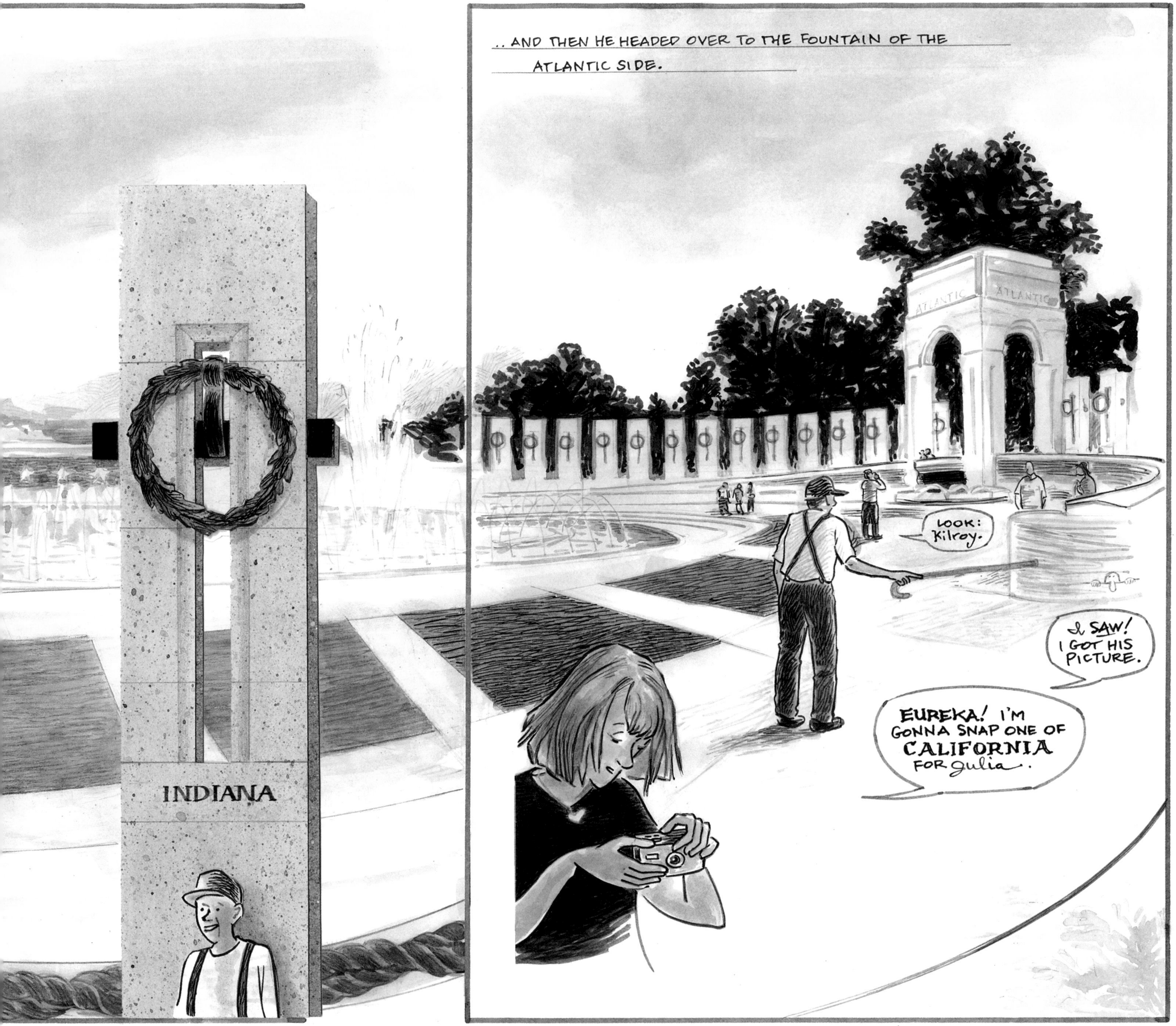
INDIANA
.. AND THEN HE HEADED OVER TO THE FOUNTAIN OF THE ATLANTIC SIDE.
ATLANTIC
ATLANTIC
LOOK: Kilroy.
I SAW! I GOT HIS PICTURE.
EUREKA! I'M GONNA SNAP ONE OF CALIFORNIA FOR Julia.

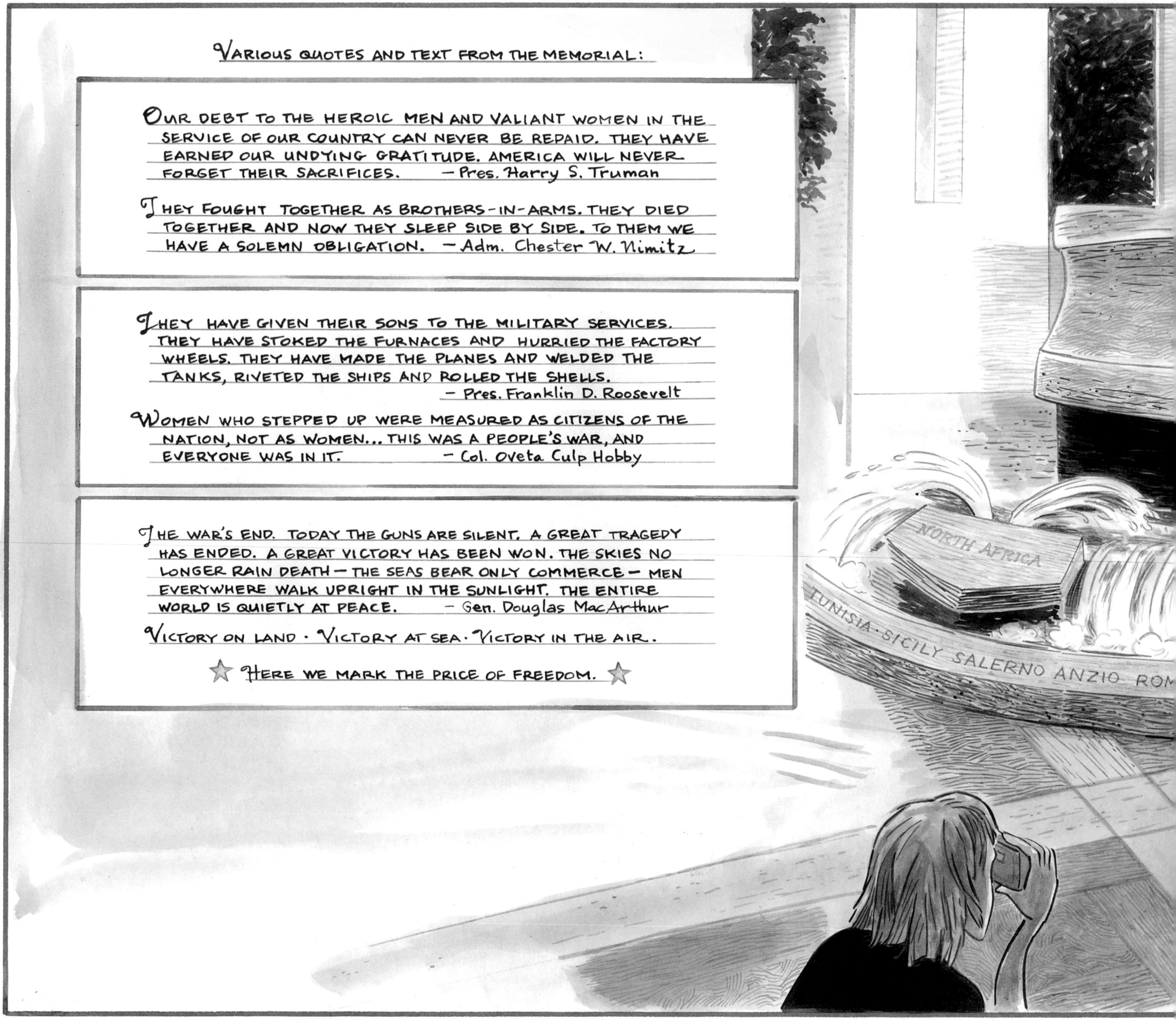
VARIOUS QUOTES AND TEXT FROM THE MEMORIAL:
OUR DEBT TO THE HEROIC MEN AND VALIANT WOMEN IN THE SERVICE OF OUR COUNTRY CAN NEVER BE REPAID. THEY HAVE EARNED OUR UNDYING GRATITUDE. AMERICA WILL NEVER FORGET THEIR SACRIFICES. – Pres. Harry S. Truman
THEY FOUGHT TOGETHER AS BROTHERS-IN-ARMS. THEY DIED TOGETHER AND NOW THEY SLEEP SIDE BY SIDE. TO THEM WE HAVE A SOLEMN OBLIGATION. – Adm. Chester W. Nimitz
THEY HAVE GIVEN THEIR SONS TO THE MILITARY SERVICES. THEY HAVE STOKED THE FURNACES AND HURRIED THE FACTORY WHEELS. THEY HAVE MADE THE PLANES AND WELDED THE TANKS, RIVETED THE SHIPS AND ROLLED THE SHELLS. – Pres. Franklin D. Roosevelt
WOMEN WHO STEPPED UP WERE MEASURED AS CITIZENS OF THE NATION, NOT AS WOMEN... THIS WAS A PEOPLE'S WAR, AND EVERYONE WAS IN IT. – Col. Oveta Culp Hobby
THE WAR'S END. TODAY THE GUNS ARE SILENT. A GREAT TRAGEDY HAS ENDED. A GREAT VICTORY HAS BEEN WON. THE SKIES NO LONGER RAIN DEATH – THE SEAS BEAR ONLY COMMERCE – MEN EVERYWHERE WALK UPRIGHT IN THE SUNLIGHT. THE ENTIRE WORLD IS QUIETLY AT PEACE. – Gen. Douglas MacArthur
VICTORY ON LAND · VICTORY AT SEA · VICTORY IN THE AIR.
HERE WE MARK THE PRICE OF FREEDOM.
NORTH AFRICA
TUNISIA · SICILY SALERNO ANZIO ROM

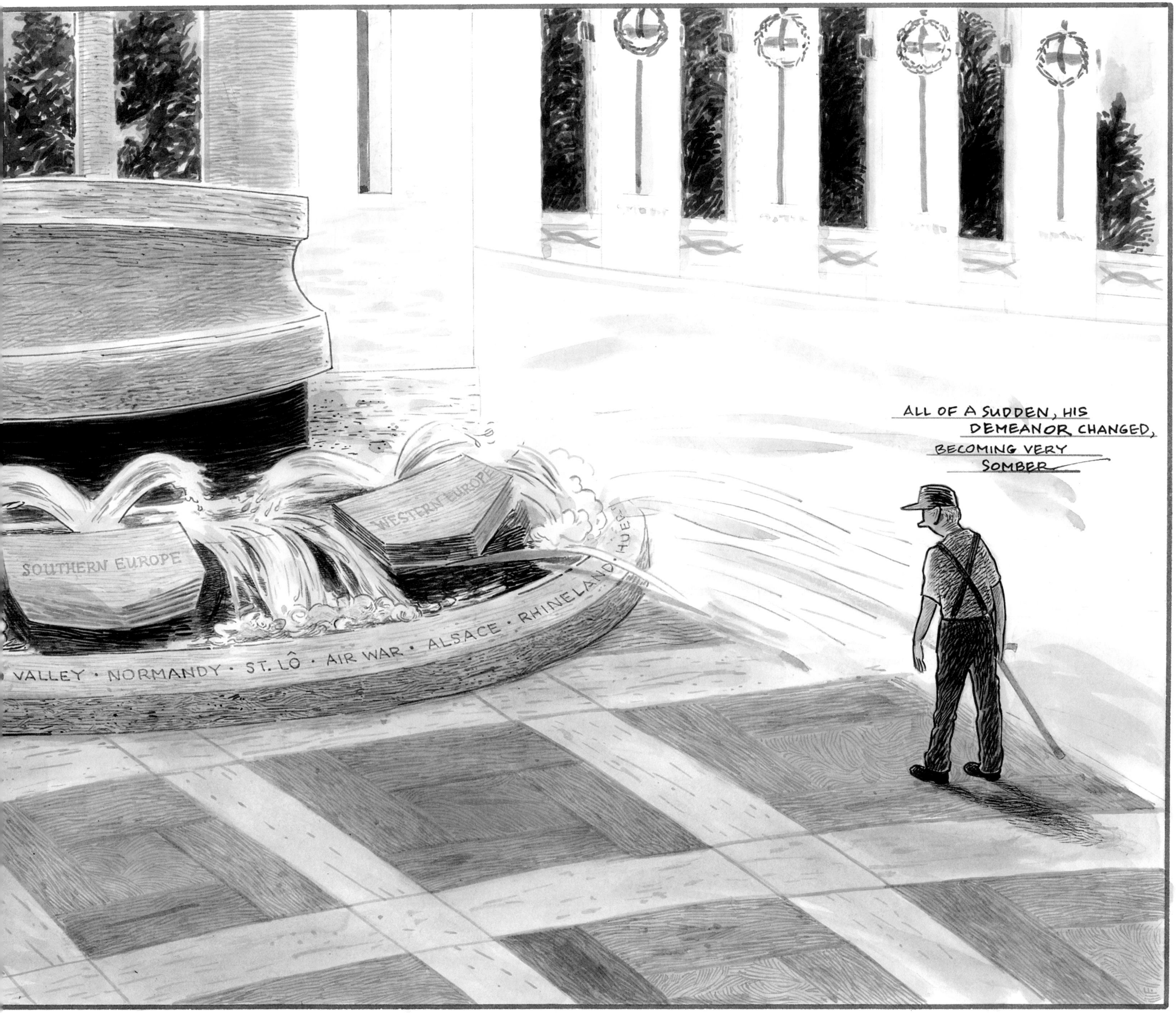
ALL OF A SUDDEN, HIS DEMEANOR CHANGED, BECOMING VERY SOMBER
SOUTHERN EUROPE
WESTERN EUROPE
VALLEY · NORMANDY · ST. LÔ · AIR WAR · ALSACE · RHINELAND ·

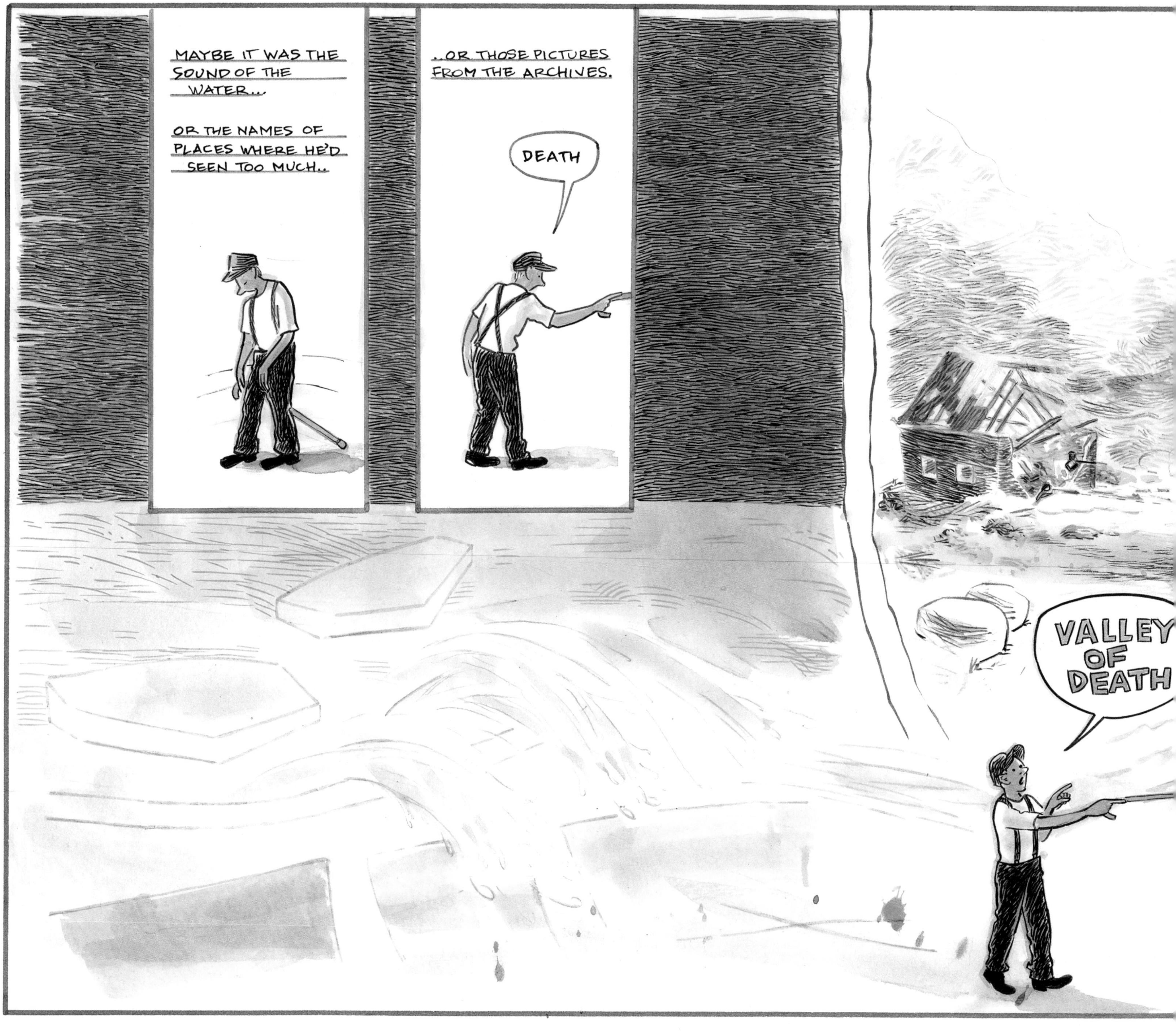
MAYBE IT WAS THE SOUND OF THE WATER...
OR THE NAMES OF PLACES WHERE HE'D SEEN TOO MUCH..
..OR THOSE PICTURES FROM THE ARCHIVES.
DEATH
VALLEY OF DEATH

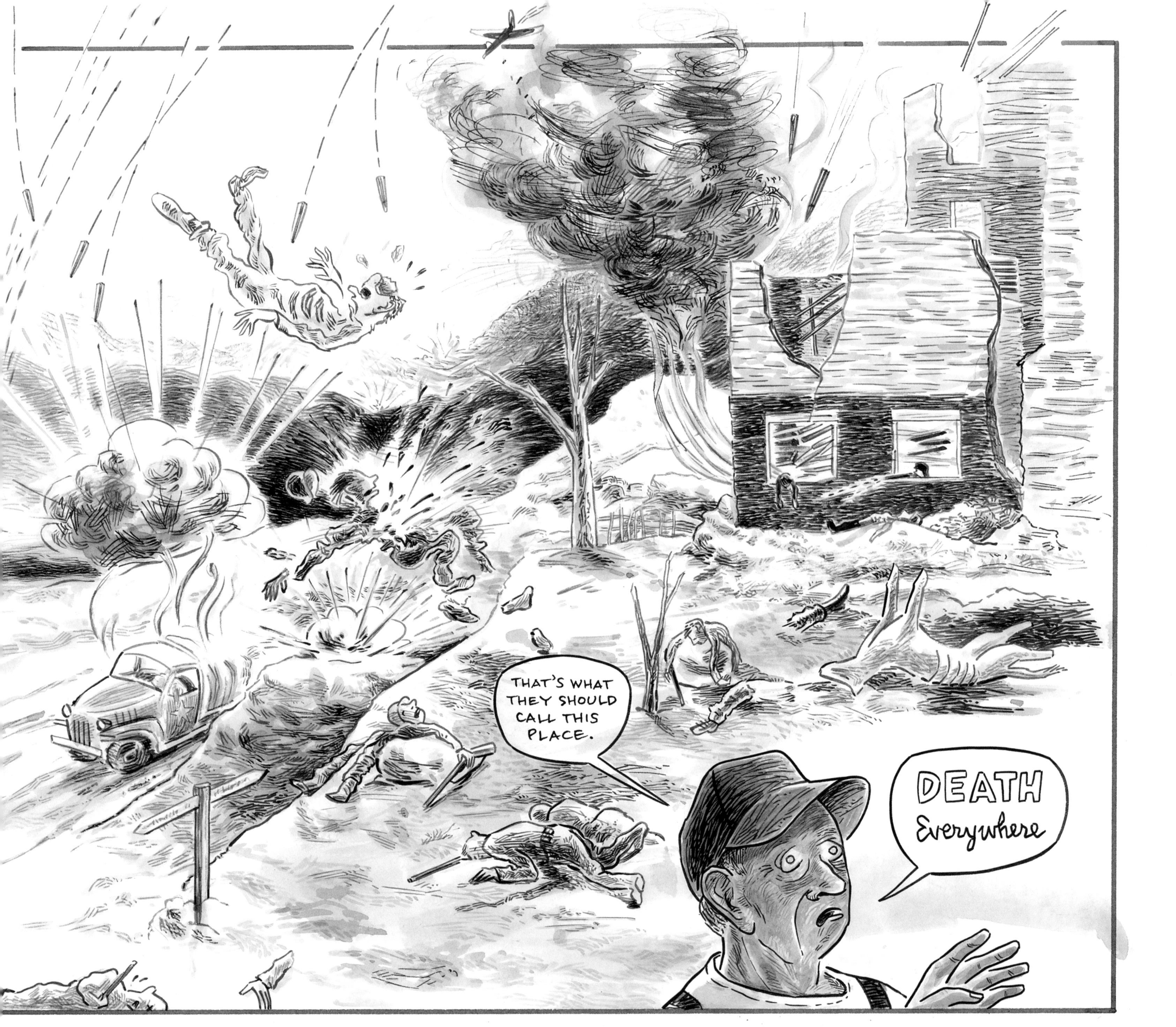
DEATH Everywhere
THAT'S WHAT THEY SHOULD CALL THIS PLACE.

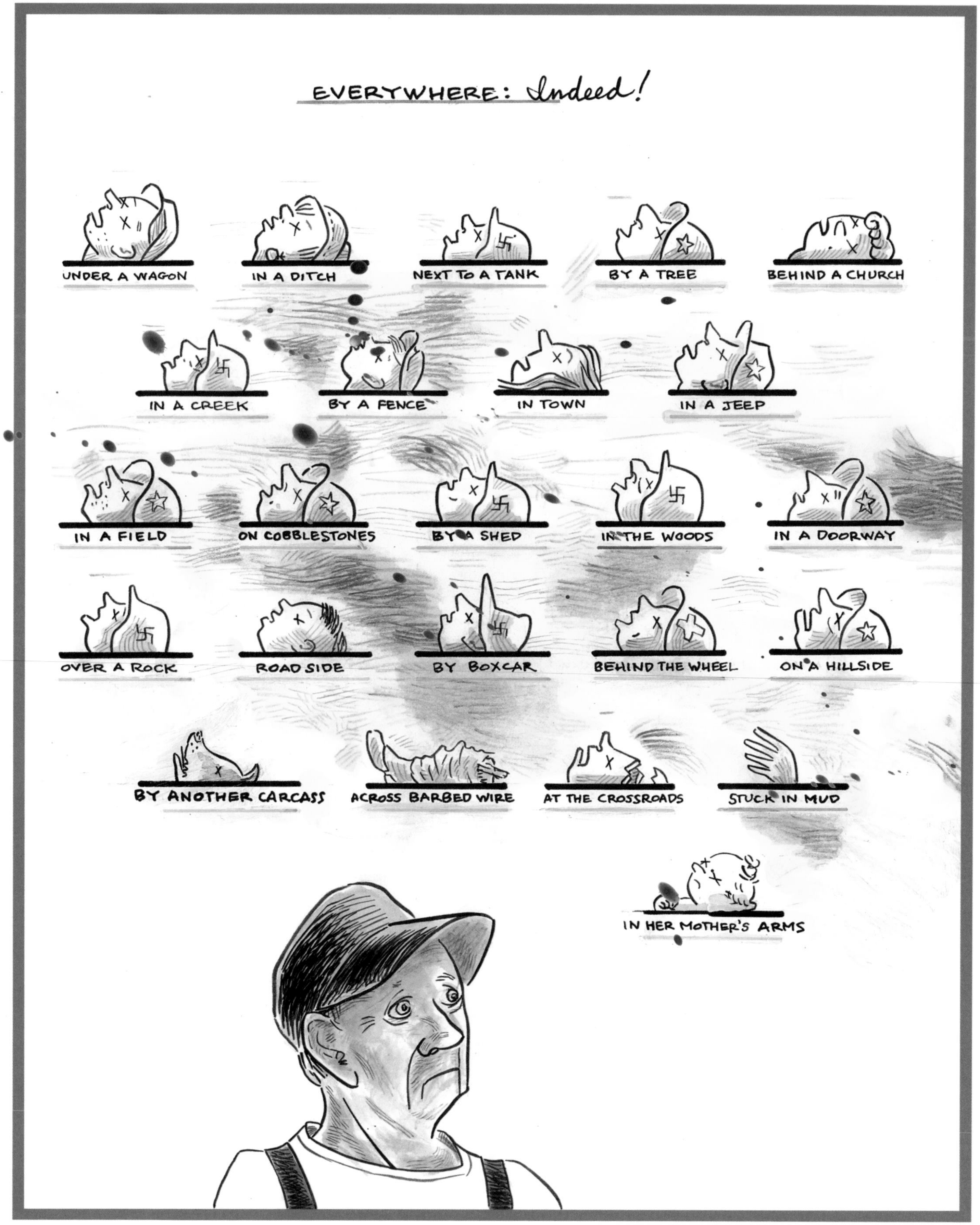
EVERYWHERE: Indeed!
UNDER A WAGON
IN A DITCH
NEXT TO A TANK
BY A TREE
BEHIND A CHURCH
IN A CREEK
BY A FENCE
IN TOWN
IN A JEEP
IN A FIELD
ON COBBLESTONES
BY A SHED
IN THE WOODS
IN A DOORWAY
OVER A ROCK
ROAD SIDE
BY BOXCAR
BEHIND THE WHEEL
ON A HILLSIDE
BY ANOTHER CARCASS
ACROSS BARBED WIRE
AT THE CROSSROADS
STUCK IN MUD
IN HER MOTHER'S ARMS

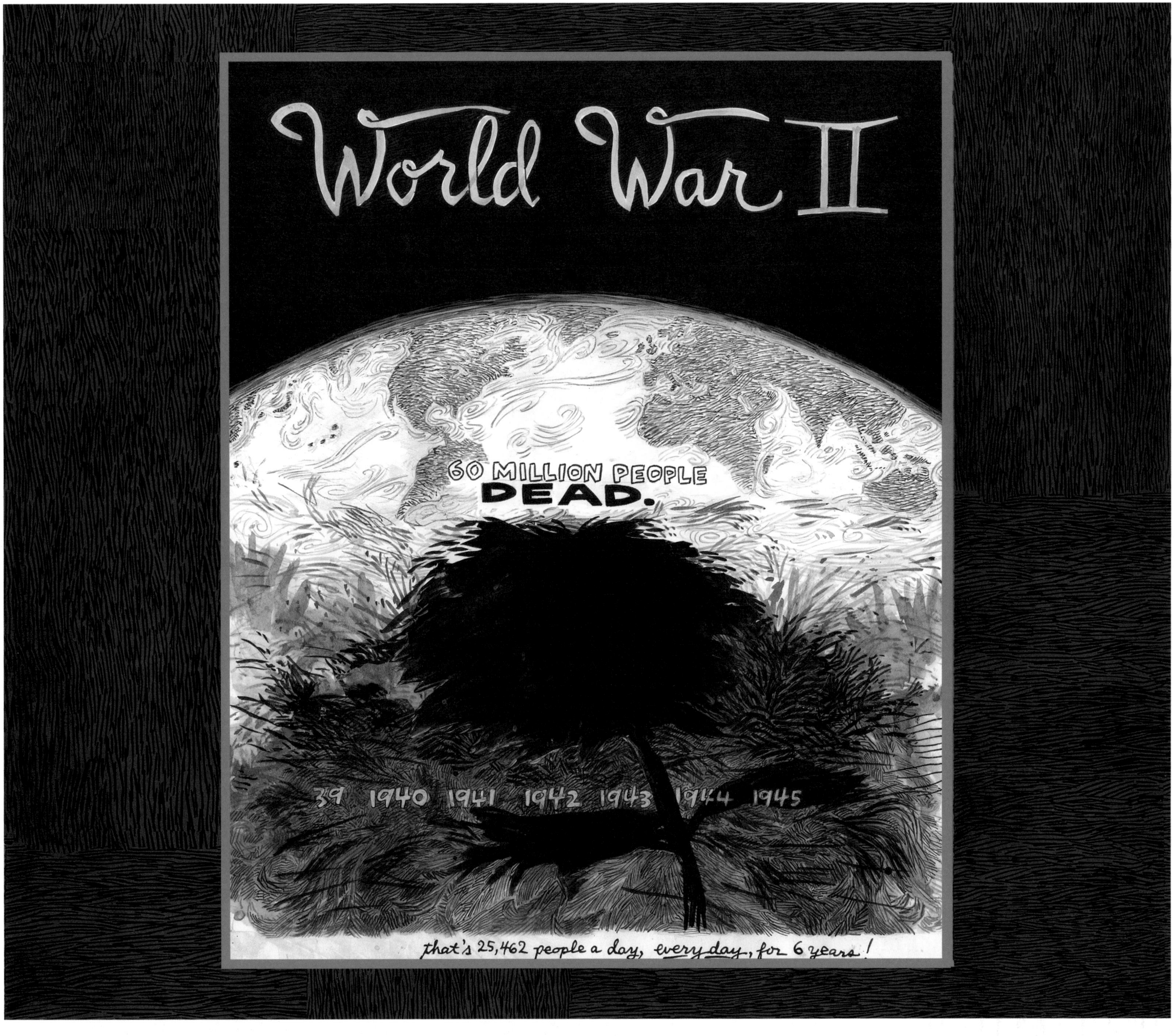

World War II
60 MILLION PEOPLE
DEAD.
39 1940 1941 1942 1943 1944 1945
that's 25,462 people a day, every day, for 6 years!

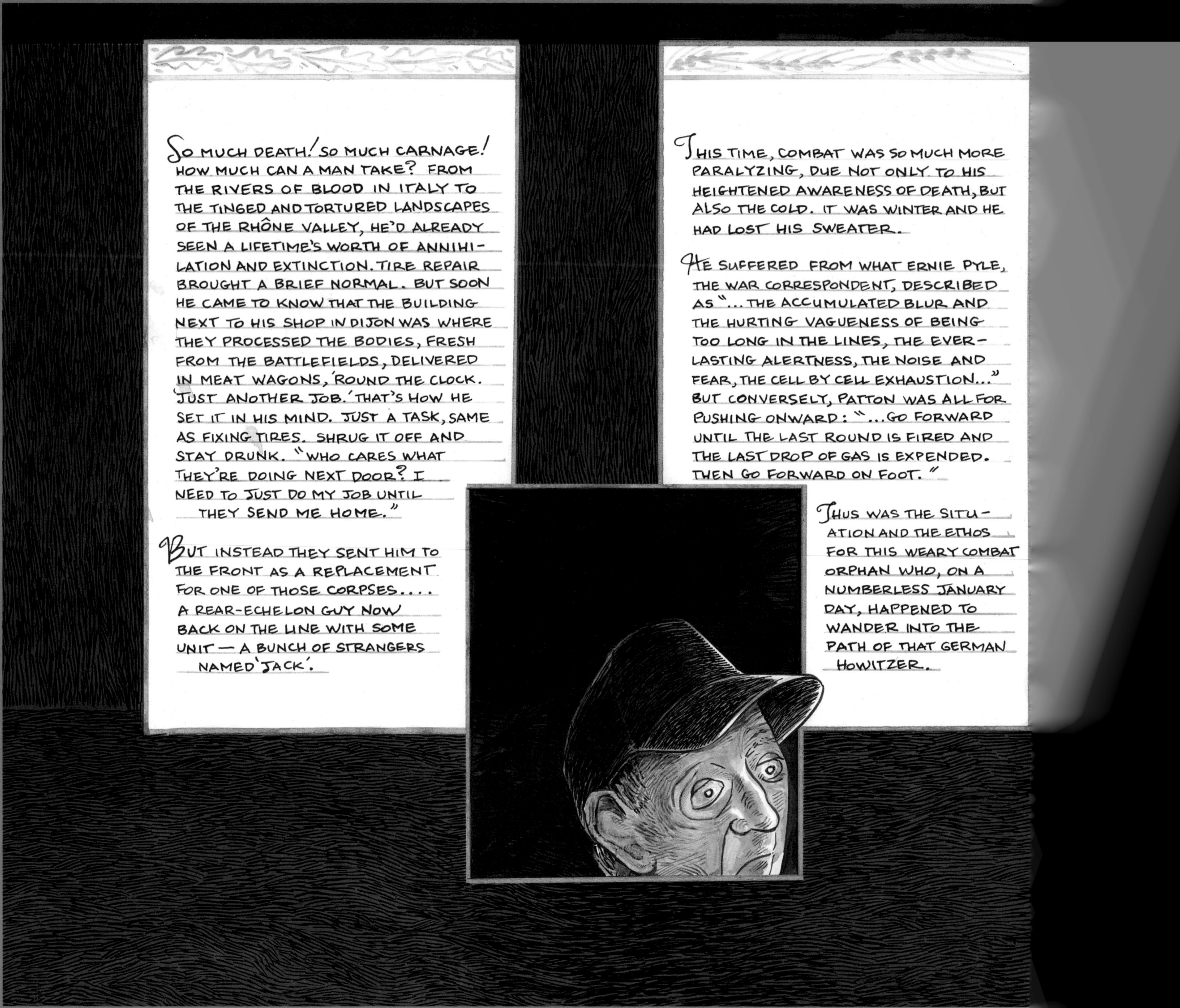
SO MUCH DEATH! SO MUCH CARNAGE! HOW MUCH CAN A MAN TAKE? FROM THE RIVERS OF BLOOD IN ITALY TO THE TINGED AND TORTURED LANDSCAPES OF THE RHÔNE VALLEY, HE'D ALREADY SEEN A LIFETIME'S WORTH OF ANNIHILATION AND EXTINCTION. TIRE REPAIR BROUGHT A BRIEF NORMAL. BUT SOON HE CAME TO KNOW THAT THE BUILDING NEXT TO HIS SHOP IN DIJON WAS WHERE THEY PROCESSED THE BODIES, FRESH FROM THE BATTLEFIELDS, DELIVERED IN MEAT WAGONS, 'ROUND THE CLOCK. 'JUST ANOTHER JOB.' THAT'S HOW HE SET IT IN HIS MIND. JUST A TASK, SAME AS FIXING TIRES. SHRUG IT OFF AND STAY DRUNK. "WHO CARES WHAT THEY'RE DOING NEXT DOOR? I NEED TO JUST DO MY JOB UNTIL THEY SEND ME HOME."
BUT INSTEAD THEY SENT HIM TO THE FRONT AS A REPLACEMENT FOR ONE OF THOSE CORPSES.... A REAR-ECHELON GUY NOW BACK ON THE LINE WITH SOME UNIT — A BUNCH OF STRANGERS NAMED 'JACK'.
THIS TIME, COMBAT WAS SO MUCH MORE PARALYZING, DUE NOT ONLY TO HIS HEIGHTENED AWARENESS OF DEATH, BUT ALSO THE COLD. IT WAS WINTER AND HE HAD LOST HIS SWEATER.
HE SUFFERED FROM WHAT ERNIE PYLE, THE WAR CORRESPONDENT, DESCRIBED AS "... THE ACCUMULATED BLUR AND THE HURTING VAGUENESS OF BEING TOO LONG IN THE LINES, THE EVERLASTING ALERTNESS, THE NOISE AND FEAR, THE CELL BY CELL EXHAUSTION..." BUT CONVERSELY, PATTON WAS ALL FOR PUSHING ONWARD: "...GO FORWARD UNTIL THE LAST ROUND IS FIRED AND THE LAST DROP OF GAS IS EXPENDED. THEN GO FORWARD ON FOOT."
THUS WAS THE SITUATION AND THE ETHOS FOR THIS WEARY COMBAT ORPHAN WHO, ON A NUMBERLESS JANUARY DAY, HAPPENED TO WANDER INTO THE PATH OF THAT GERMAN HOWITZER.

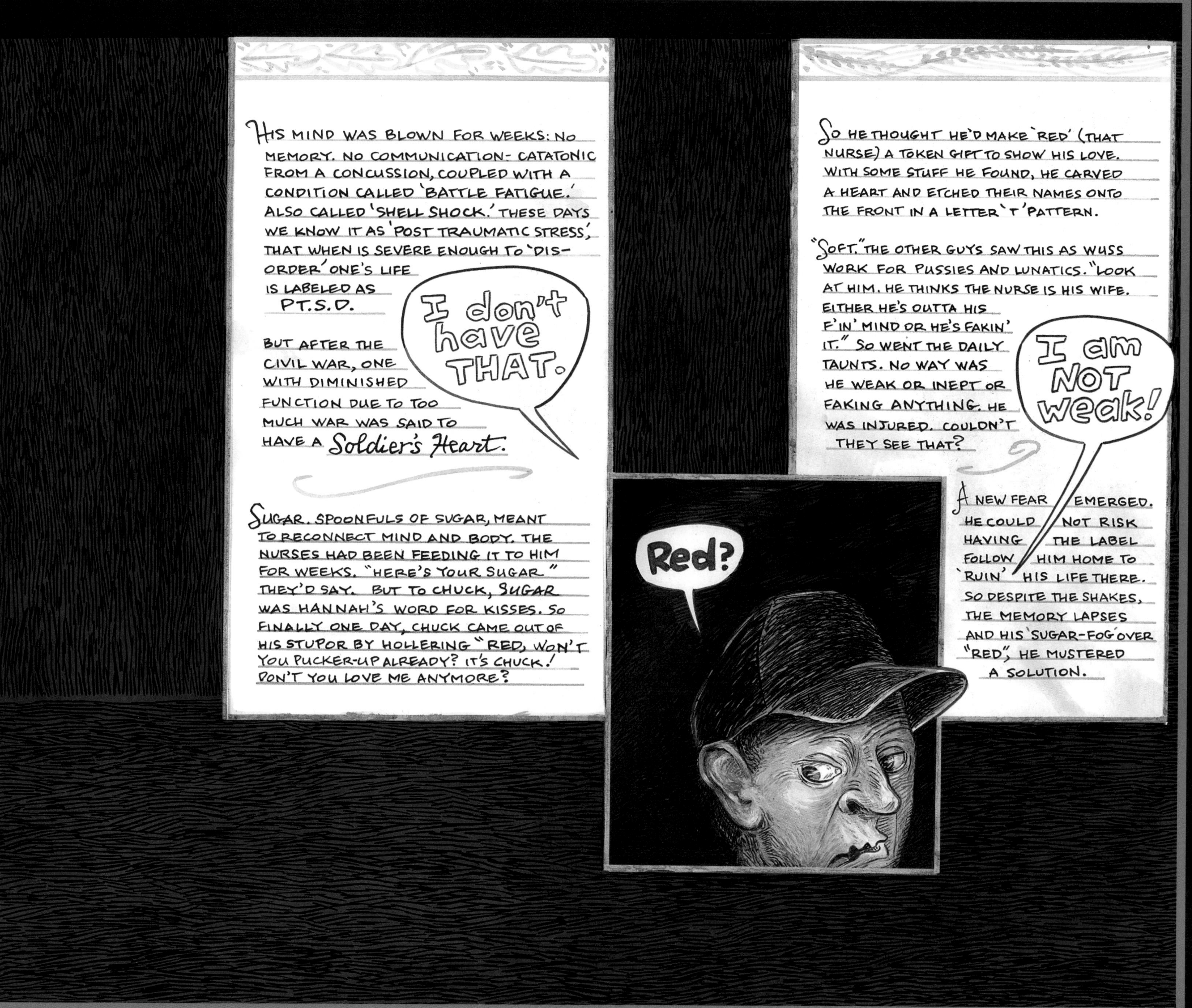
HIS MIND WAS BLOWN FOR WEEKS: NO MEMORY. NO COMMUNICATION- CATATONIC FROM A CONCUSSION, COUPLED WITH A CONDITION CALLED 'BATTLE FATIGUE.' ALSO CALLED 'SHELL SHOCK.' THESE DAYS WE KNOW IT AS 'POST TRAUMATIC STRESS', THAT WHEN IS SEVERE ENOUGH TO 'DIS-ORDER' ONE'S LIFE IS LABELED AS PT.S.D.
BUT AFTER THE CIVIL WAR, ONE WITH DIMINISHED FUNCTION DUE TO TOO MUCH WAR WAS SAID TO HAVE A Soldier's Heart.
I don't have THAT.
SUGAR. SPOONFULS OF SUGAR, MEANT TO RECONNECT MIND AND BODY. THE NURSES HAD BEEN FEEDING IT TO HIM FOR WEEKS. "HERE'S YOUR SUGAR" THEY'D SAY. BUT TO CHUCK, SUGAR WAS HANNAH'S WORD FOR KISSES. SO FINALLY ONE DAY, CHUCK CAME OUT OF HIS STUPOR BY HOLLERING "RED, WON'T YOU PUCKER-UP ALREADY? IT'S CHUCK! DON'T YOU LOVE ME ANYMORE?
SO HE THOUGHT HE'D MAKE 'RED' (THAT NURSE) A TOKEN GIFT TO SHOW HIS LOVE. WITH SOME STUFF HE FOUND, HE CARVED A HEART AND ETCHED THEIR NAMES ONTO THE FRONT IN A LETTER 'T' PATTERN.
"SOFT." THE OTHER GUYS SAW THIS AS WUSS WORK FOR PUSSIES AND LUNATICS. "LOOK AT HIM. HE THINKS THE NURSE IS HIS WIFE. EITHER HE'S OUTTA HIS F'IN' MIND OR HE'S FAKIN' IT." SO WENT THE DAILY TAUNTS. NO WAY WAS HE WEAK OR INEPT OR FAKING ANYTHING. HE WAS INJURED. COULDN'T THEY SEE THAT?
I am NOT weak!
Red?
A NEW FEAR EMERGED. HE COULD NOT RISK HAVING THE LABEL FOLLOW HIM HOME TO 'RUIN' HIS LIFE THERE. SO DESPITE THE SHAKES, THE MEMORY LAPSES AND HIS 'SUGAR-FOG' OVER "RED", HE MUSTERED A SOLUTION.

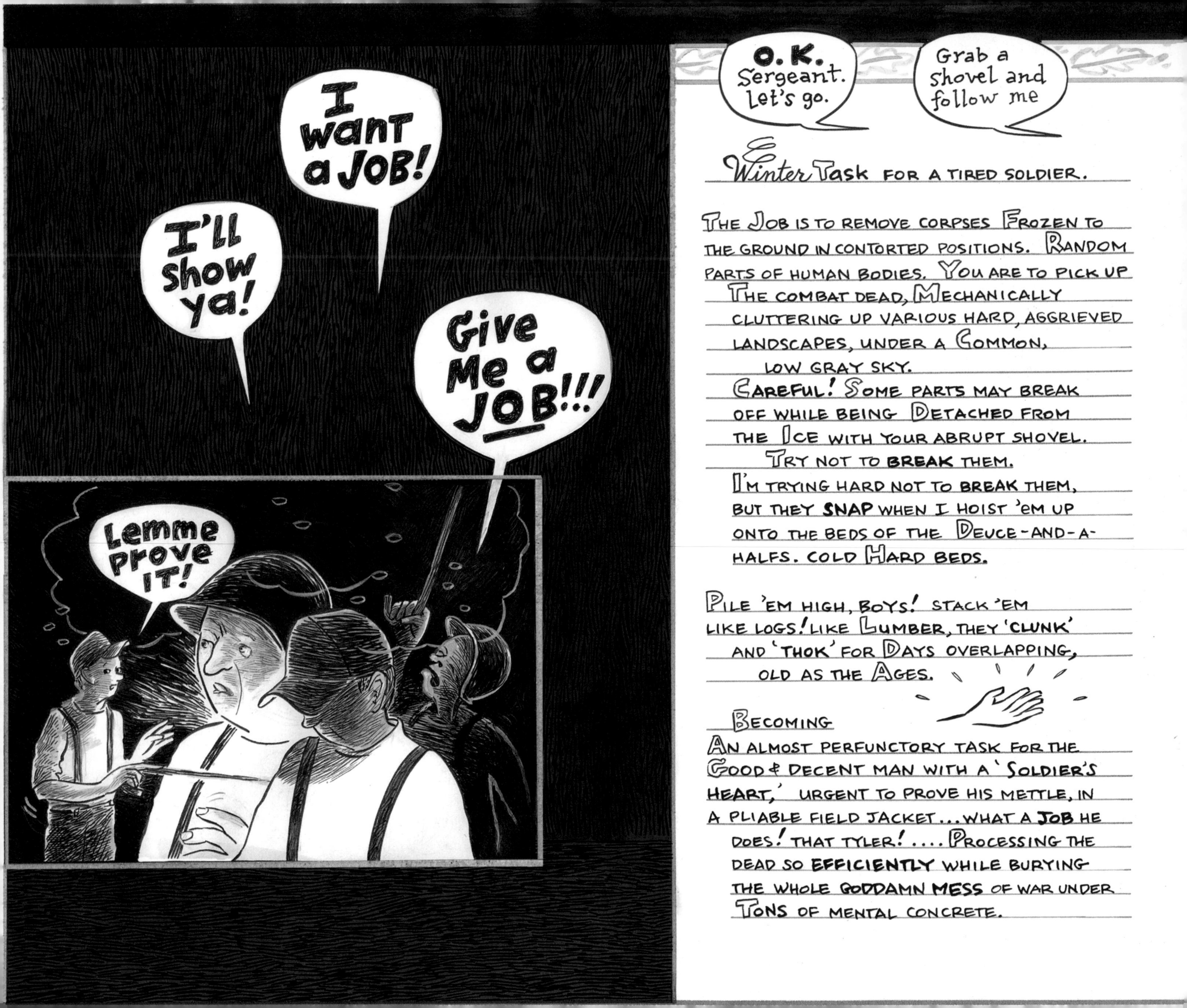
I want a JOB!
I'll Show ya!
Give Me a JOB!!!
Lemme prove IT!
O.K. Sergeant. Let's go.
Grab a shovel and follow me
Winter Task FOR A TIRED SOLDIER.
THE JOB IS TO REMOVE CORPSES FROZEN TO THE GROUND IN CONTORTED POSITIONS. RANDOM PARTS OF HUMAN BODIES. YOU ARE TO PICK UP THE COMBAT DEAD, MECHANICALLY CLUTTERING UP VARIOUS HARD, AGGRIEVED LANDSCAPES, UNDER A COMMON, LOW GRAY SKY.
CAREFUL! SOME PARTS MAY BREAK OFF WHILE BEING DETACHED FROM THE ICE WITH YOUR ABRUPT SHOVEL.
TRY NOT TO BREAK THEM.
I'M TRYING HARD NOT TO BREAK THEM, BUT THEY SNAP WHEN I HOIST 'EM UP ONTO THE BEDS OF THE DEUCE-AND-A-HALFS. COLD HARD BEDS.
PILE 'EM HIGH, BOYS! STACK 'EM LIKE LOGS! LIKE LUMBER, THEY 'CLUNK' AND 'THOK' FOR DAYS OVERLAPPING, OLD AS THE AGES.
BECOMING
AN ALMOST PERFUNCTORY TASK FOR THE GOOD & DECENT MAN WITH A 'SOLDIER'S HEART,' URGENT TO PROVE HIS METTLE, IN A PLIABLE FIELD JACKET... WHAT A JOB HE DOES! THAT TYLER! .... PROCESSING THE DEAD SO EFFICIENTLY WHILE BURYING THE WHOLE GODDAMN MESS OF WAR UNDER TONS OF MENTAL CONCRETE.

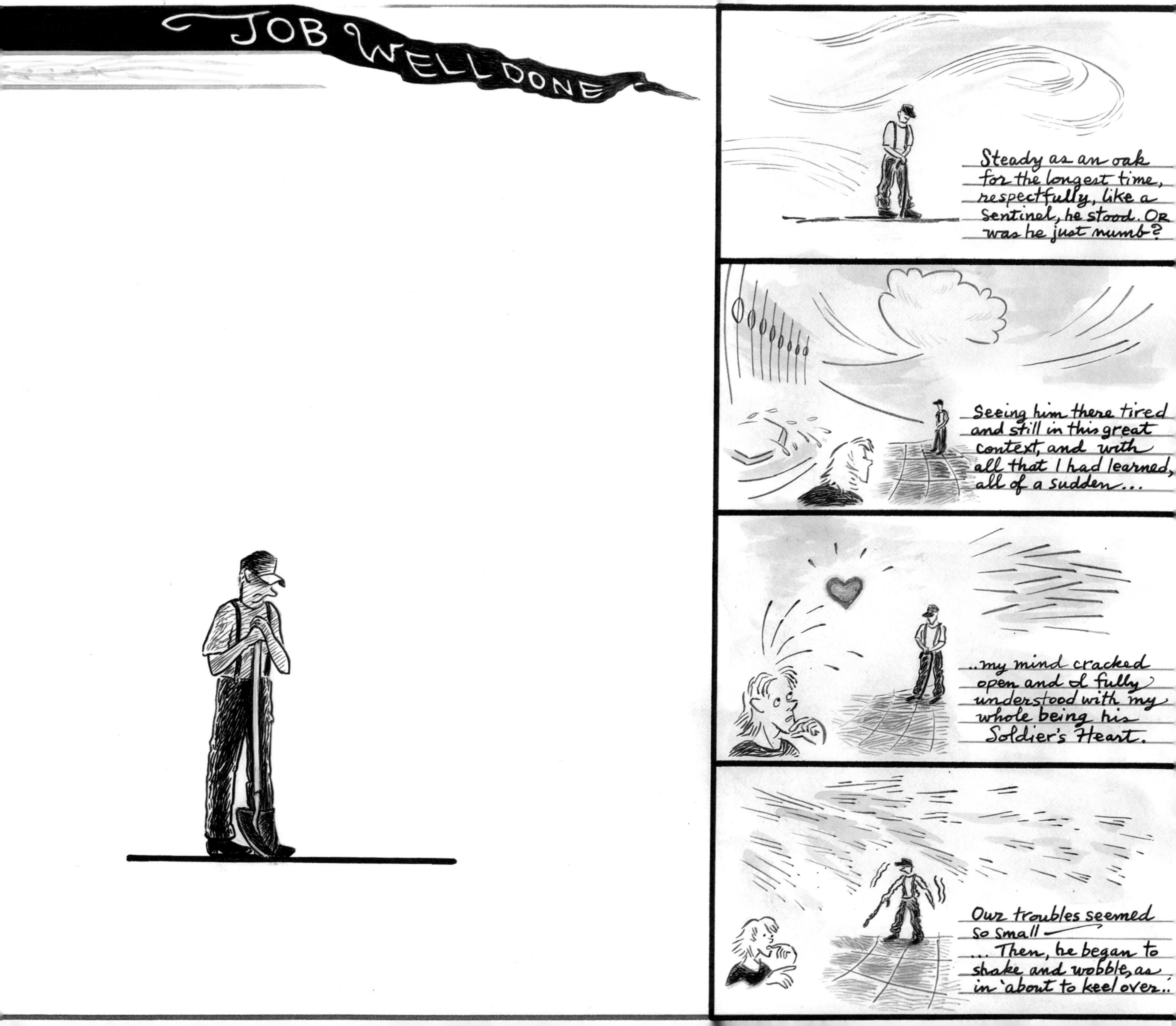
JOB WELL DONE
Steady as an oak for the longest time, respectfully, like a Sentinel, he stood. OR was he just numb?
Seeing him there tired and still in this great context, and with all that I had learned, all of a sudden...
..my mind cracked open and I fully understood with my whole being his Soldier's Heart.
Our troubles seemed so small
... Then, he began to shake and wobble, as in 'about to keel over.'

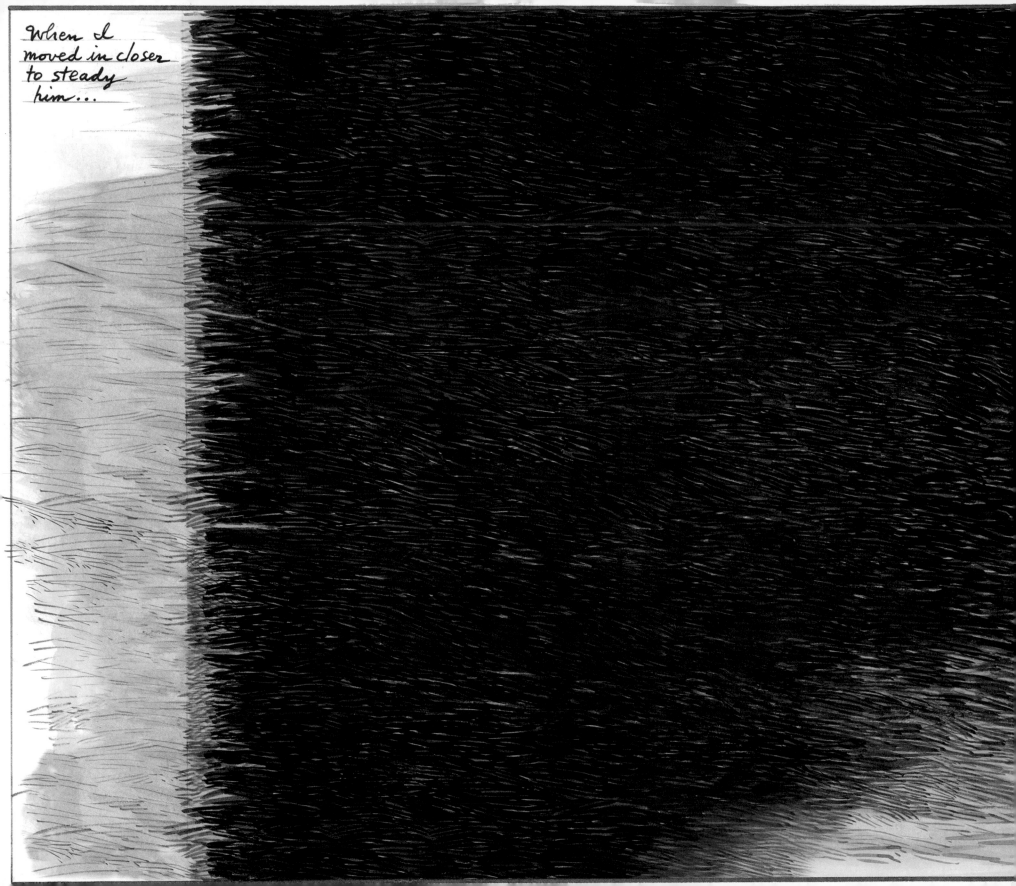

When I
moved in closer
to steady
him...

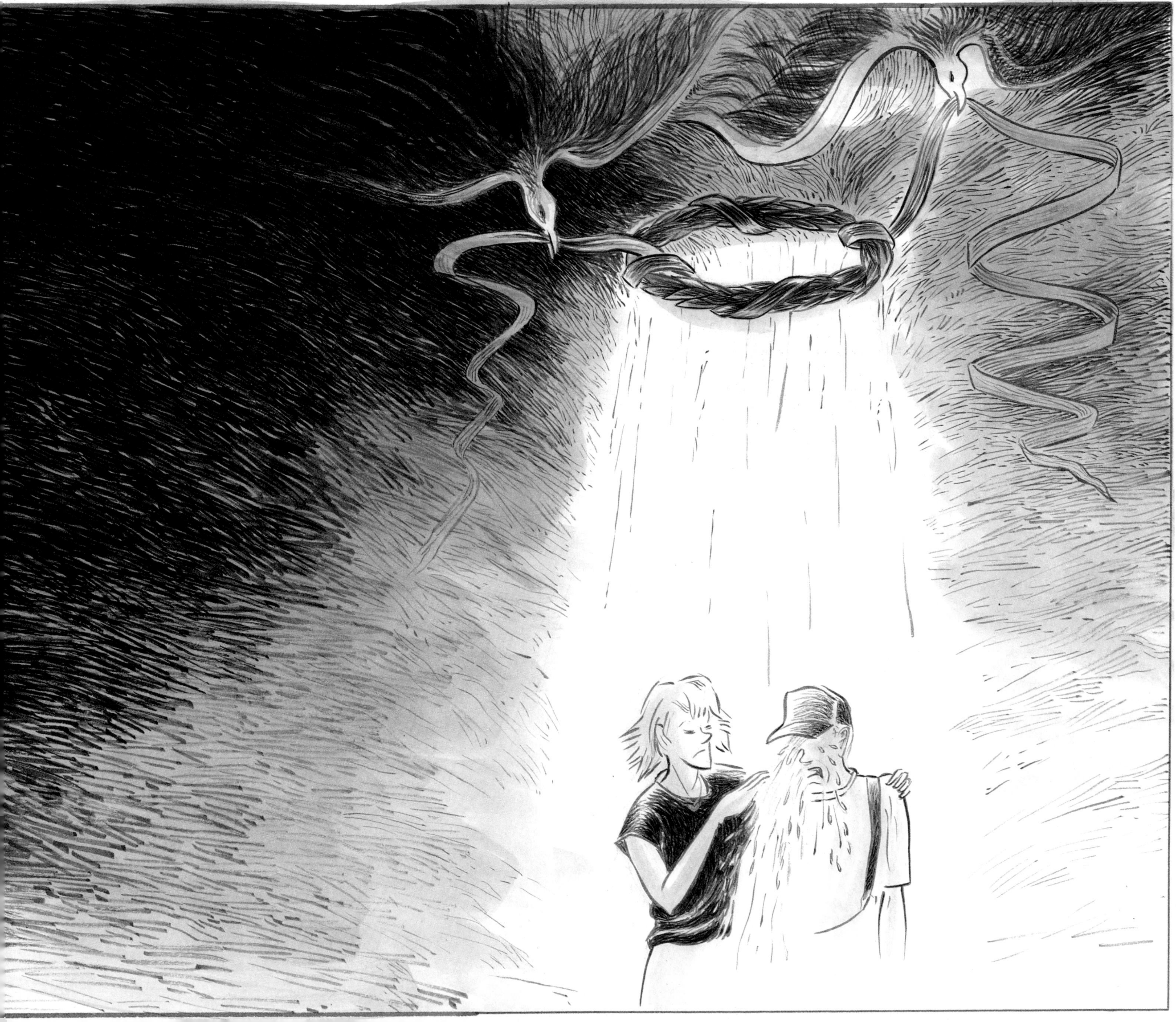

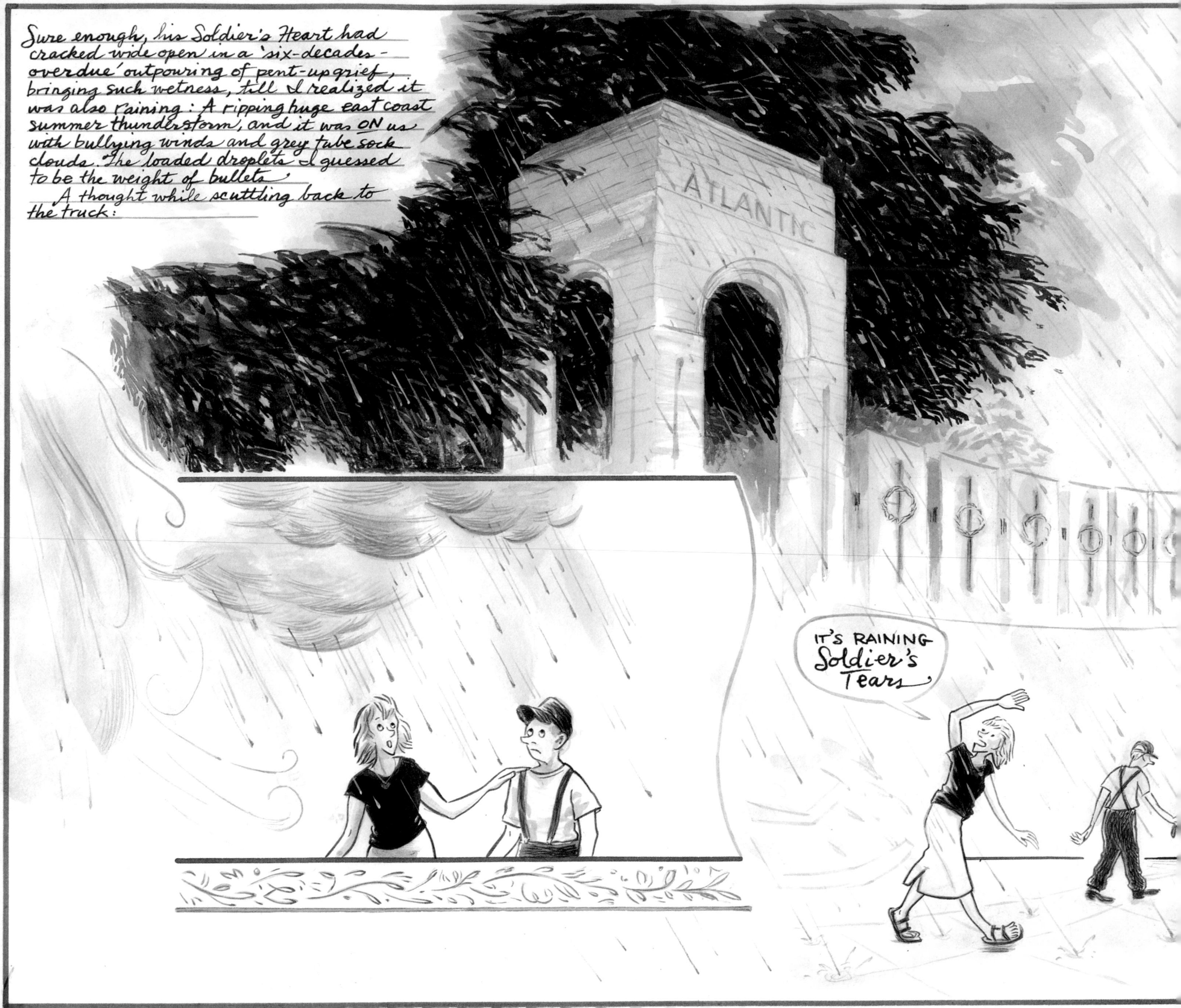
Sure enough, his Soldier's Heart had cracked wide open in a 'six-decades-overdue' outpouring of pent-up grief, bringing such wetness, till I realized it was also raining: A ripping huge east coast summer thunderstorm, and it was ON us with bullying winds and grey tube sock clouds. The loaded droplets I guessed to be the weight of bullets.
A thought while scuttling back to the truck:
ATLANTIC
IT'S RAINING Soldier's Tears

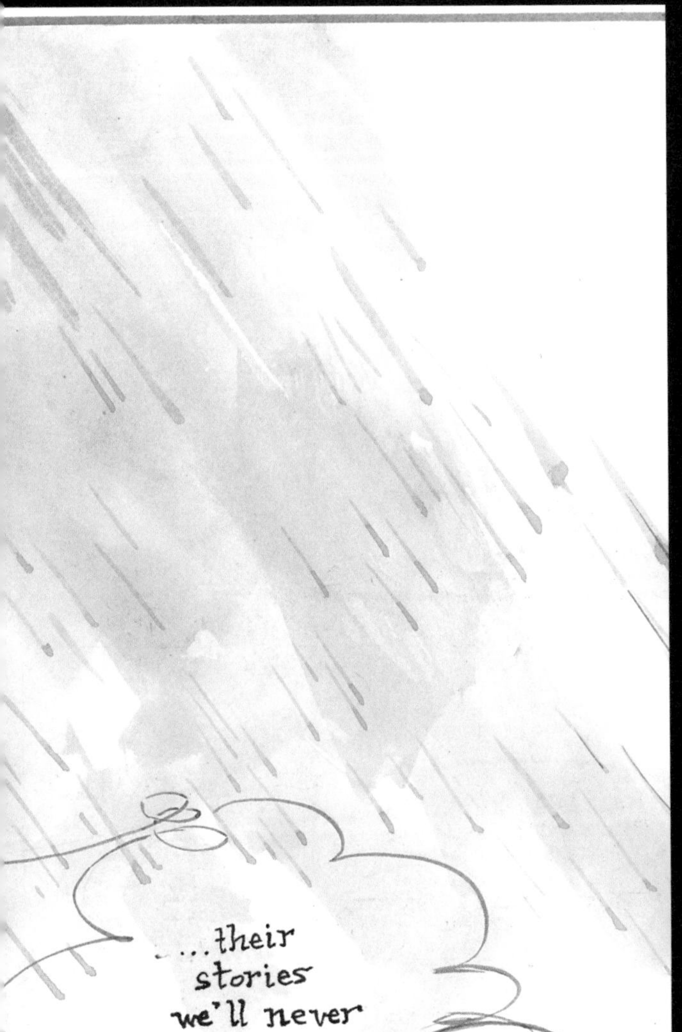
...their stories we'll never know.

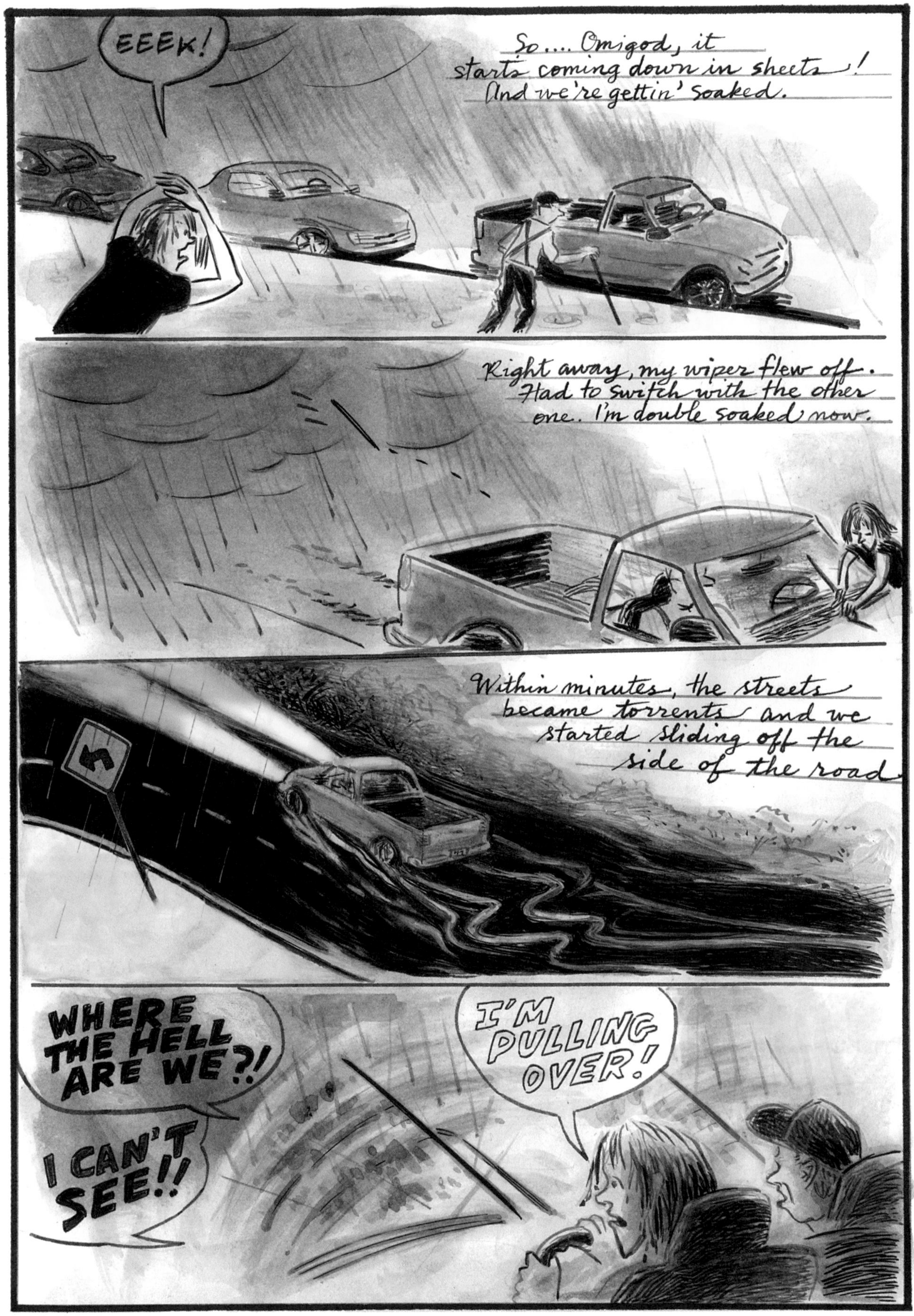
EEEK!
So.... Omigod, it starts coming down in sheets! And we're gettin' soaked.
Right away, my wiper flew off. Had to switch with the other one. I'm double soaked now.
Within minutes, the streets became torrents and we started sliding off the side of the road.
WHERE THE HELL ARE WE?!
I CAN'T SEE!!
I'M PULLING OVER!

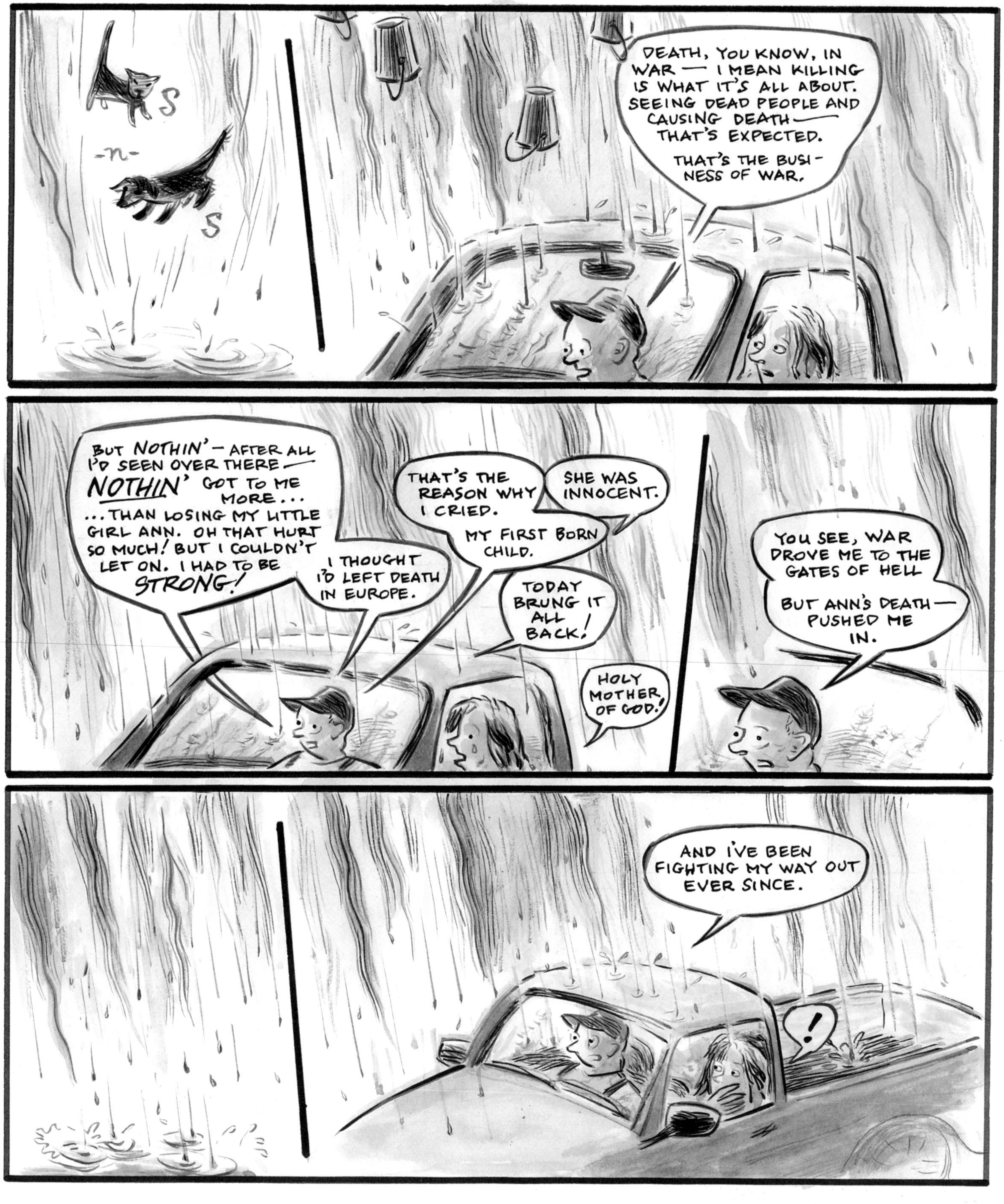
S
-n-
S
DEATH, YOU KNOW, IN WAR — I MEAN KILLING IS WHAT IT'S ALL ABOUT. SEEING DEAD PEOPLE AND CAUSING DEATH — THAT'S EXPECTED.
THAT'S THE BUSINESS OF WAR.
BUT NOTHIN' — AFTER ALL I'D SEEN OVER THERE — NOTHIN' GOT TO ME MORE...
...THAN LOSING MY LITTLE GIRL ANN. OH THAT HURT SO MUCH! BUT I COULDN'T LET ON. I HAD TO BE STRONG!
I THOUGHT I'D LEFT DEATH IN EUROPE.
THAT'S THE REASON WHY I CRIED.
SHE WAS INNOCENT.
MY FIRST BORN CHILD.
TODAY BRUNG IT ALL BACK!
HOLY MOTHER OF GOD!
YOU SEE, WAR DROVE ME TO THE GATES OF HELL
BUT ANN'S DEATH — PUSHED ME IN.
AND I'VE BEEN FIGHTING MY WAY OUT EVER SINCE.
!

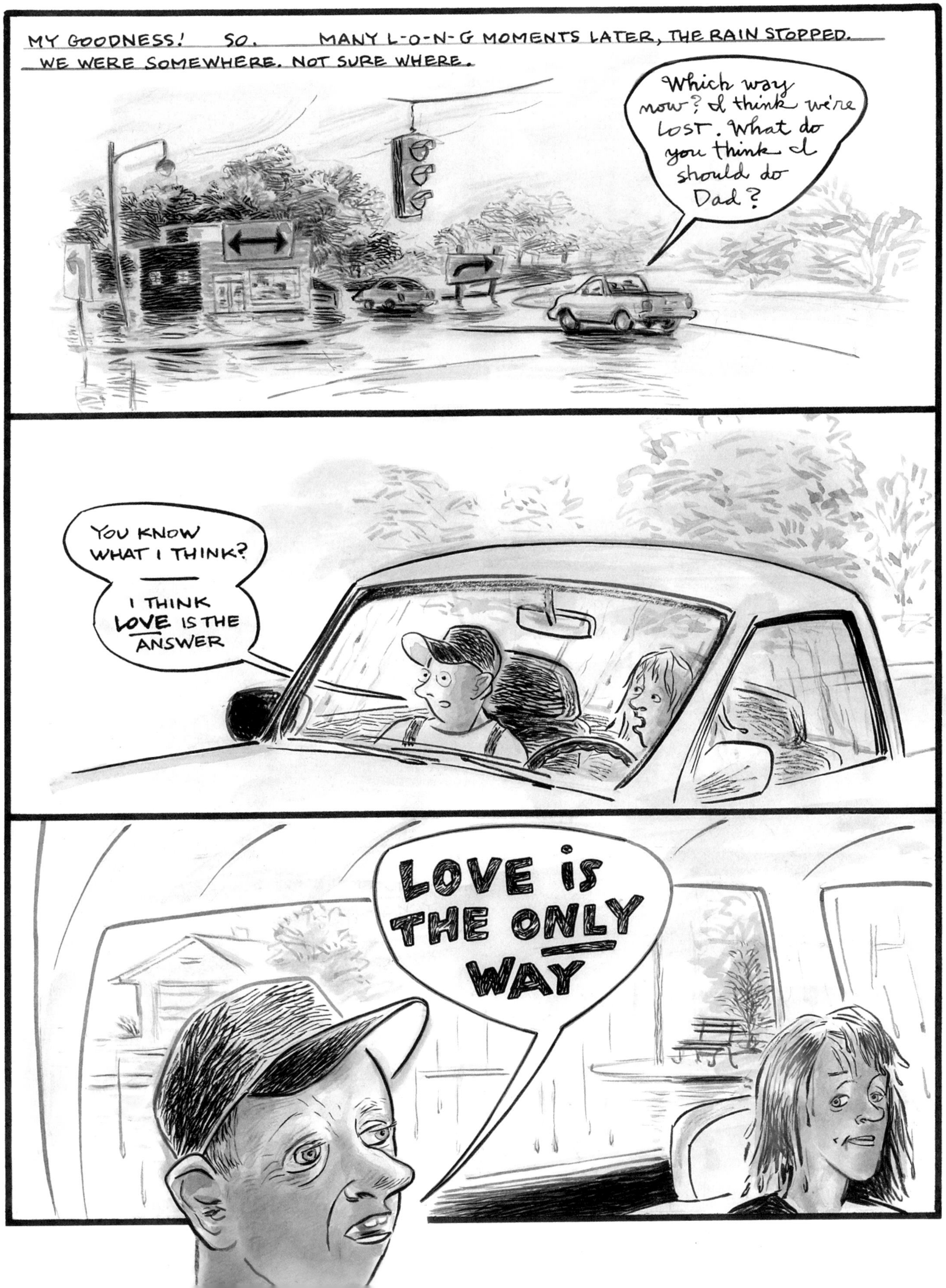
MY GOODNESS! SO. MANY L-O-N-G MOMENTS LATER, THE RAIN STOPPED.
WE WERE SOMEWHERE. NOT SURE WHERE.
Which way now? I think we're lost. What do you think I should do Dad?
YOU KNOW WHAT I THINK?
I THINK LOVE IS THE ANSWER
LOVE IS THE ONLY WAY

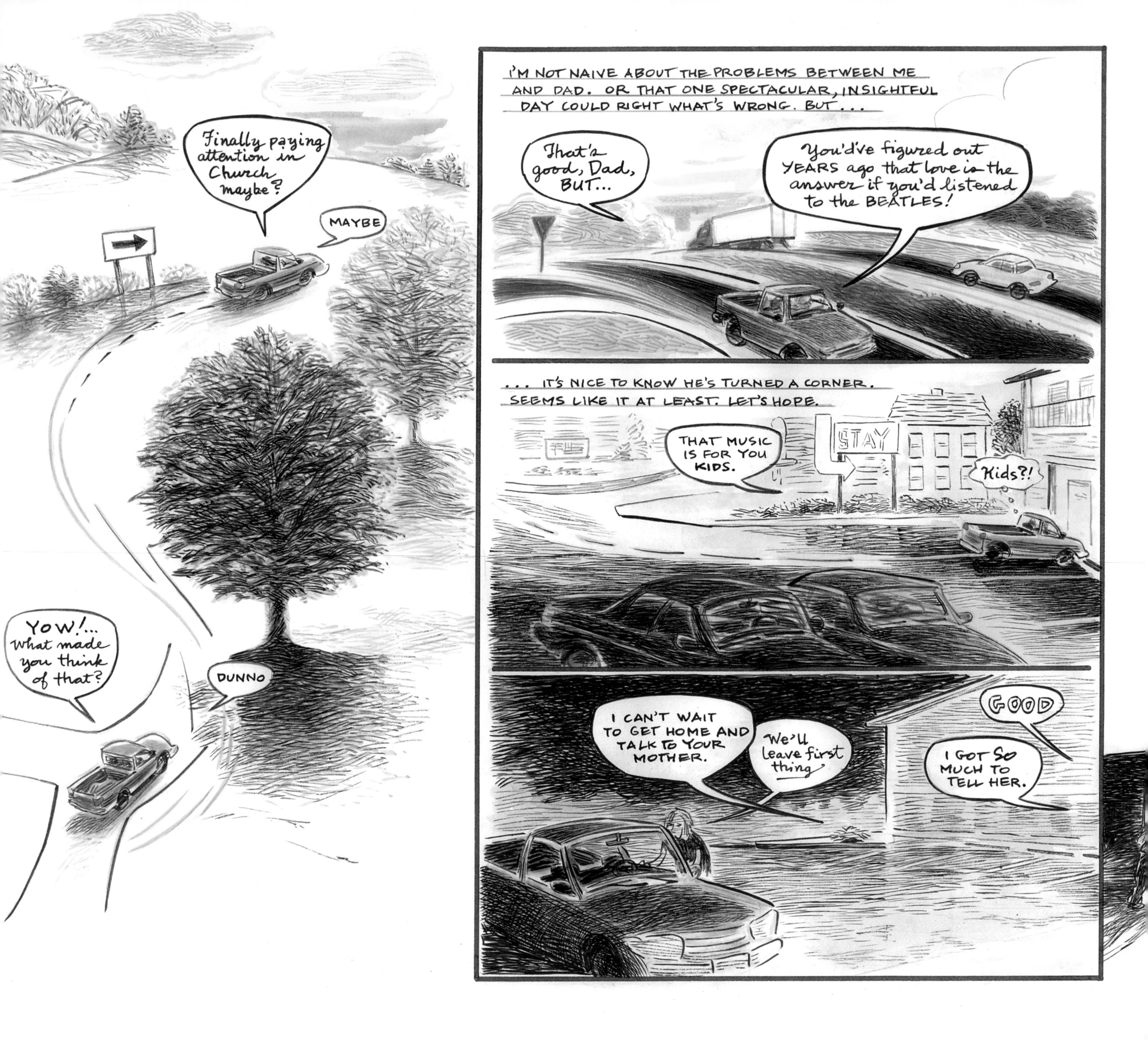
Finally paying attention in Church maybe?
MAYBE
YOW!... What made you think of that?
DUNNO
I'M NOT NAIVE ABOUT THE PROBLEMS BETWEEN ME AND DAD. OR THAT ONE SPECTACULAR, INSIGHTFUL DAY COULD RIGHT WHAT'S WRONG. BUT...
That's good, Dad, BUT...
You'd've figured out YEARS ago that love is the answer if you'd listened to the BEATLES!
... IT'S NICE TO KNOW HE'S TURNED A CORNER. SEEMS LIKE IT AT LEAST. LET'S HOPE.
STAY
THAT MUSIC IS FOR YOU KIDS.
Kids?!
I CAN'T WAIT TO GET HOME AND TALK TO YOUR MOTHER.
We'll leave first thing
GOOD
I GOT SO MUCH TO TELL HER.

NEXT DAY, ON THE WAY HOME, HE HAD ME STOP AT A FLORIST.
R-R-ED-D!
RED I'M BACK FROM THE WAR! I'M FINALLY HOME!
OH MY GOODNESS LOOKEY HERE.
Welcome Home!
WHEN I GOT BACK TO MY HOUSE, AN ENTIRELY DIFFERENT SITUATION.. NO 'WELCOME HOME' HERE!
4
C.
"Julia is with her new friend Matilda
and I'm in my studio.
Sorry about the mess."
J.
E
S
N
W
So...
LONELY SELF HEADED TOWARD PROJECT ON THE HUMBLE PLANK, BUT THEN REMEMBERED:
IT'S NOT HERE

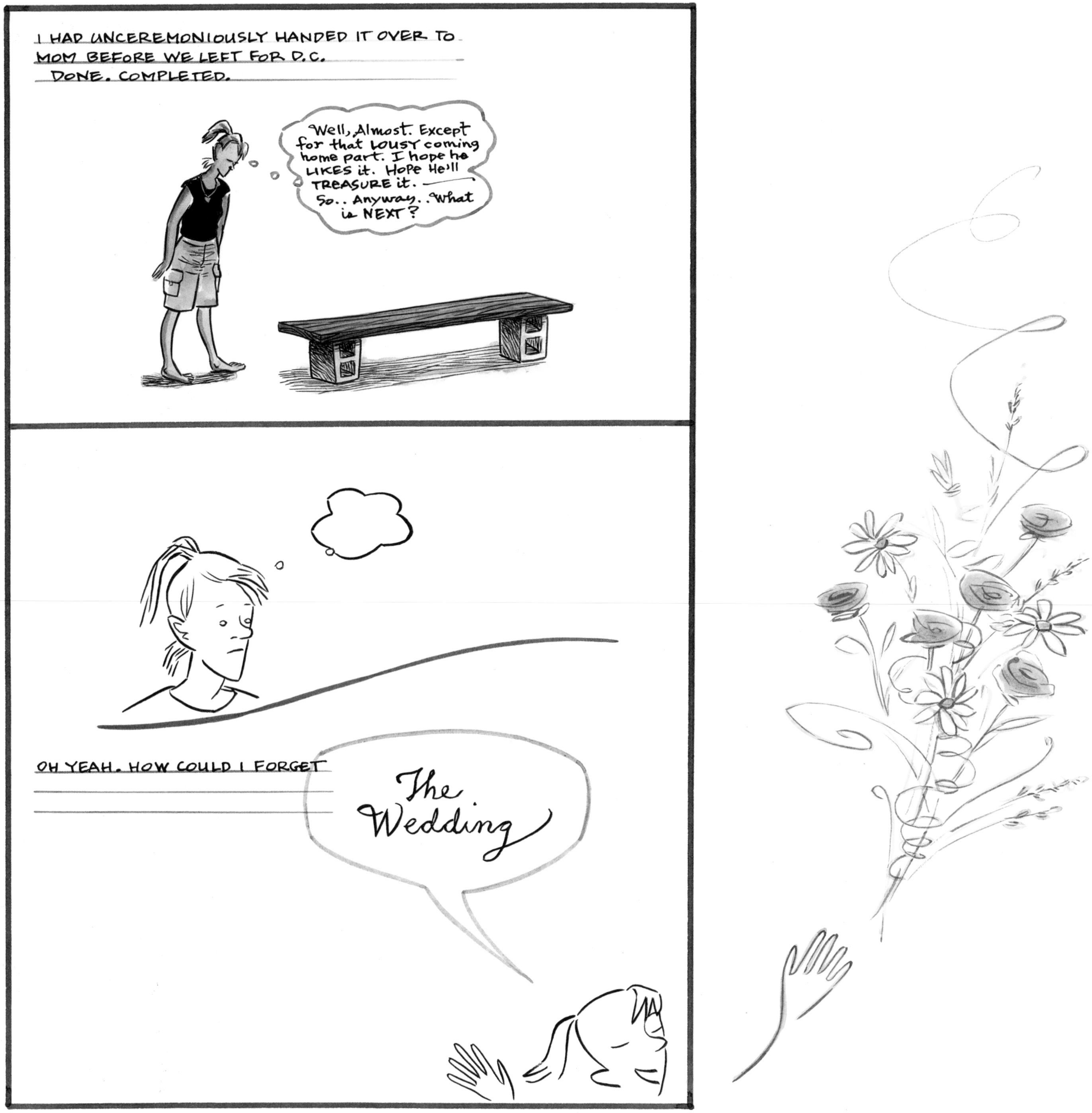
I HAD UNCEREMONIOUSLY HANDED IT OVER TO MOM BEFORE WE LEFT FOR D.C.
DONE. COMPLETED.
Well, Almost. Except for that LOUSY coming home part. I hope he LIKES it. Hope He'll TREASURE it. So.. Anyway.. What is NEXT?
OH YEAH. HOW COULD I FORGET
The Wedding

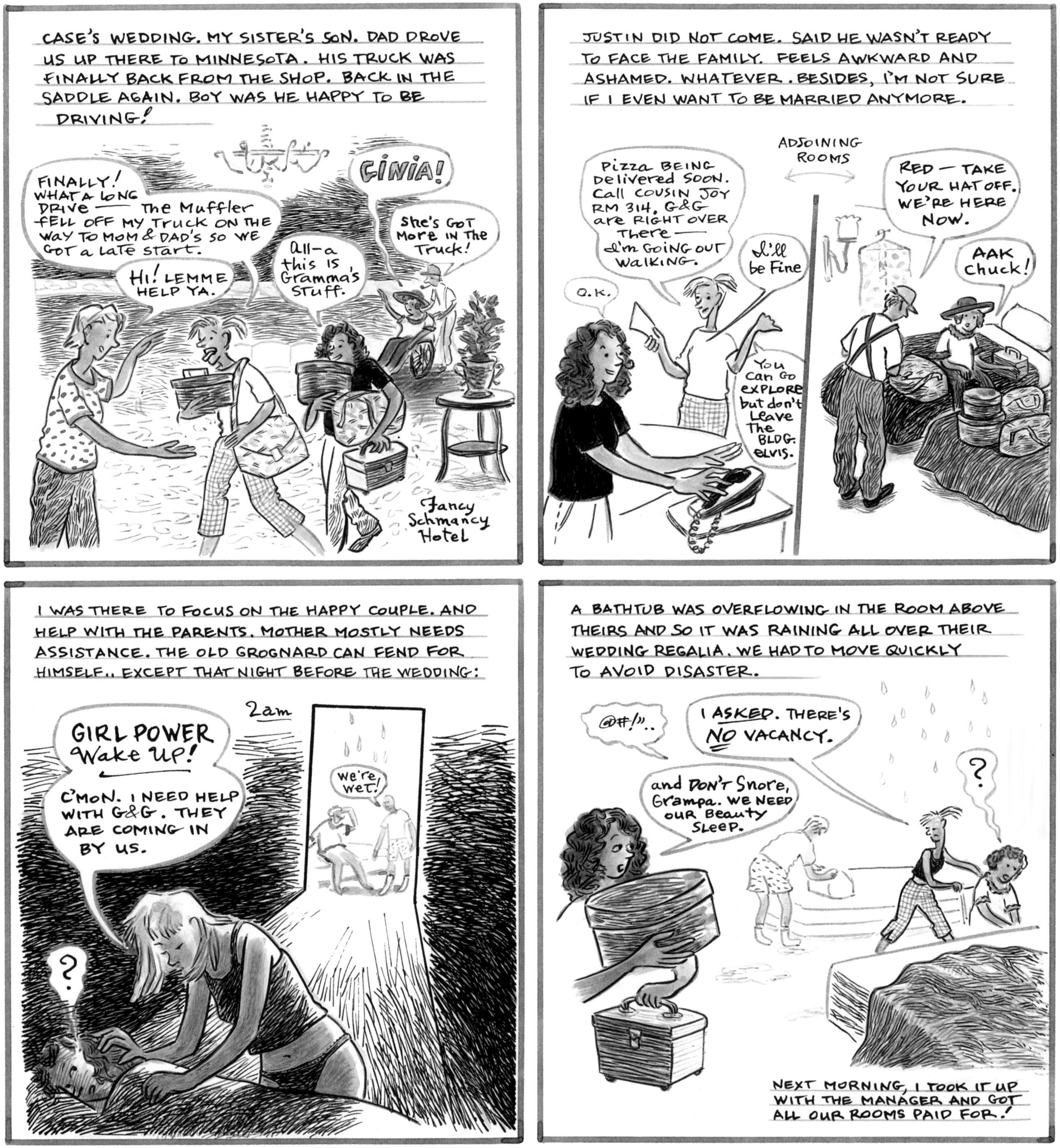
CASE'S WEDDING. MY SISTER'S SON. DAD DROVE US UP THERE TO MINNESOTA. HIS TRUCK WAS FINALLY BACK FROM THE SHOP. BACK IN THE SADDLE AGAIN. BOY WAS HE HAPPY TO BE DRIVING!
FINALLY! WHAT A LONG DRIVE — The Muffler fell off my truck on the way to Mom & Dad's so we got a late start.
CINIA!
Hi! LEMME HELP YA.
All-a this is Gramma's Stuff.
She's got more in the Truck!
Fancy Schmancy Hotel
JUSTIN DID NOT COME. SAID HE WASN'T READY TO FACE THE FAMILY. FEELS AWKWARD AND ASHAMED. WHATEVER. BESIDES, I'M NOT SURE IF I EVEN WANT TO BE MARRIED ANYMORE.
ADJOINING ROOMS
Pizza BEING Delivered Soon. Call COUSIN JOY RM 314. G&G are RIGHT OVER There — I'm GOING OUT WALKING.
O.K.
I'll be Fine
You can go EXPLORE but don't Leave The BLDG. ELVIS.
RED — TAKE YOUR HAT OFF. WE'RE HERE NOW.
AAK Chuck!
I WAS THERE TO FOCUS ON THE HAPPY COUPLE. AND HELP WITH THE PARENTS. MOTHER MOSTLY NEEDS ASSISTANCE. THE OLD GROGNARD CAN FEND FOR HIMSELF.. EXCEPT THAT NIGHT BEFORE THE WEDDING:
2am
GIRL POWER Wake Up!
C'MON. I NEED HELP WITH G&G. THEY ARE COMING IN BY US.
We're wet!
?
A BATHTUB WAS OVERFLOWING IN THE ROOM ABOVE THEIRS AND SO IT WAS RAINING ALL OVER THEIR WEDDING REGALIA. WE HAD TO MOVE QUICKLY TO AVOID DISASTER.
@#!"..
I ASKED. THERE'S NO VACANCY.
and DON'T Snore, Grampa. WE NEED our Beauty Sleep.
?
NEXT MORNING, I TOOK IT UP WITH THE MANAGER AND GOT ALL OUR ROOMS PAID FOR!

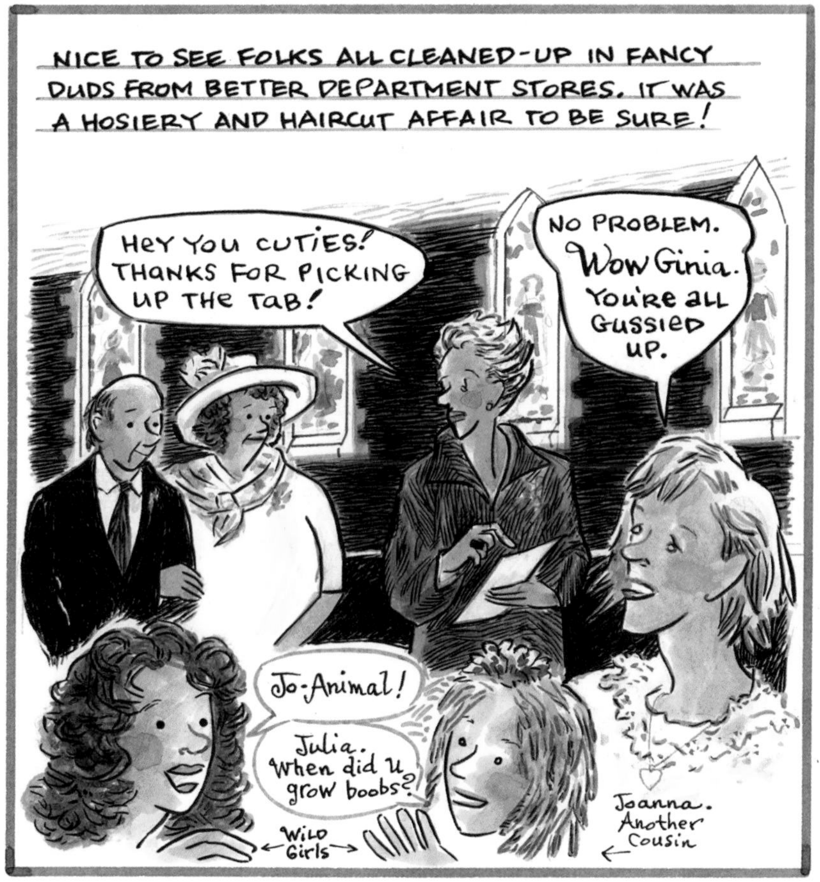
NICE TO SEE FOLKS ALL CLEANED-UP IN FANCY DUDS FROM BETTER DEPARTMENT STORES. IT WAS A HOSIERY AND HAIRCUT AFFAIR TO BE SURE!
HEY YOU CUTIES! THANKS FOR PICKING UP THE TAB!
NO PROBLEM. Wow Ginia. You're all gussied up.
Jo-Animal!
Julia. When did u grow boobs?
Wild Girls
Joanna. Another Cousin

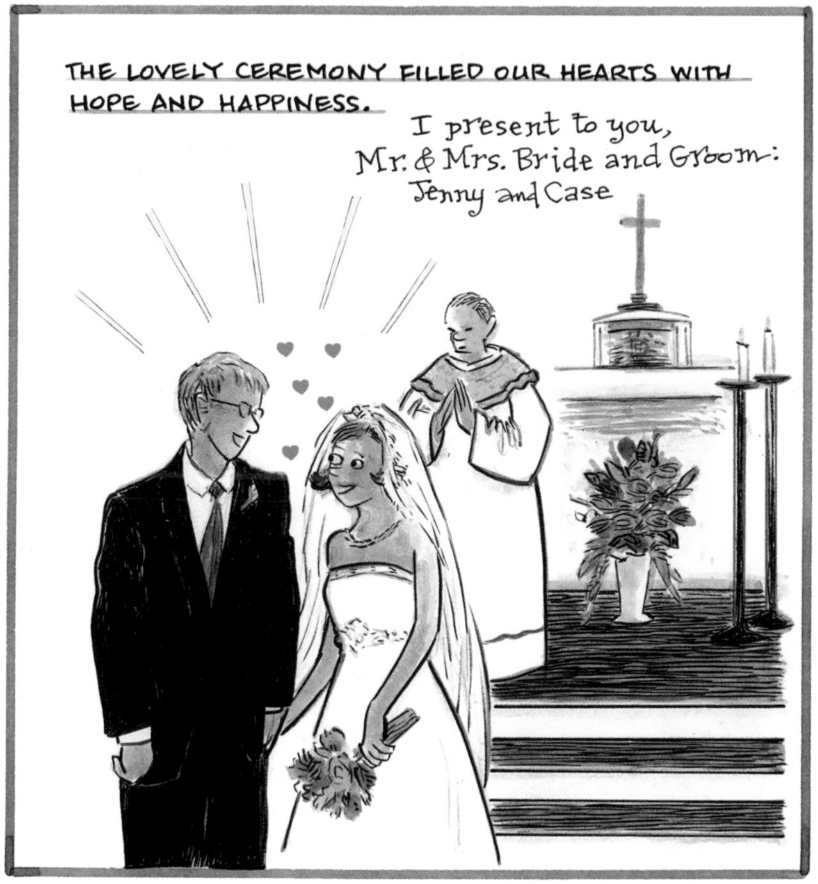
THE LOVELY CEREMONY FILLED OUR HEARTS WITH HOPE AND HAPPINESS.
I present to you, Mr. & Mrs. Bride and Groom: Jenny and Case

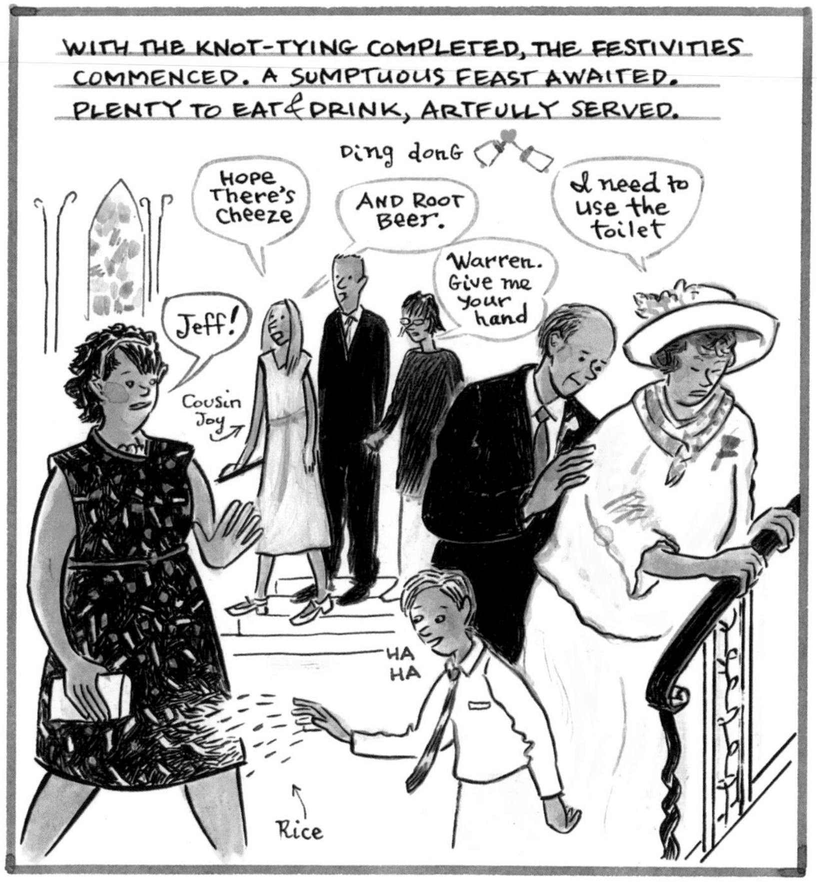
WITH THE KNOT-TYING COMPLETED, THE FESTIVITIES COMMENCED. A SUMPTUOUS FEAST AWAITED. PLENTY TO EAT & DRINK, ARTFULLY SERVED.
Ding dong
Hope There's Cheeze
AND ROOT BEER.
I need to use the toilet
Warren. Give me your hand
Jeff!
Cousin Joy
HA HA
Rice

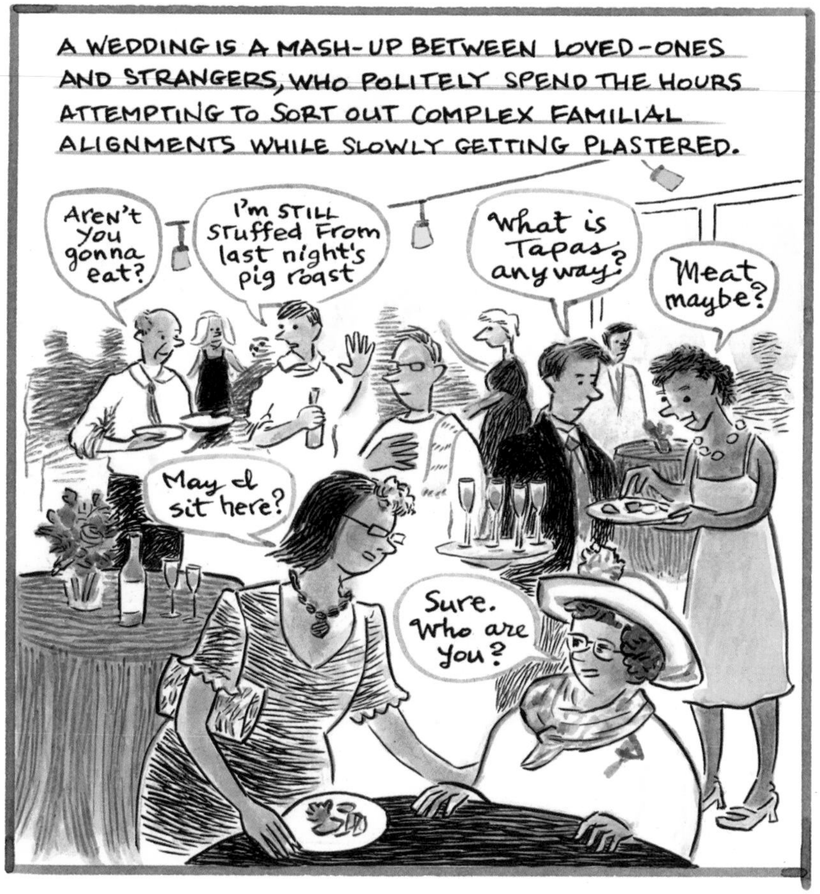
A WEDDING IS A MASH-UP BETWEEN LOVED-ONES AND STRANGERS, WHO POLITELY SPEND THE HOURS ATTEMPTING TO SORT OUT COMPLEX FAMILIAL ALIGNMENTS WHILE SLOWLY GETTING PLASTERED.
Aren't you gonna eat?
I'm STILL stuffed from last night's pig roast
What is Tapas anyway?
Meat maybe?
May I sit here?
Sure. Who are you?

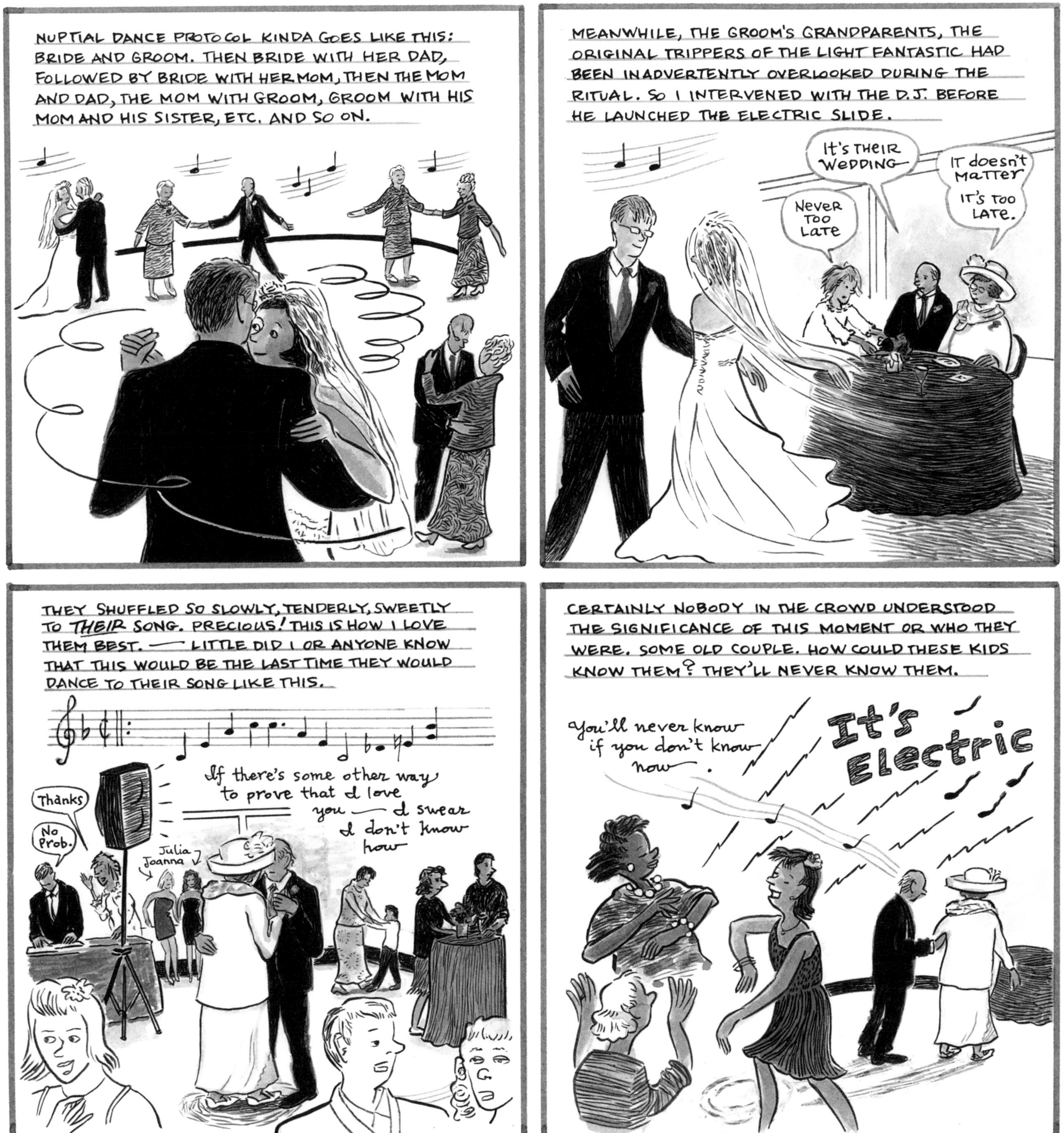
NUPTIAL DANCE PROTOCOL KINDA GOES LIKE THIS: BRIDE AND GROOM. THEN BRIDE WITH HER DAD, FOLLOWED BY BRIDE WITH HER MOM, THEN THE MOM AND DAD, THE MOM WITH GROOM, GROOM WITH HIS MOM AND HIS SISTER, ETC. AND SO ON.
MEANWHILE, THE GROOM'S GRANDPARENTS, THE ORIGINAL TRIPPERS OF THE LIGHT FANTASTIC HAD BEEN INADVERTENTLY OVERLOOKED DURING THE RITUAL. SO I INTERVENED WITH THE D.J. BEFORE HE LAUNCHED THE ELECTRIC SLIDE.
It's THEIR WEDDING—
Never Too Late
IT doesn't Matter
IT's Too LATE.
THEY SHUFFLED SO SLOWLY, TENDERLY, SWEETLY TO THEIR SONG. PRECIOUS! THIS IS HOW I LOVE THEM BEST. — LITTLE DID I OR ANYONE KNOW THAT THIS WOULD BE THE LAST TIME THEY WOULD DANCE TO THEIR SONG LIKE THIS.
If there's some other way to prove that I love you — I swear I don't know how
Thanks
No Prob.
Julia
Joanna
CERTAINLY NOBODY IN THE CROWD UNDERSTOOD THE SIGNIFICANCE OF THIS MOMENT OR WHO THEY WERE. SOME OLD COUPLE. HOW COULD THESE KIDS KNOW THEM? THEY'LL NEVER KNOW THEM.
You'll never know if you don't know now.
It's Electric

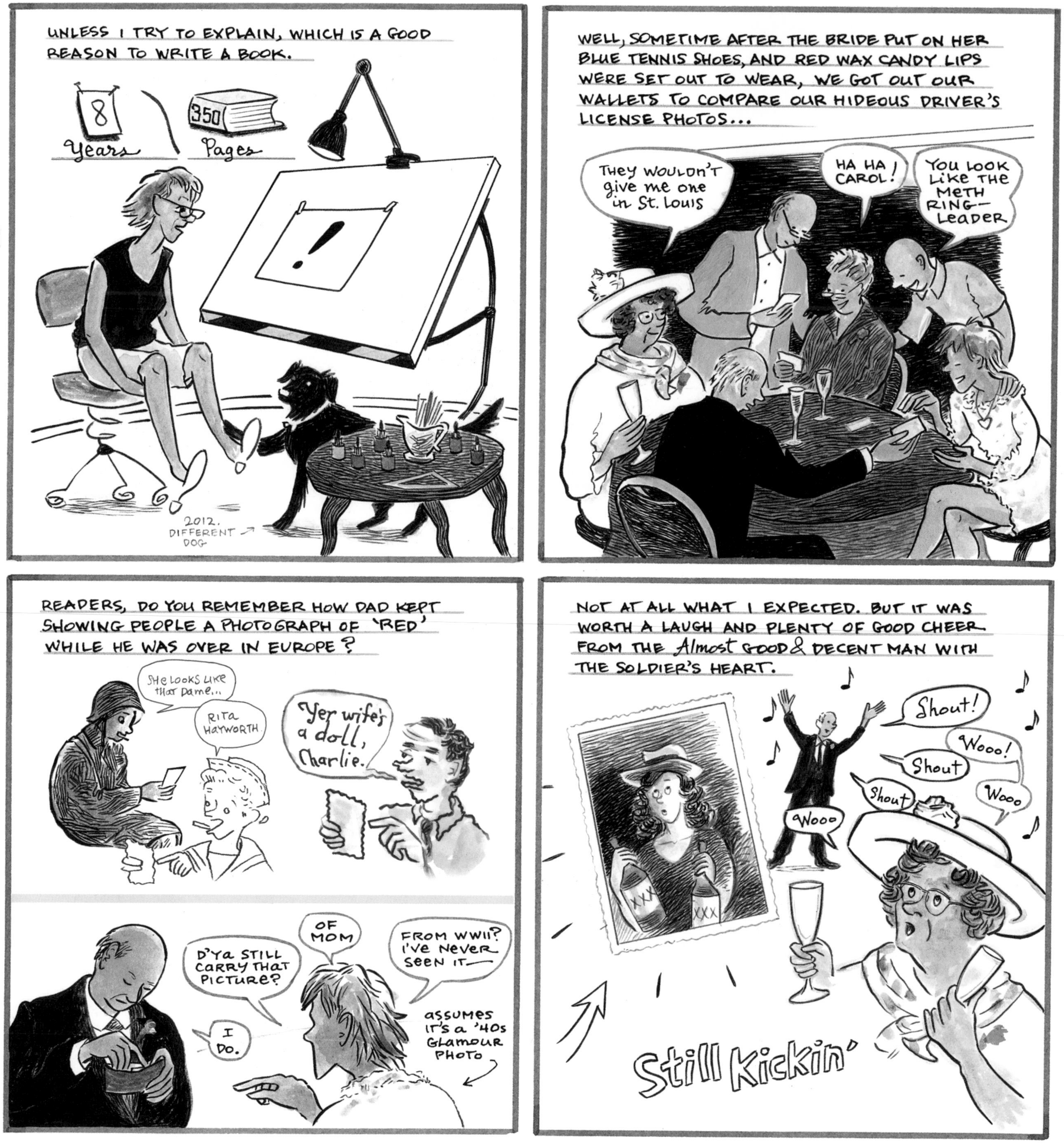
UNLESS I TRY TO EXPLAIN, WHICH IS A GOOD REASON TO WRITE A BOOK.
8 Years
350 Pages
!
2012. DIFFERENT DOG
WELL, SOMETIME AFTER THE BRIDE PUT ON HER BLUE TENNIS SHOES, AND RED WAX CANDY LIPS WERE SET OUT TO WEAR, WE GOT OUT OUR WALLETS TO COMPARE OUR HIDEOUS DRIVER'S LICENSE PHOTOS...
They wouldn't give me one in St. Louis
HA HA CAROL!
You look like the METH RING-LEADER
READERS, DO YOU REMEMBER HOW DAD KEPT SHOWING PEOPLE A PHOTOGRAPH OF 'RED' WHILE HE WAS OVER IN EUROPE?
She looks like that Dame...
RITA HAYWORTH.
Yer wife's a doll, Charlie.
D'ya STILL CARRY THAT PICTURE?
OF MOM
FROM WWII? I've NEVER SEEN IT—
I DO.
assumes it's a '40s GLAMOUR PHOTO
NOT AT ALL WHAT I EXPECTED. BUT IT WAS WORTH A LAUGH AND PLENTY OF GOOD CHEER FROM THE Almost GOOD & DECENT MAN WITH THE SOLDIER'S HEART.
Shout!
Wooo!
Shout
Wooo
Shout
Wooo
XXX
XXX
Still Kickin'

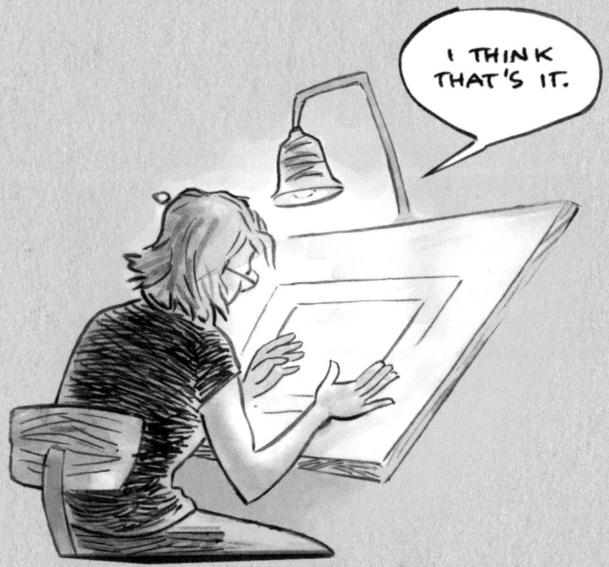
I THINK THAT'S IT.

OH WAIT—

Epilogue

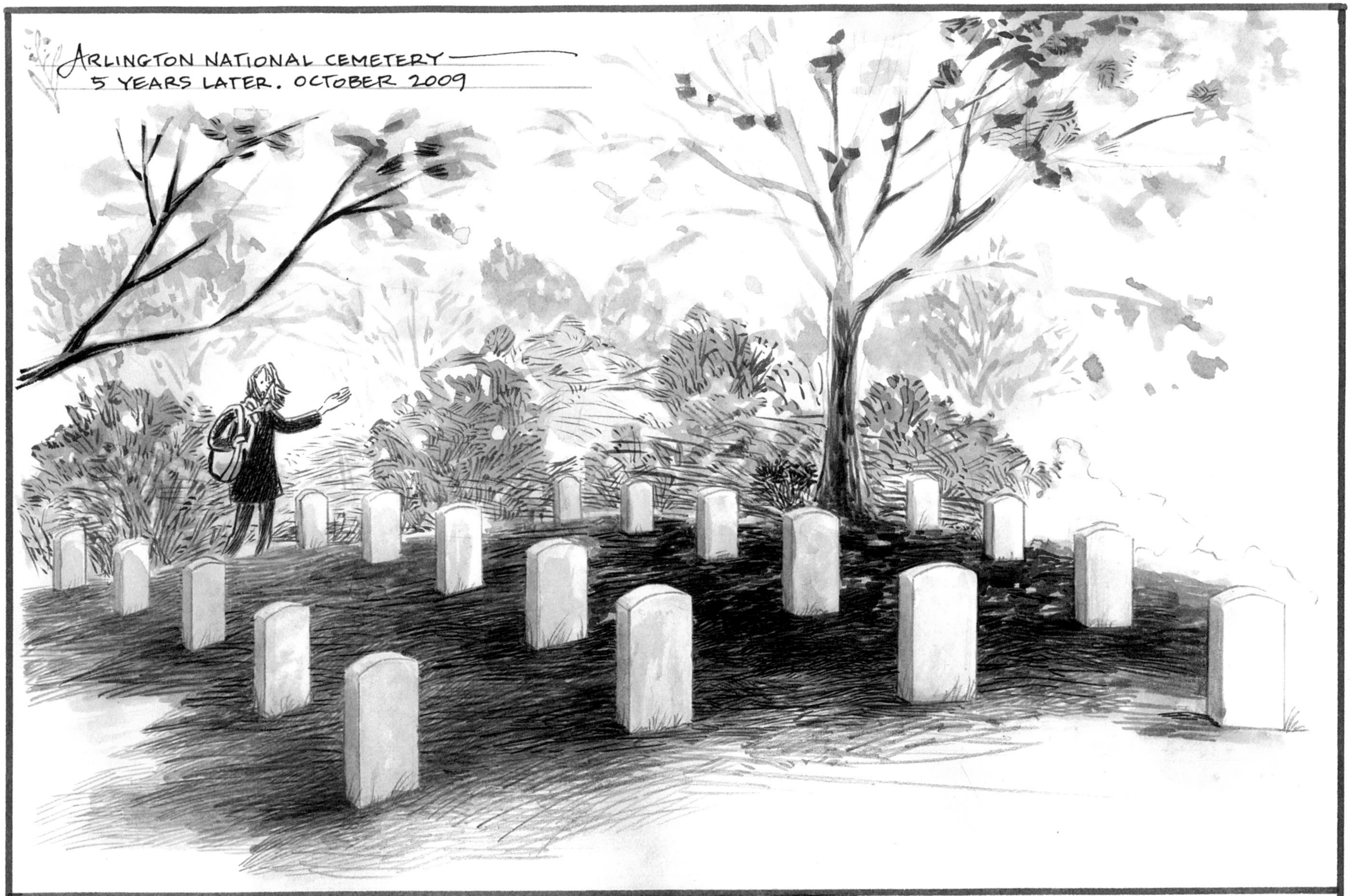
ARLINGTON NATIONAL CEMETERY
5 YEARS LATER. OCTOBER 2009

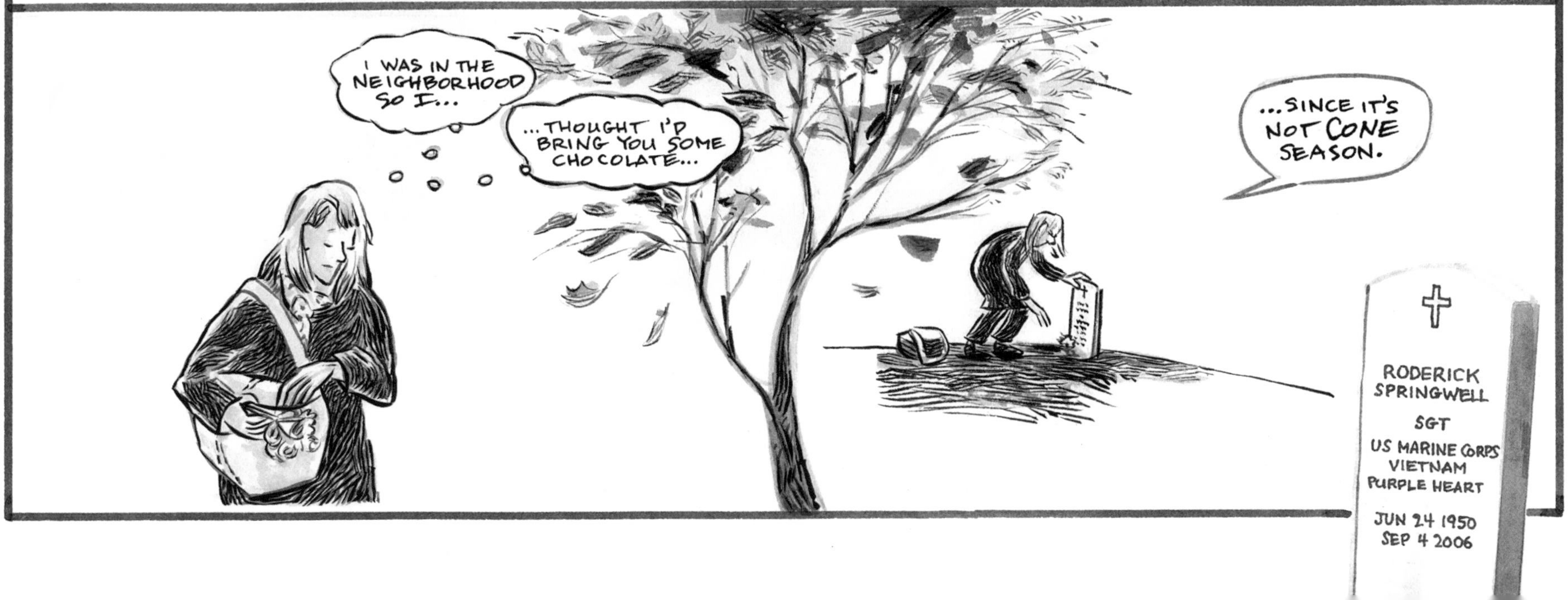
I WAS IN THE NEIGHBORHOOD SO I...
...THOUGHT I'D BRING YOU SOME CHOCOLATE...
...SINCE IT'S NOT CONE SEASON.
RODERICK SPRINGWELL
SGT
US MARINE CORPS
VIETNAM
PURPLE HEART
JUN 24 1950
SEP 4 2006

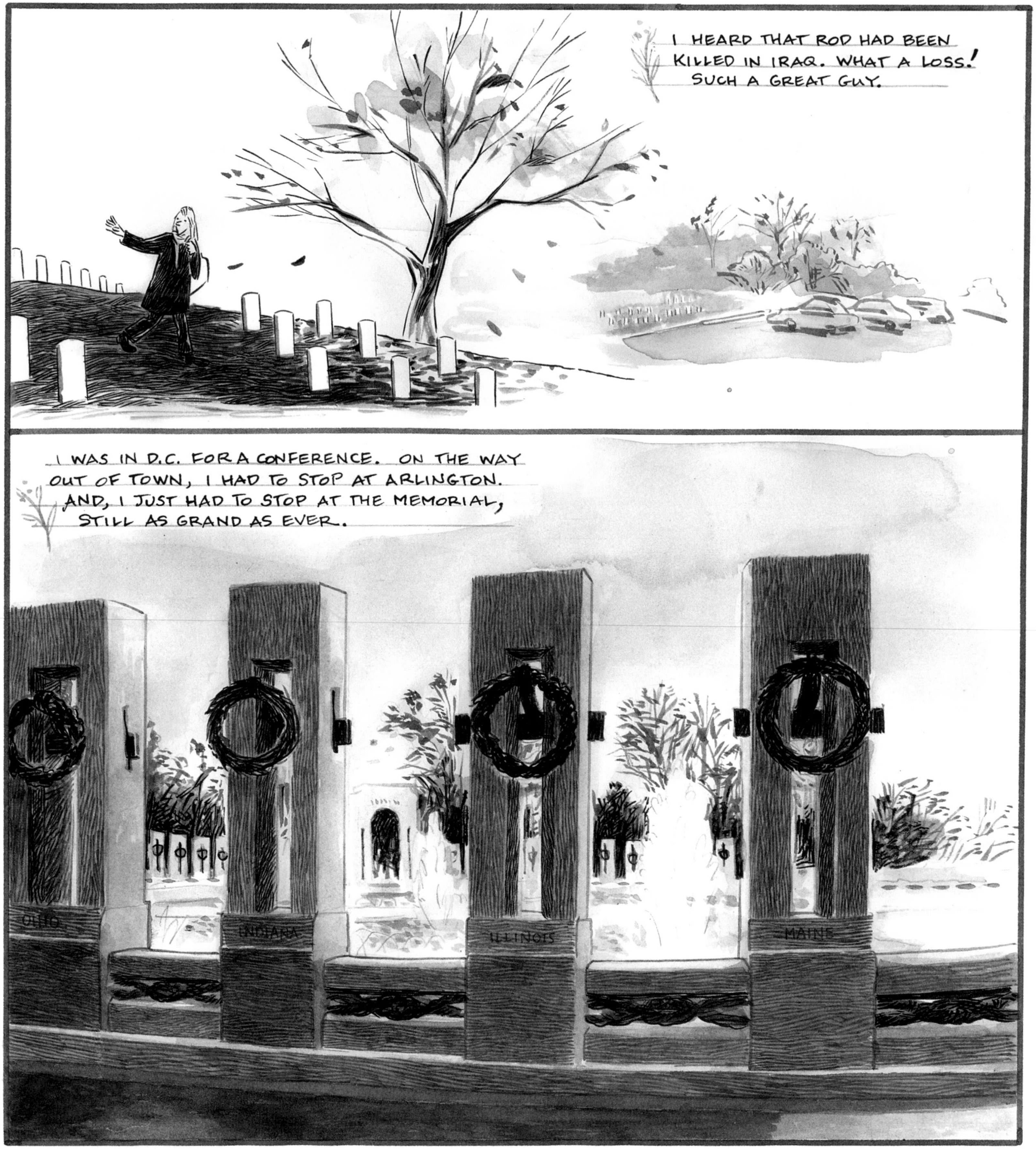
I HEARD THAT ROD HAD BEEN KILLED IN IRAQ. WHAT A LOSS! SUCH A GREAT GUY.
I WAS IN D.C. FOR A CONFERENCE. ON THE WAY OUT OF TOWN, I HAD TO STOP AT ARLINGTON. AND, I JUST HAD TO STOP AT THE MEMORIAL, STILL AS GRAND AS EVER.
OHIO
INDIANA
ILLINOIS
MAINE

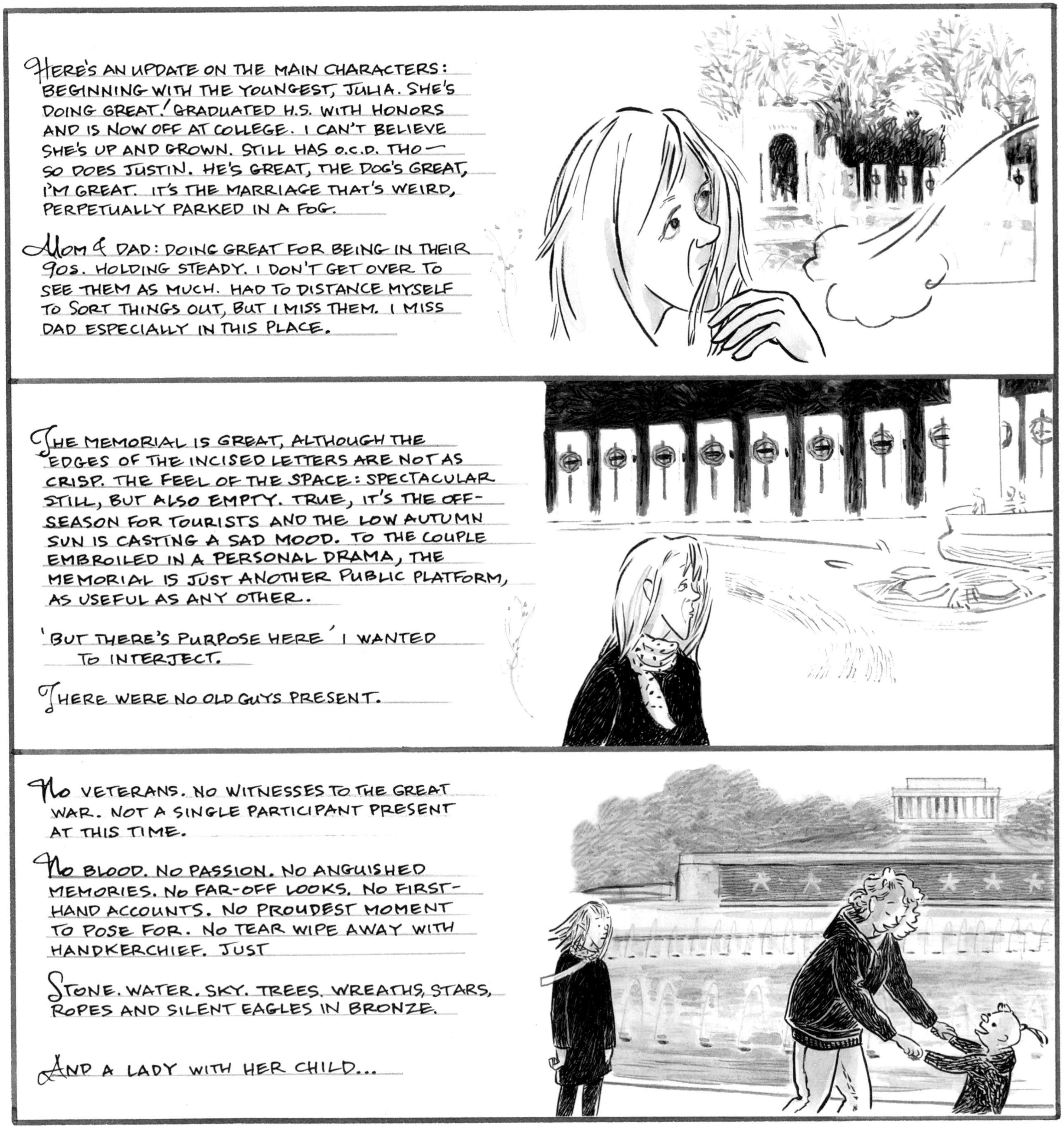
HERE'S AN UPDATE ON THE MAIN CHARACTERS: BEGINNING WITH THE YOUNGEST, JULIA. SHE'S DOING GREAT! GRADUATED H.S. WITH HONORS AND IS NOW OFF AT COLLEGE. I CAN'T BELIEVE SHE'S UP AND GROWN. STILL HAS O.C.D. THO— SO DOES JUSTIN. HE'S GREAT, THE DOG'S GREAT, I'M GREAT. IT'S THE MARRIAGE THAT'S WEIRD, PERPETUALLY PARKED IN A FOG.
MOM & DAD: DOING GREAT FOR BEING IN THEIR 90S. HOLDING STEADY. I DON'T GET OVER TO SEE THEM AS MUCH. HAD TO DISTANCE MYSELF TO SORT THINGS OUT, BUT I MISS THEM. I MISS DAD ESPECIALLY IN THIS PLACE.
THE MEMORIAL IS GREAT, ALTHOUGH THE EDGES OF THE INCISED LETTERS ARE NOT AS CRISP. THE FEEL OF THE SPACE: SPECTACULAR STILL, BUT ALSO EMPTY. TRUE, IT'S THE OFF-SEASON FOR TOURISTS AND THE LOW AUTUMN SUN IS CASTING A SAD MOOD. TO THE COUPLE EMBROILED IN A PERSONAL DRAMA, THE MEMORIAL IS JUST ANOTHER PUBLIC PLATFORM, AS USEFUL AS ANY OTHER.
'BUT THERE'S PURPOSE HERE' I WANTED TO INTERJECT.
THERE WERE NO OLD GUYS PRESENT.
NO VETERANS. NO WITNESSES TO THE GREAT WAR. NOT A SINGLE PARTICIPANT PRESENT AT THIS TIME.
NO BLOOD. NO PASSION. NO ANGUISHED MEMORIES. NO FAR-OFF LOOKS. NO FIRST-HAND ACCOUNTS. NO PROUDEST MOMENT TO POSE FOR. NO TEAR WIPE AWAY WITH HANDKERCHIEF. JUST
STONE. WATER. SKY. TREES. WREATHS, STARS, ROPES AND SILENT EAGLES IN BRONZE.
AND A LADY WITH HER CHILD...

They were having the time of their lives!